GRIMM UNIVERSE CRE
**JOE BRUSHA AND RALF**

# Grimm Fairy Tales presents:

# ROBYN HOOD
## ORIGIN

---

## ROBYN HOOD TRILOGY: PART 1 OF 3

---

zenescope
WWW.ZENESCOPE.COM
FACEBOOK.COM/ZENESCOPE

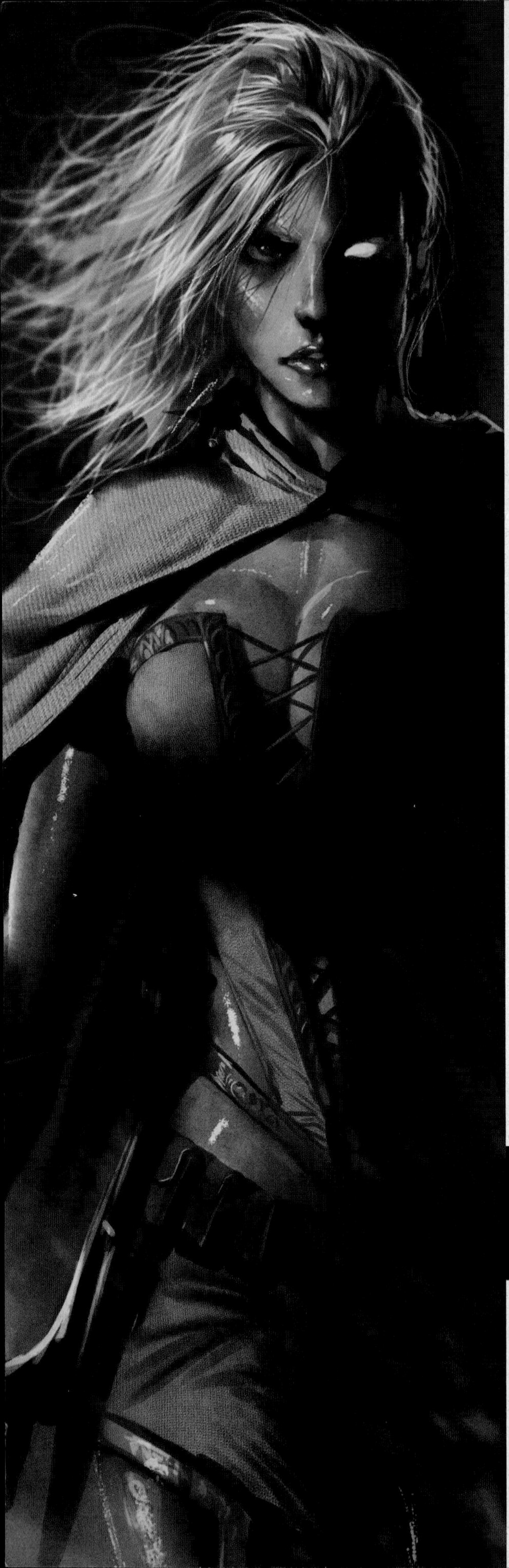

Grimm Fairy Tales presents

# ROBYN HOOD ORIGIN

STORY
**JOE BRUSHA**
**RAVEN GREGORY**
**RALPH TEDESCO**
**PAT SHAND**

WRITER
**PAT SHAND**

TRADE DESIGN
**CHRISTOPHER COTE**

EDITOR
**RALPH TEDESCO**

ASSISTANT EDITORS
**PAT SHAND**
**HANNAH GORFINKEL**

THIS VOLUME REPRINTS THE COMIC SERIES GRIMM FAIRY TALES PRESENTS ROBYN HOOD #1-5 PUBLISHED BY ZENESCOPE ENTERTAINMENT.

WWW.ZENESCOPE.COM

SECOND EDITION, FEBRUARY 2015
ISBN: 978-1-937068-79-0

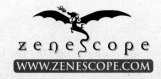

zenescope
WWW.ZENESCOPE.COM

ZENESCOPE ENTERTAINMENT, INC.

**Joe Brusha** • President & Chief Creative Officer
**Ralph Tedesco** • Editor-in-Chief
**Jennifer Bermel** • General Manager
**Christopher Cote** • Art Director
**Jen Sells** • Marketing Manager
**Jason Condeelis** • Direct Market Sales & Customer Service

Grimm Fairy Tales presents Robyn Hood: Origin Trade Paperback Vol. 1, February, 2015. Second Printing. Published by Zenescope Entertainment Inc., 433 Caredean Drive, Ste. C, Horsham, Pennsylvania 19044.

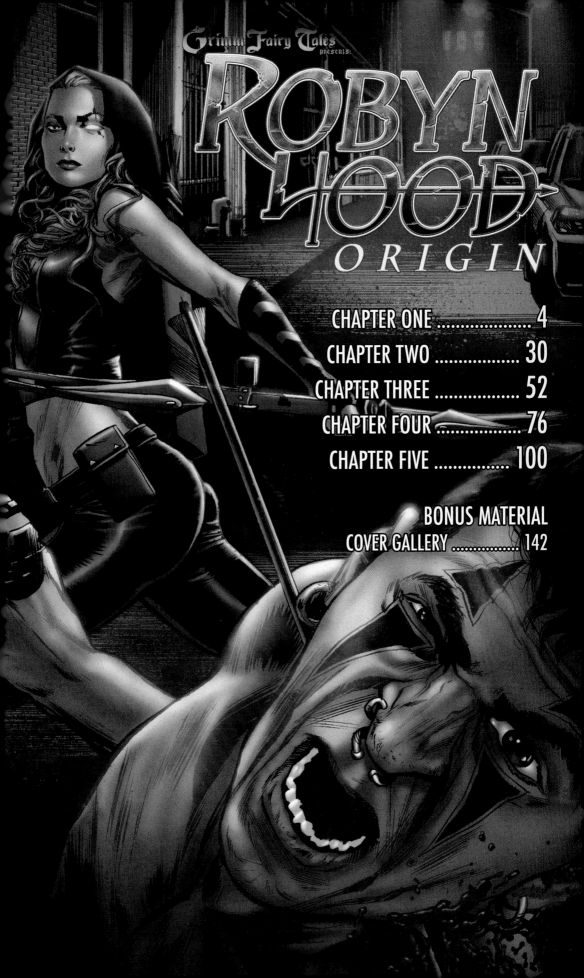

Grimm Fairy Tales
presents:

# ROBYN HOOD
## ORIGIN

# CHAPTER ONE

*Writer* Pat Shand
*Artwork* Dan Glasl
*Colors* Tom Mullin & Jason Embury
*Letters* Jim Campbell

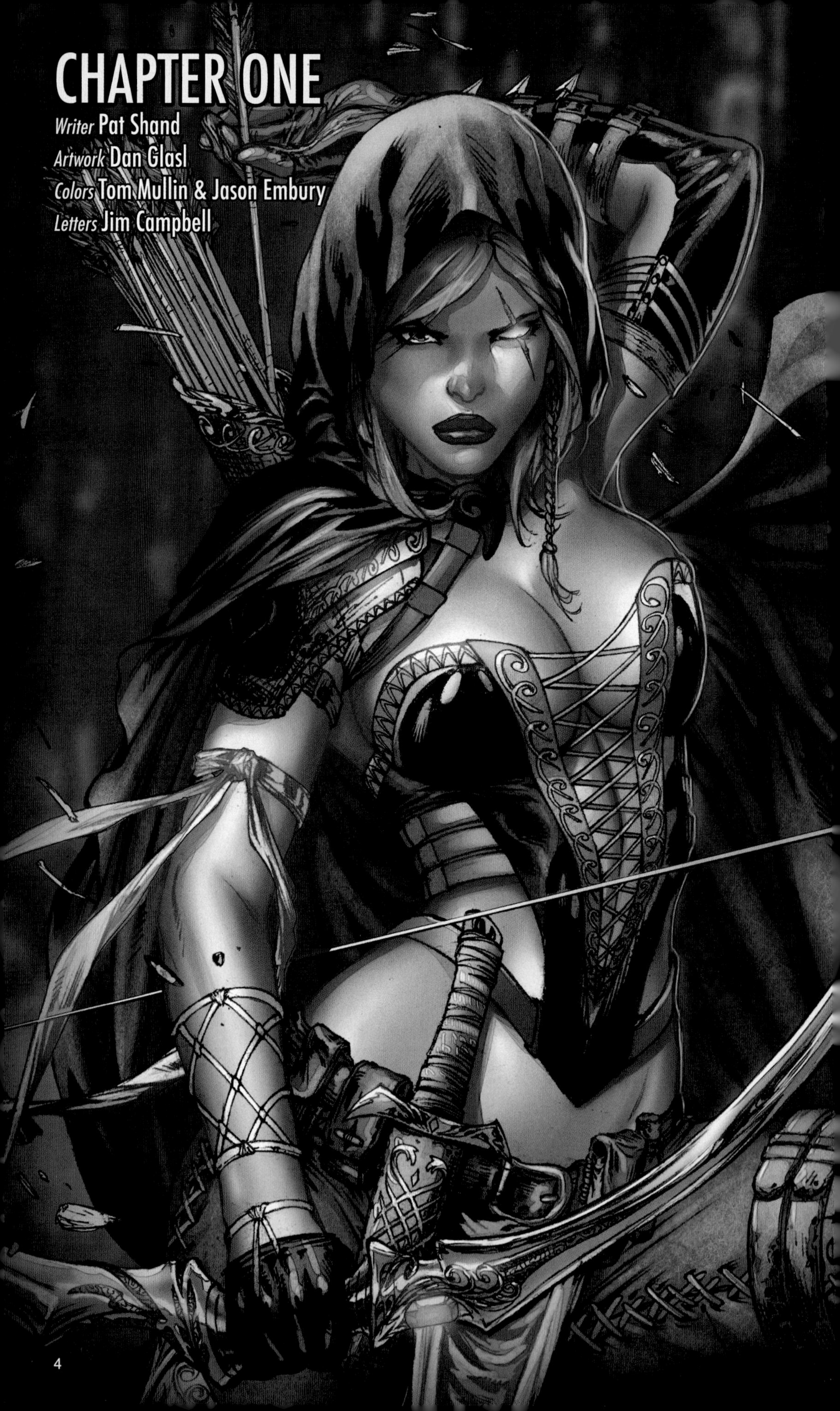

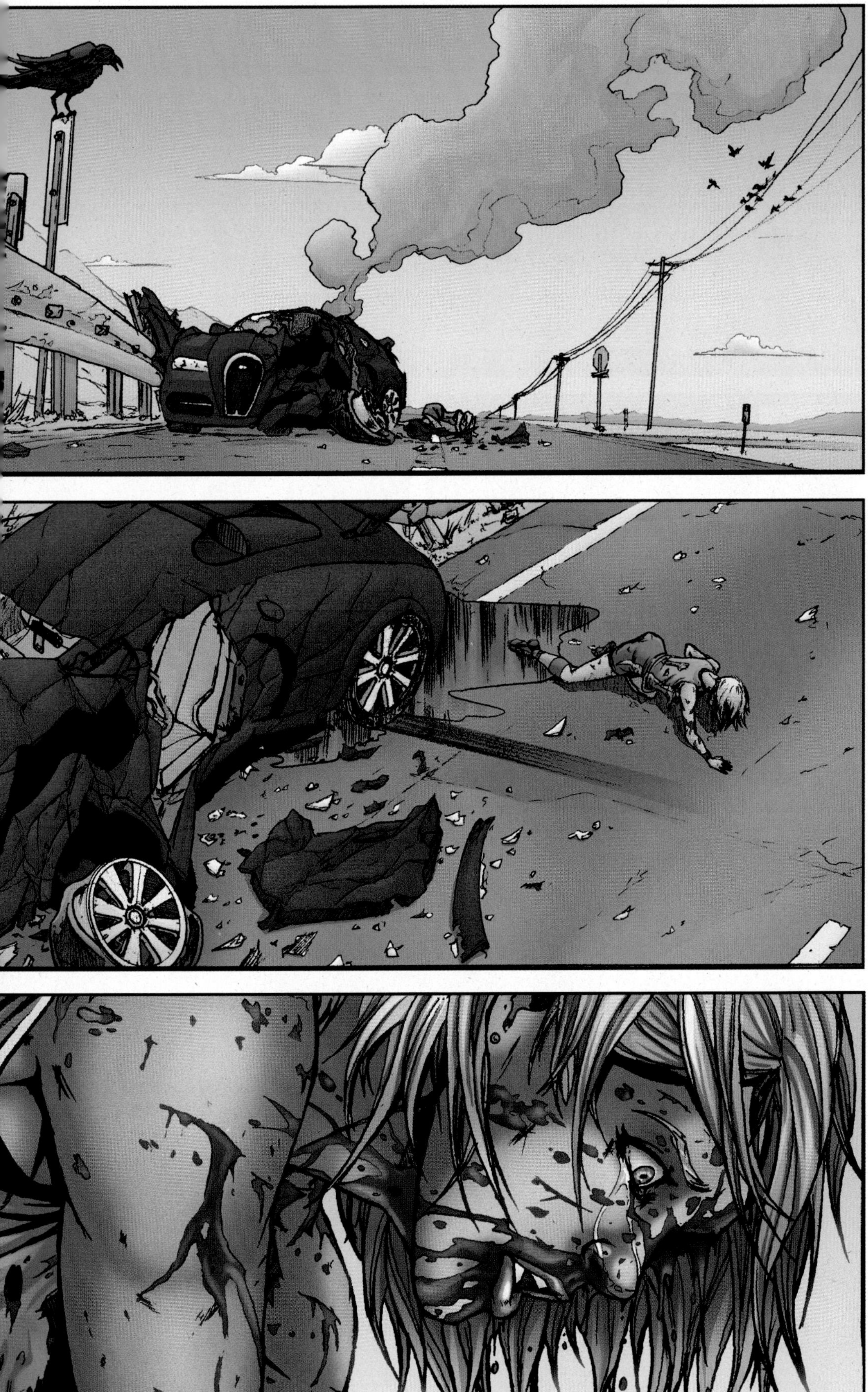
THIS IS HOW IT STARTS.

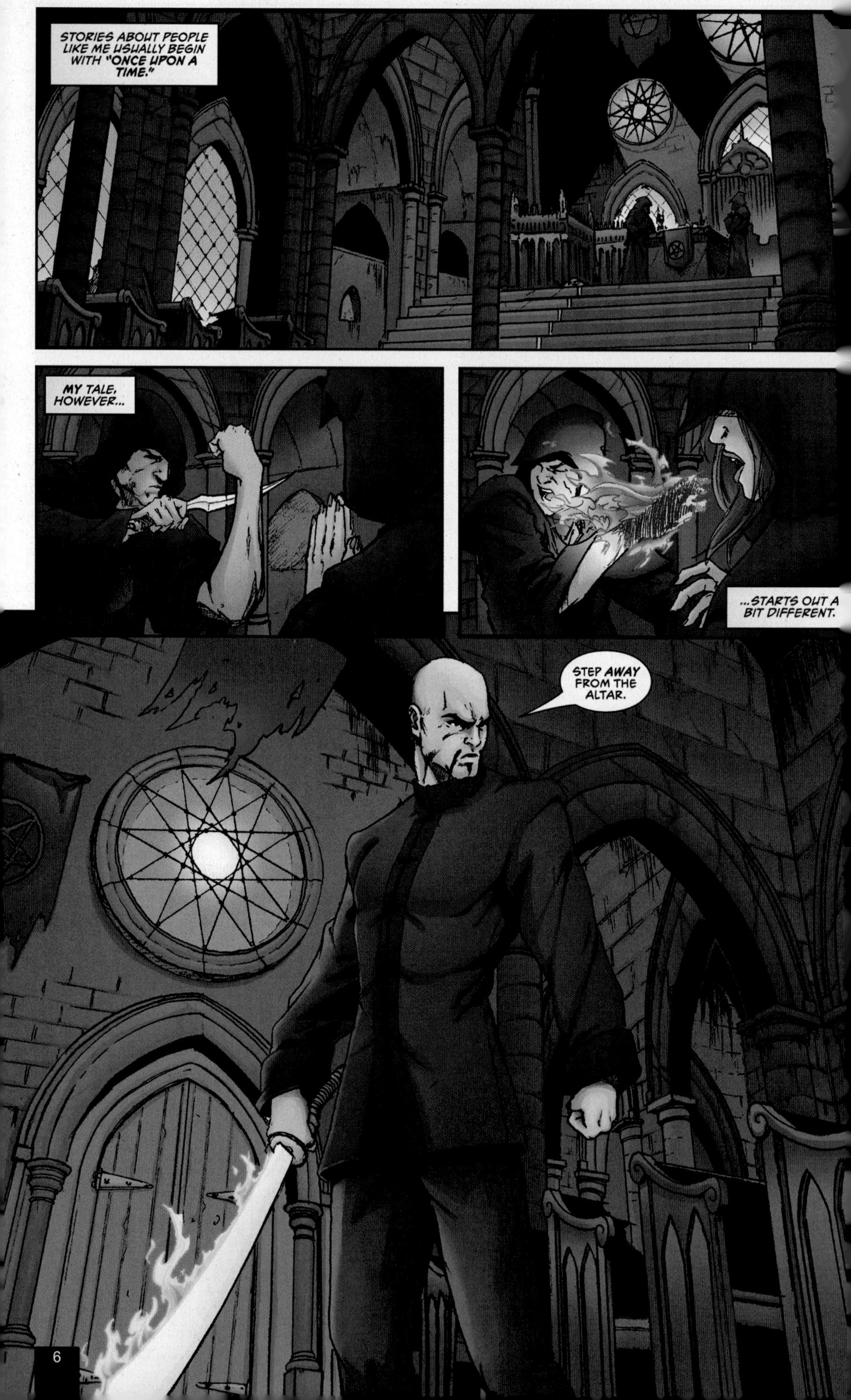
STORIES ABOUT PEOPLE LIKE ME USUALLY BEGIN WITH "ONCE UPON A TIME."
MY TALE, HOWEVER...
...STARTS OUT A BIT DIFFERENT.
STEP AWAY FROM THE ALTAR.

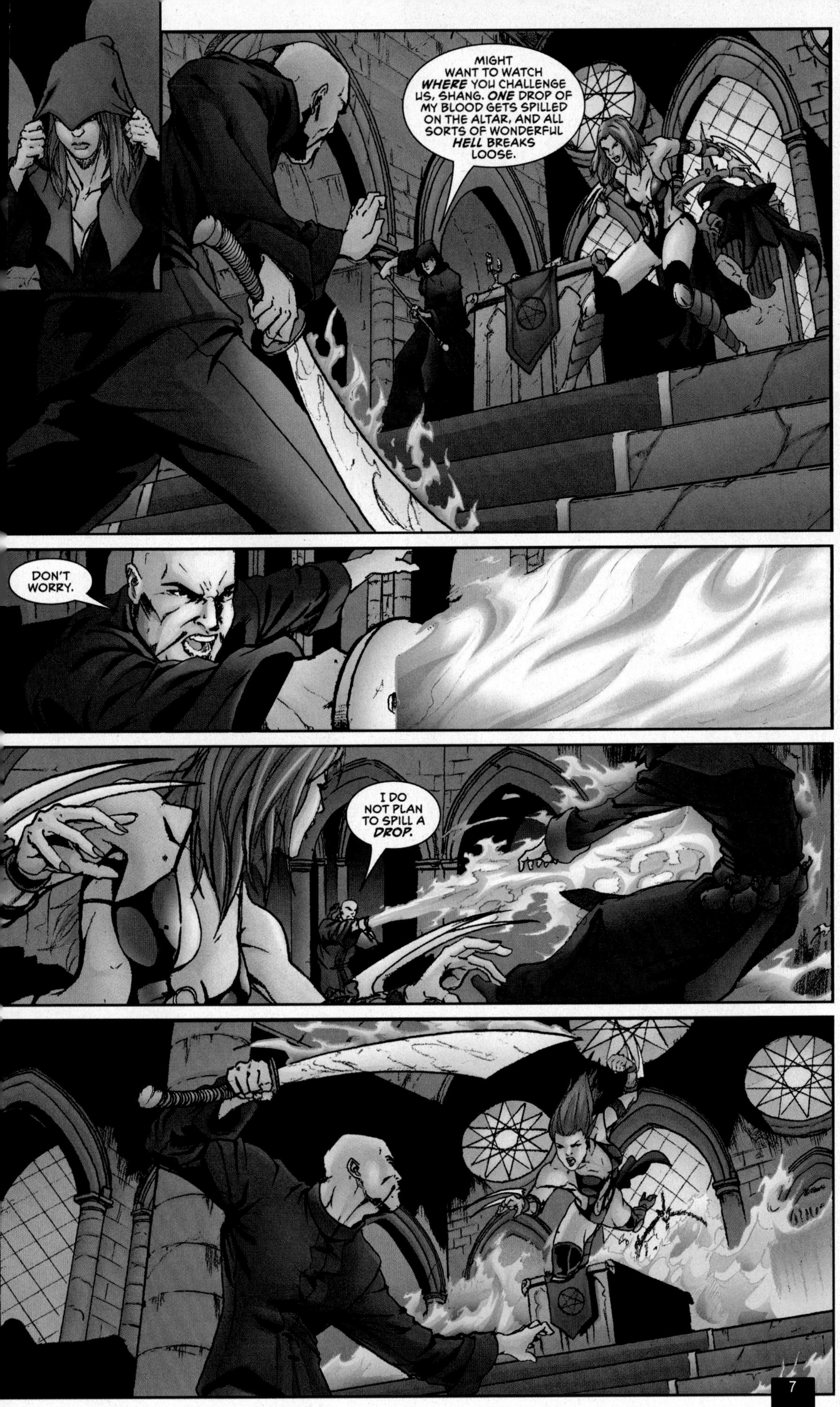
MIGHT WANT TO WATCH WHERE YOU CHALLENGE US, SHANG. ONE DROP OF MY BLOOD GETS SPILLED ON THE ALTAR, AND ALL SORTS OF WONDERFUL HELL BREAKS LOOSE.
DON'T WORRY.
I DO NOT PLAN TO SPILL A DROP.

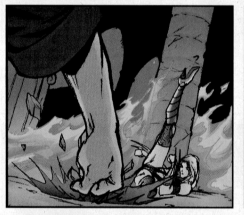

UHF.

FOR A MAN SO INTENT ON BRINGING *PEACE* TO THIS REALM, THE TRAIL OF *BODIES* YOU LEAVE BEHIND IS *REMARKABLE*.

VIOLENCE IS *NEVER* MY FIRST CHOICE.

KRAASH

WE ALL START OUT THE SAME.

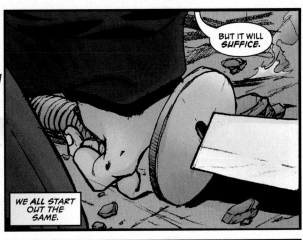

BUT IT WILL SUFFICE.

WAAAAAAH!

EVERYONE IS *PUSHED* INTO THIS WORLD, KICKING AND SCREAMING, COVERED IN *BLOOD*. FIGHTING SOMETHING WE HAVE NO *HOPE* OF BEATING.

SOME OF US NEVER ESCAPE THE BLOOD.

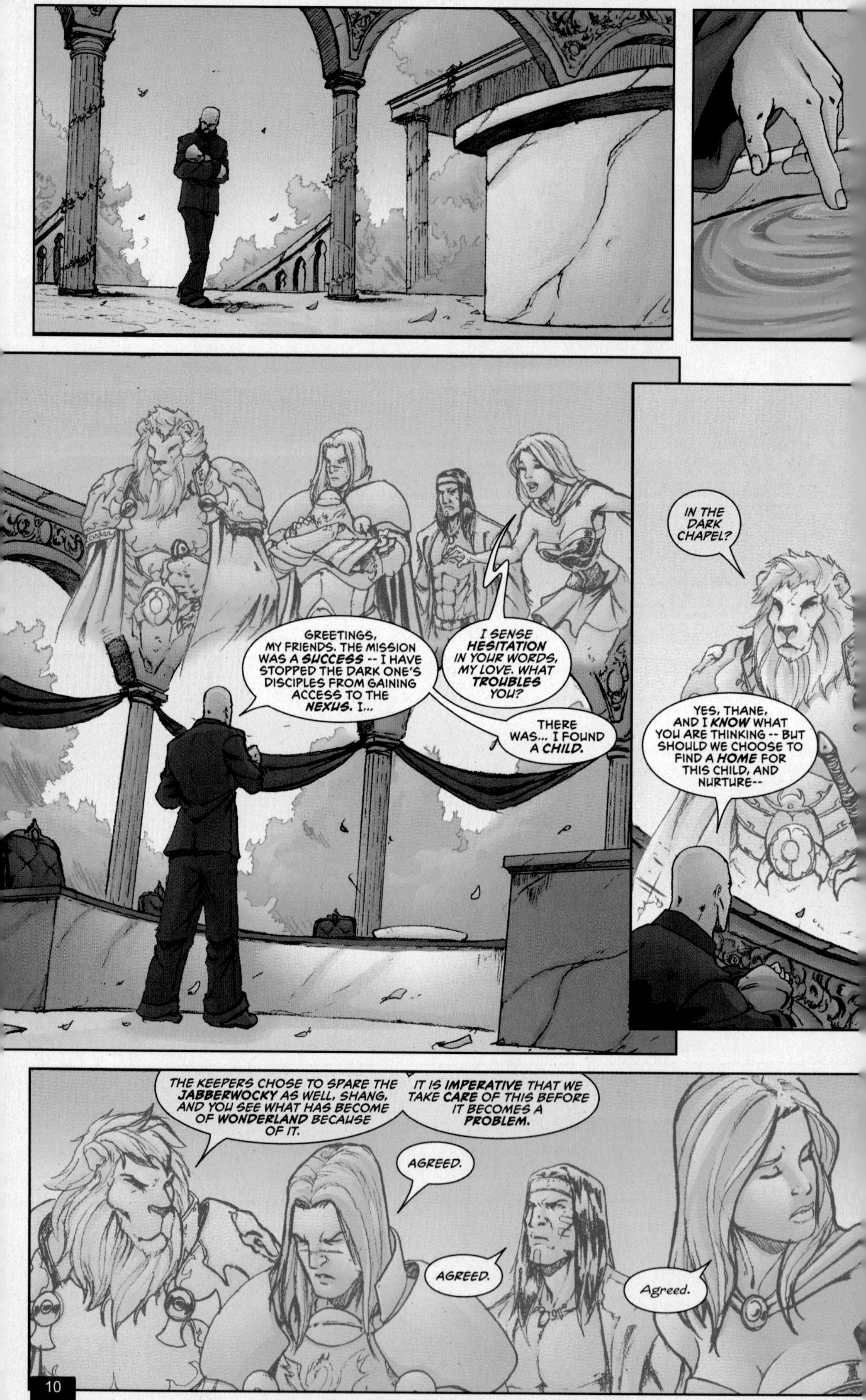
IN THE DARK CHAPEL?
GREETINGS, MY FRIENDS. THE MISSION WAS A SUCCESS -- I HAVE STOPPED THE DARK ONE'S DISCIPLES FROM GAINING ACCESS TO THE NEXUS. I...
I SENSE HESITATION IN YOUR WORDS, MY LOVE. WHAT TROUBLES YOU?
THERE WAS... I FOUND A CHILD.
YES, THANE, AND I KNOW WHAT YOU ARE THINKING -- BUT SHOULD WE CHOOSE TO FIND A HOME FOR THIS CHILD, AND NURTURE--
THE KEEPERS CHOSE TO SPARE THE JABBERWOCKY AS WELL, SHANG, AND YOU SEE WHAT HAS BECOME OF WONDERLAND BECAUSE OF IT.
IT IS IMPERATIVE THAT WE TAKE CARE OF THIS BEFORE IT BECOMES A PROBLEM.
AGREED.
AGREED.
Agreed.

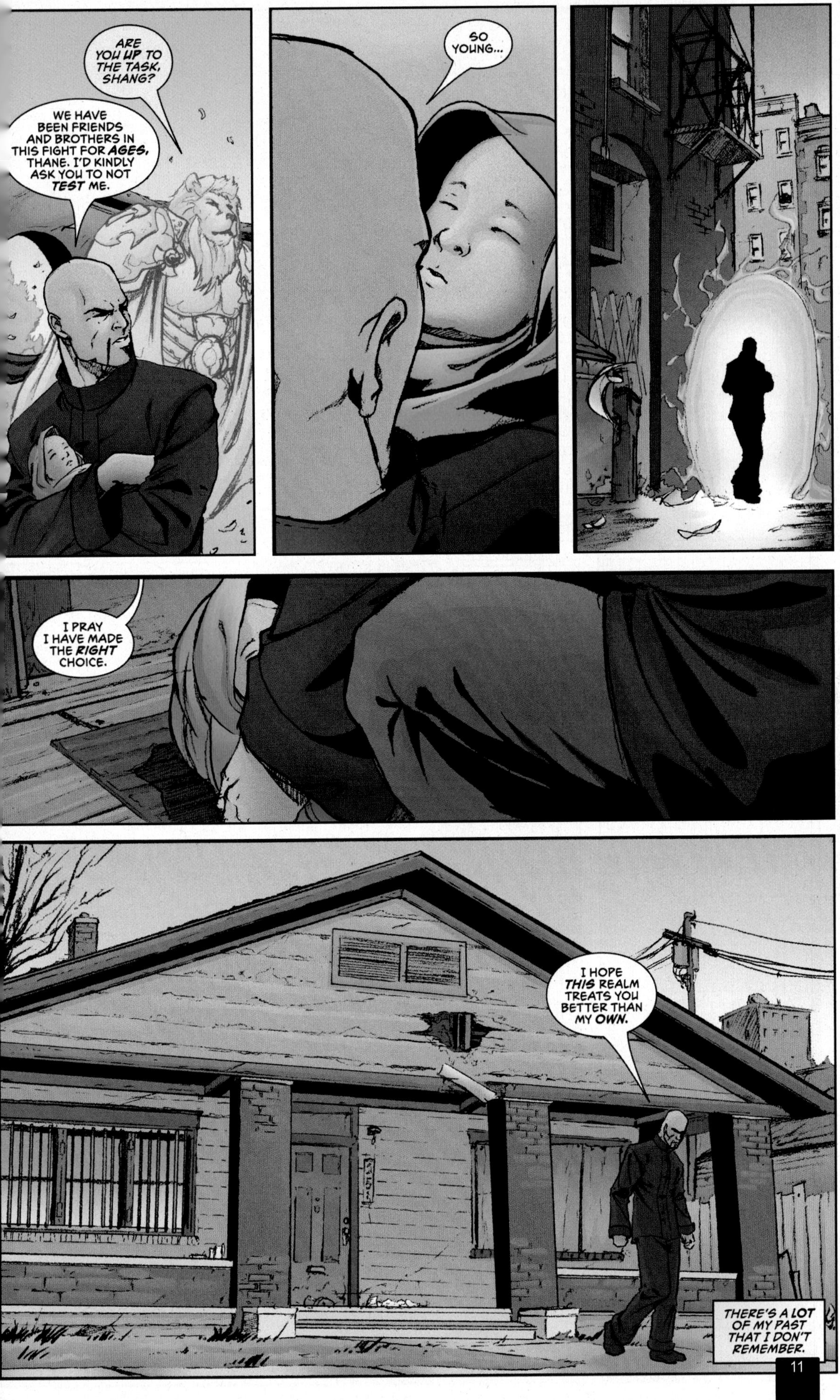
ARE YOU UP TO THE TASK, SHANG?
WE HAVE BEEN FRIENDS AND BROTHERS IN THIS FIGHT FOR AGES, THANE. I'D KINDLY ASK YOU TO NOT TEST ME.
SO YOUNG...
I PRAY I HAVE MADE THE RIGHT CHOICE.
I HOPE THIS REALM TREATS YOU BETTER THAN MY OWN.
THERE'S A LOT OF MY PAST THAT I DON'T REMEMBER.

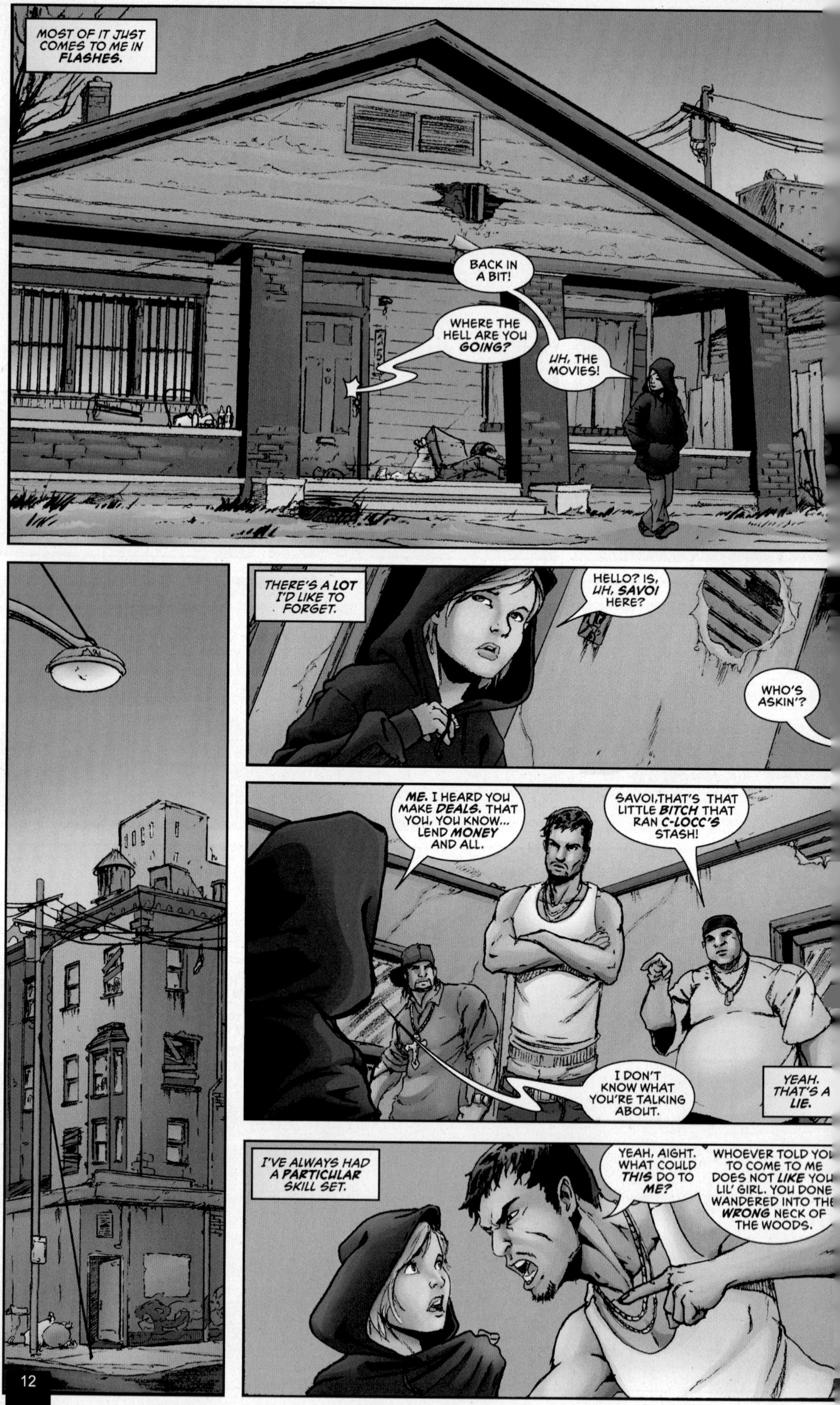

MOST OF IT JUST COMES TO ME IN FLASHES.
BACK IN A BIT!
WHERE THE HELL ARE YOU GOING?
UH, THE MOVIES!
THERE'S A LOT I'D LIKE TO FORGET.
HELLO? IS, UH, SAVOI HERE?
WHO'S ASKIN'?
ME. I HEARD YOU MAKE DEALS. THAT YOU, YOU KNOW... LEND MONEY AND ALL.
SAVOI,THAT'S THAT LITTLE BITCH THAT RAN C-LOCC'S STASH!
I DON'T KNOW WHAT YOU'RE TALKING ABOUT.
YEAH. THAT'S A LIE.
I'VE ALWAYS HAD A PARTICULAR SKILL SET.
YEAH, AIGHT. WHAT COULD THIS DO TO ME?
WHOEVER TOLD YOU TO COME TO ME DOES NOT LIKE YOU LIL' GIRL. YOU DONE WANDERED INTO THE WRONG NECK OF THE WOODS.

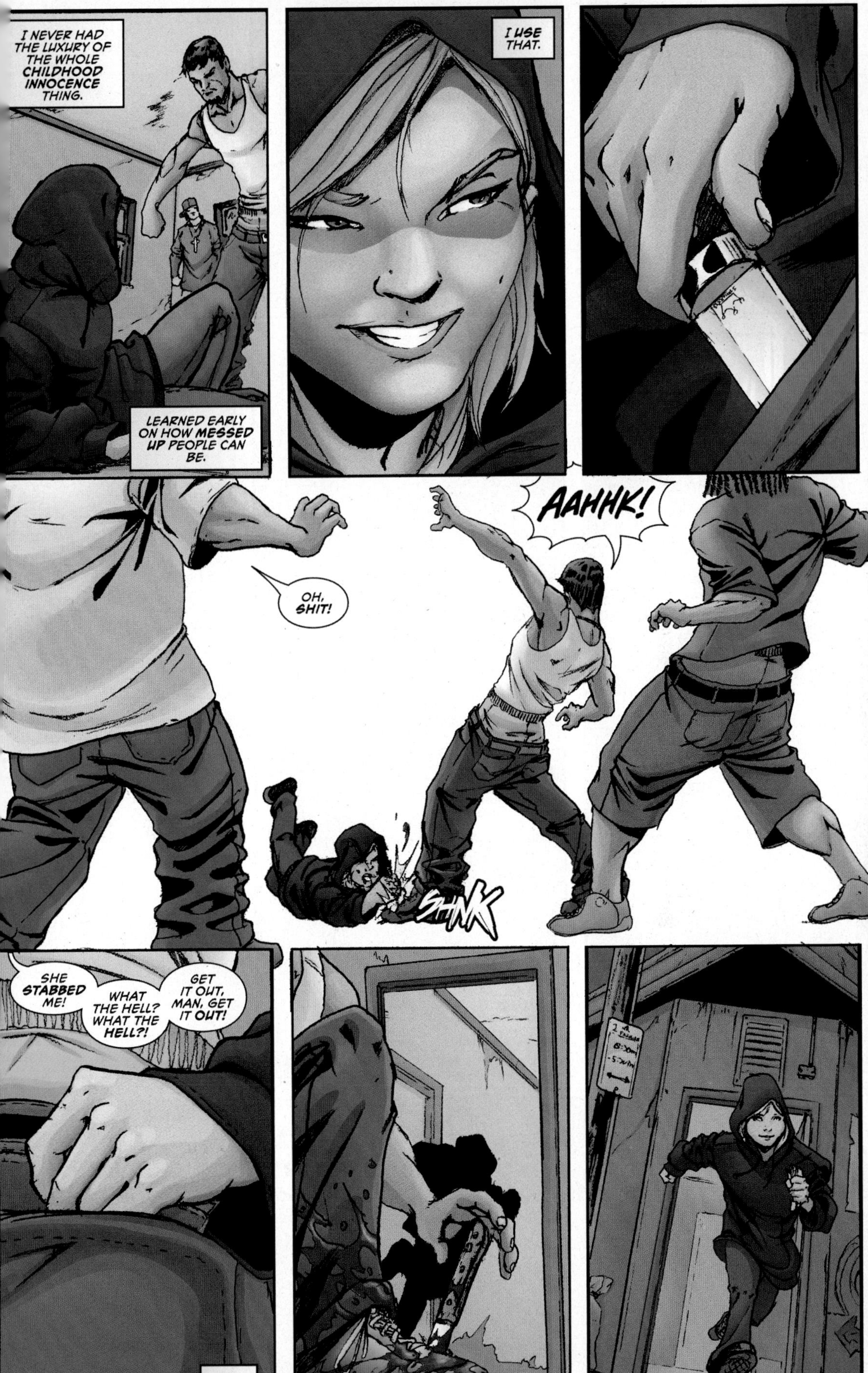
I NEVER HAD THE LUXURY OF THE WHOLE CHILDHOOD INNOCENCE THING.
LEARNED EARLY ON HOW MESSED UP PEOPLE CAN BE.
I USE THAT.
OH, SHIT!
AAHHK!
SHNK
SHE STABBED ME!
WHAT THE HELL? WHAT THE HELL?!
GET IT OUT, MAN, GET IT OUT!
MINE.

THANK YOU.

SPARE SOME CHANGE GOD BLESS

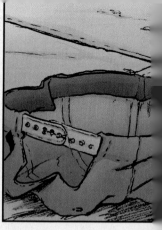

SPARE SOME CHANGE GOD BLESS

AND THAT'S HOW IT WAS FOR A WHILE. I DON'T REMEMBER MOST OF THE DETAILS.

I GOT YOUR MEDICINE, MOM.

OH, MY SWEET GIRL... HOW DID YOU MANAGE?

WHICH IS MOSTLY A GOOD THING.

HERE I AM WONDERING THE SAME GODDAMN THING.

I REMEMBER THINKING I WAS SUPPOSED TO FEEL BAD WHEN I STOLE FROM PEOPLE.

I DIDN'.

I REMEMBER WHEN MY "FATHER" KICKED ME AND MY MOTHER OUT. AT TEN YEARS OLD, I TOLD MY MOM THAT I'D KILL HIM FOR IT ONE DAY. SHE LAUGHED IT OFF AS THE SILLINESS OF A CHILD.

IT WASN'T.

14

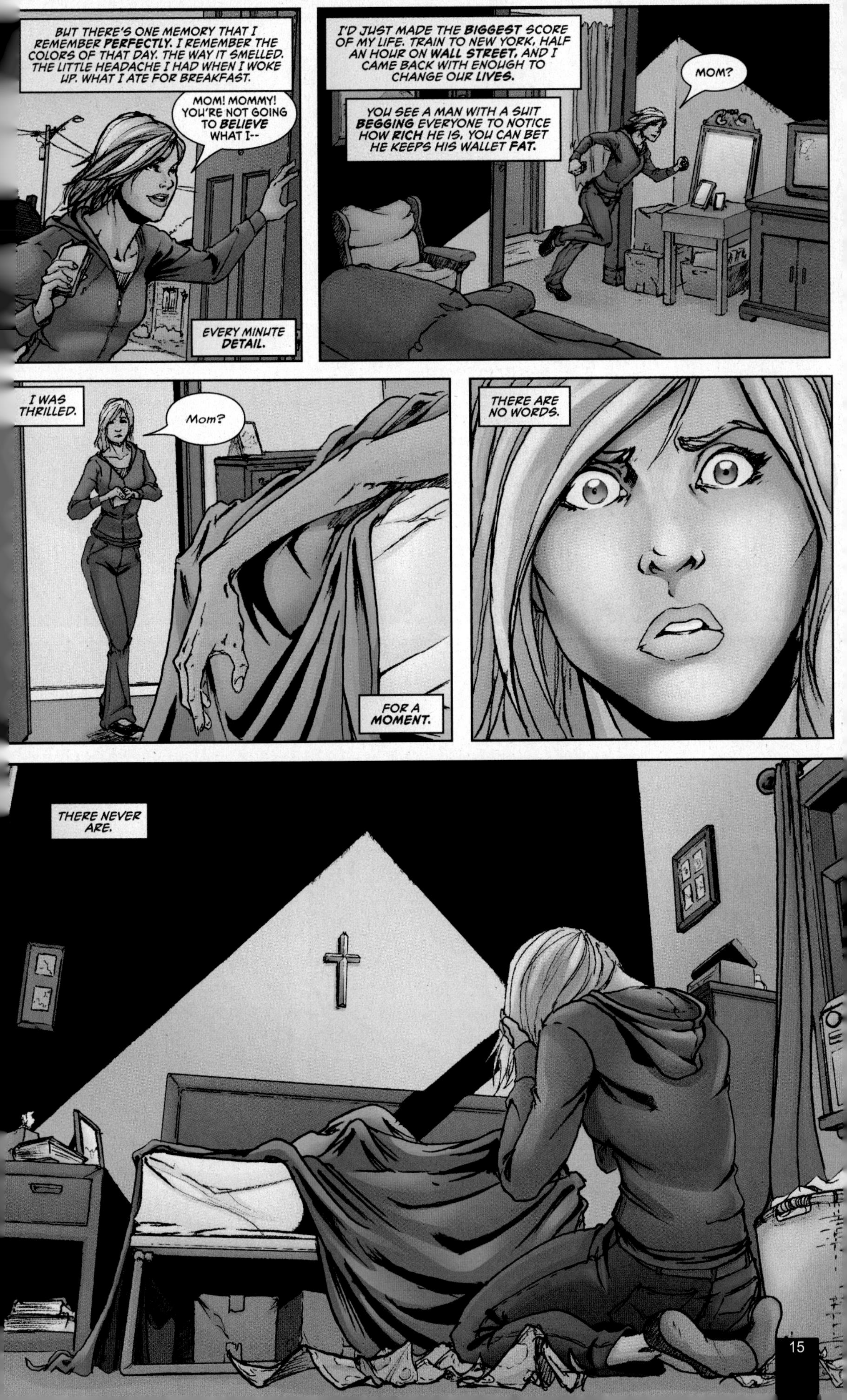
BUT THERE'S ONE MEMORY THAT I REMEMBER PERFECTLY. I REMEMBER THE COLORS OF THAT DAY. THE WAY IT SMELLED. THE LITTLE HEADACHE I HAD WHEN I WOKE UP. WHAT I ATE FOR BREAKFAST.
MOM! MOMMY! YOU'RE NOT GOING TO BELIEVE WHAT I--
EVERY MINUTE DETAIL.
I'D JUST MADE THE BIGGEST SCORE OF MY LIFE. TRAIN TO NEW YORK, HALF AN HOUR ON WALL STREET, AND I CAME BACK WITH ENOUGH TO CHANGE OUR LIVES.
YOU SEE A MAN WITH A SUIT BEGGING EVERYONE TO NOTICE HOW RICH HE IS, YOU CAN BET HE KEEPS HIS WALLET FAT.
MOM?
I WAS THRILLED.
Mom?
FOR A MOMENT.
THERE ARE NO WORDS.
THERE NEVER ARE.

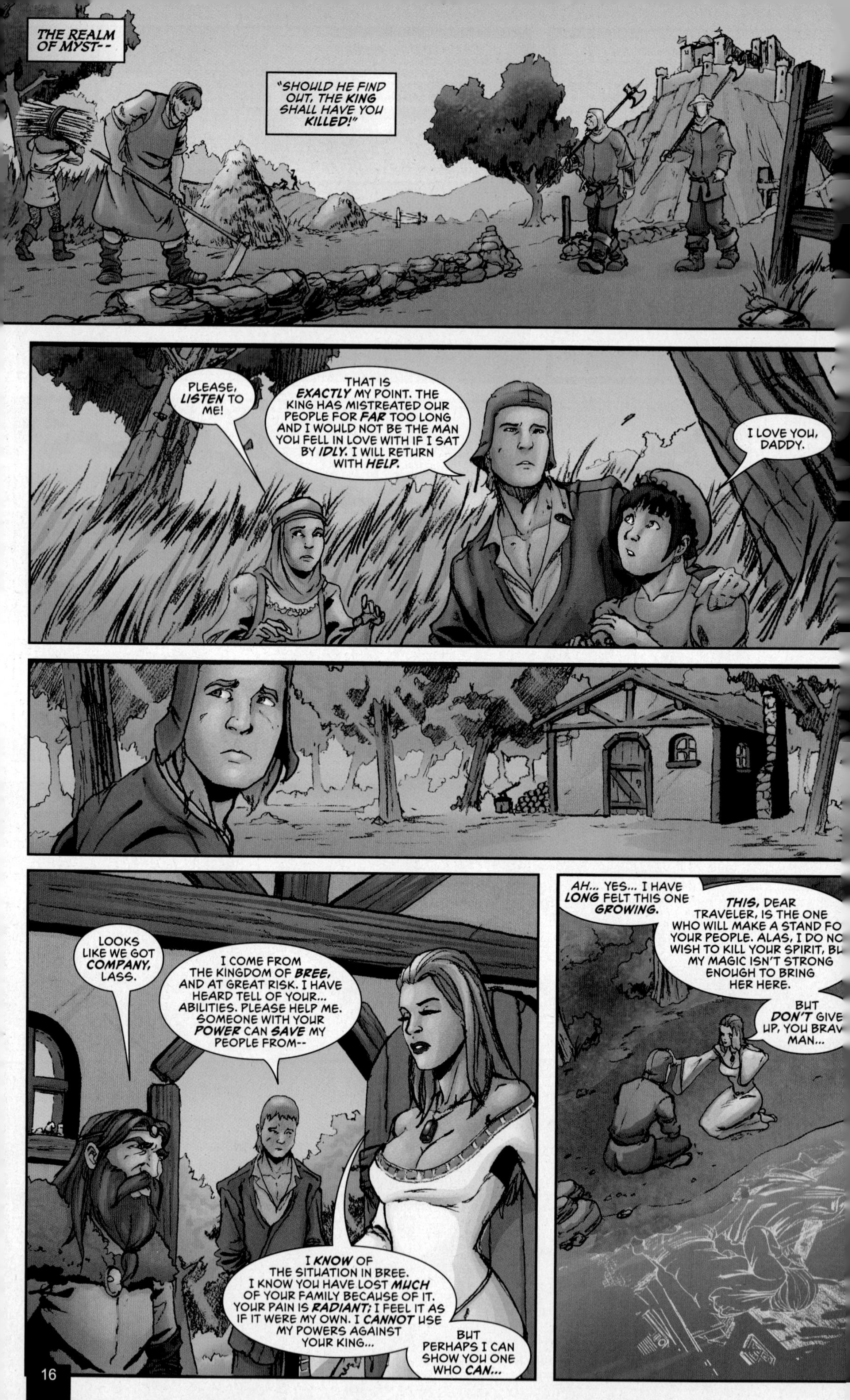
THE REALM OF MYST--
"SHOULD HE FIND OUT, THE KING SHALL HAVE YOU KILLED!"
PLEASE, LISTEN TO ME!
THAT IS EXACTLY MY POINT. THE KING HAS MISTREATED OUR PEOPLE FOR FAR TOO LONG AND I WOULD NOT BE THE MAN YOU FELL IN LOVE WITH IF I SAT BY IDLY. I WILL RETURN WITH HELP.
I LOVE YOU, DADDY.
LOOKS LIKE WE GOT COMPANY, LASS.
I COME FROM THE KINGDOM OF BREE, AND AT GREAT RISK. I HAVE HEARD TELL OF YOUR... ABILITIES. PLEASE HELP ME. SOMEONE WITH YOUR POWER CAN SAVE MY PEOPLE FROM--
I KNOW OF THE SITUATION IN BREE. I KNOW YOU HAVE LOST MUCH OF YOUR FAMILY BECAUSE OF IT. YOUR PAIN IS RADIANT; I FEEL IT AS IF IT WERE MY OWN. I CANNOT USE MY POWERS AGAINST YOUR KING...
BUT PERHAPS I CAN SHOW YOU ONE WHO CAN...
AH... YES... I HAVE LONG FELT THIS ONE GROWING.
THIS, DEAR TRAVELER, IS THE ONE WHO WILL MAKE A STAND FO YOUR PEOPLE. ALAS, I DO NO WISH TO KILL YOUR SPIRIT, BU MY MAGIC ISN'T STRONG ENOUGH TO BRING HER HERE.
BUT DON'T GIVE UP, YOU BRAV MAN...

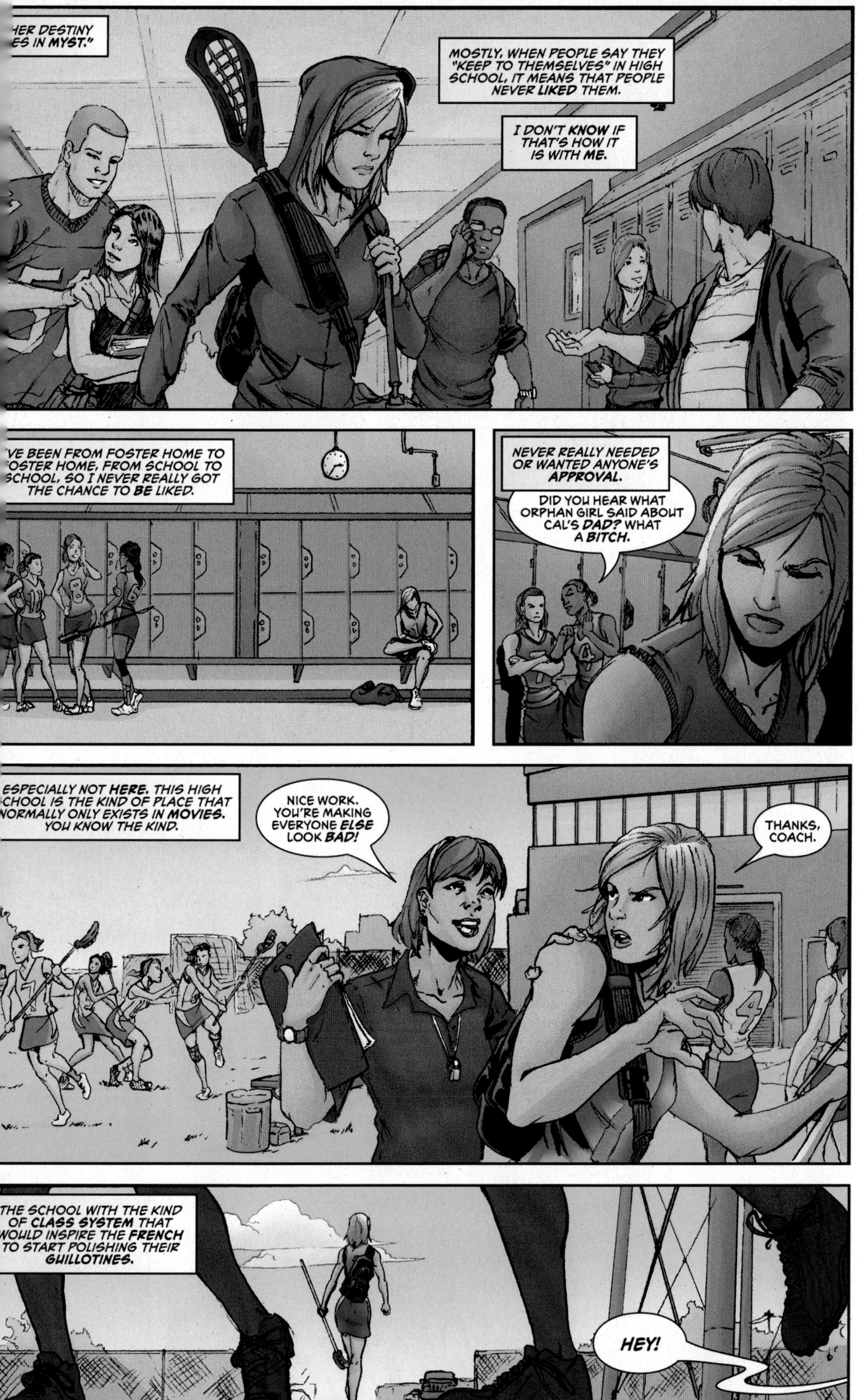
HER DESTINY ES IN MYST."
MOSTLY, WHEN PEOPLE SAY THEY "KEEP TO THEMSELVES" IN HIGH SCHOOL, IT MEANS THAT PEOPLE NEVER LIKED THEM.
I DON'T KNOW IF THAT'S HOW IT IS WITH ME.
'VE BEEN FROM FOSTER HOME TO FOSTER HOME, FROM SCHOOL TO SCHOOL, SO I NEVER REALLY GOT THE CHANCE TO BE LIKED.
NEVER REALLY NEEDED OR WANTED ANYONE'S APPROVAL.
DID YOU HEAR WHAT ORPHAN GIRL SAID ABOUT CAL'S DAD? WHAT A BITCH.
ESPECIALLY NOT HERE. THIS HIGH SCHOOL IS THE KIND OF PLACE THAT NORMALLY ONLY EXISTS IN MOVIES. YOU KNOW THE KIND.
NICE WORK. YOU'RE MAKING EVERYONE ELSE LOOK BAD!
THANKS, COACH.
THE SCHOOL WITH THE KIND OF CLASS SYSTEM THAT WOULD INSPIRE THE FRENCH TO START POLISHING THEIR GUILLOTINES.
HEY!

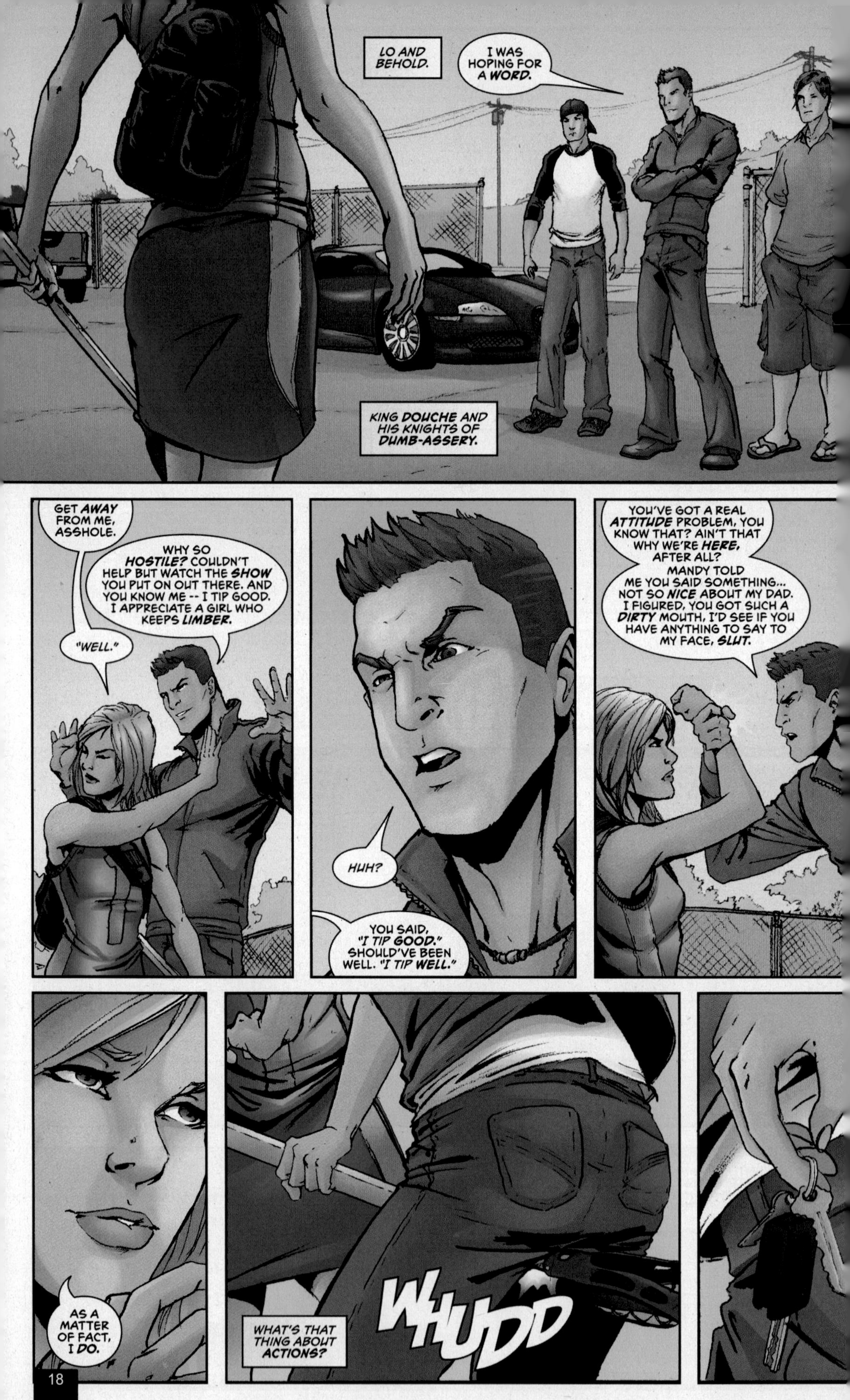
LO AND BEHOLD.
I WAS HOPING FOR A WORD.
KING DOUCHE AND HIS KNIGHTS OF DUMB-ASSERY.
GET AWAY FROM ME, ASSHOLE.
WHY SO HOSTILE? COULDN'T HELP BUT WATCH THE SHOW YOU PUT ON OUT THERE. AND YOU KNOW ME -- I TIP GOOD. I APPRECIATE A GIRL WHO KEEPS LIMBER.
"WELL."
HUH?
YOU SAID, "I TIP GOOD." SHOULD'VE BEEN WELL. "I TIP WELL."
YOU'VE GOT A REAL ATTITUDE PROBLEM, YOU KNOW THAT? AIN'T THAT WHY WE'RE HERE, AFTER ALL?
MANDY TOLD ME YOU SAID SOMETHING... NOT SO NICE ABOUT MY DAD. I FIGURED, YOU GOT SUCH A DIRTY MOUTH, I'D SEE IF YOU HAVE ANYTHING TO SAY TO MY FACE, SLUT.
AS A MATTER OF FACT, I DO.
WHAT'S THAT THING ABOUT ACTIONS?
WHUDD

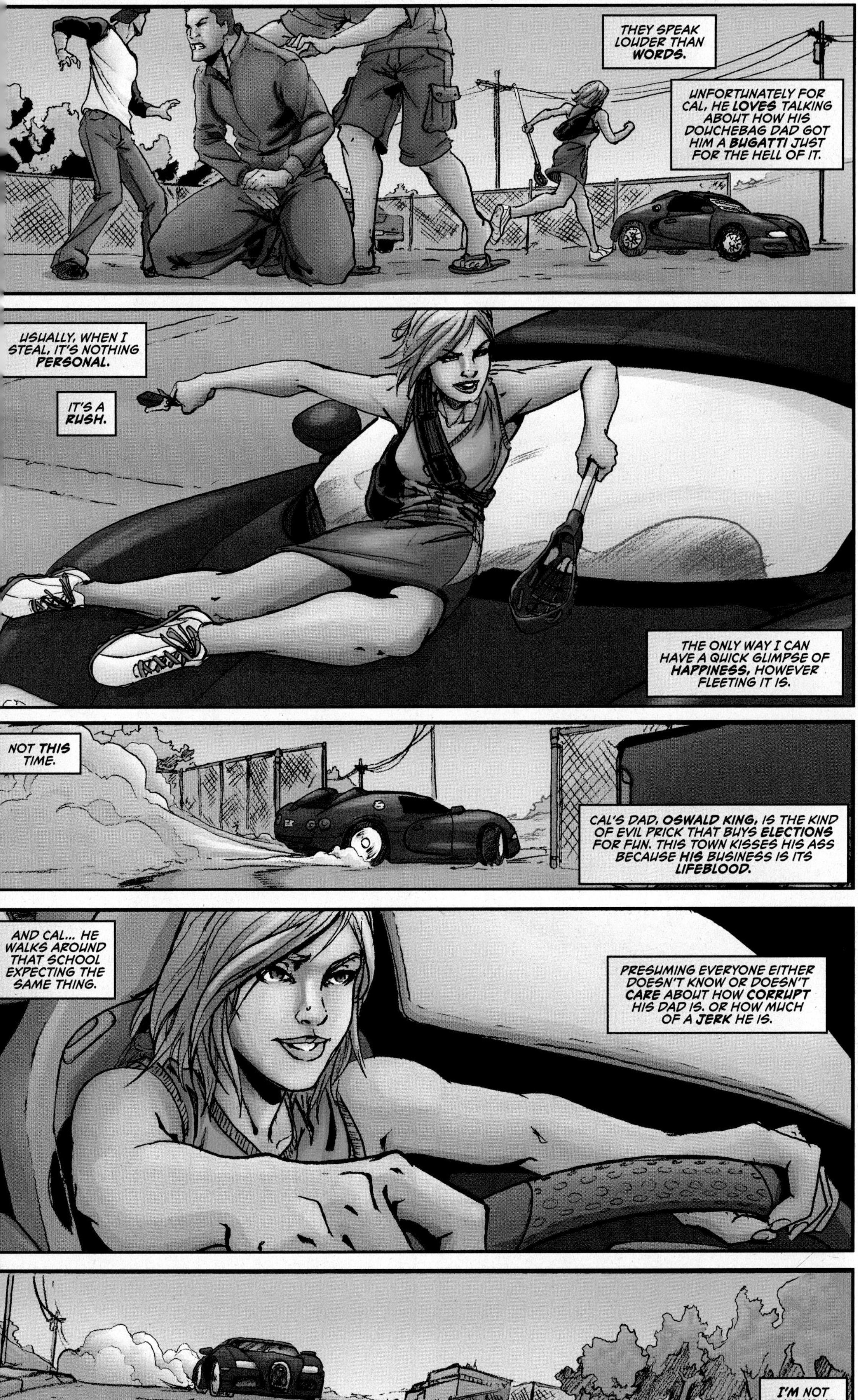
THEY SPEAK LOUDER THAN WORDS.
UNFORTUNATELY FOR CAL, HE LOVES TALKING ABOUT HOW HIS DOUCHEBAG DAD GOT HIM A BUGATTI JUST FOR THE HELL OF IT.
USUALLY, WHEN I STEAL, IT'S NOTHING PERSONAL.
IT'S A RUSH.
THE ONLY WAY I CAN HAVE A QUICK GLIMPSE OF HAPPINESS, HOWEVER FLEETING IT IS.
NOT THIS TIME.
CAL'S DAD, OSWALD KING, IS THE KIND OF EVIL PRICK THAT BUYS ELECTIONS FOR FUN. THIS TOWN KISSES HIS ASS BECAUSE HIS BUSINESS IS ITS LIFEBLOOD.
AND CAL... HE WALKS AROUND THAT SCHOOL EXPECTING THE SAME THING.
PRESUMING EVERYONE EITHER DOESN'T KNOW OR DOESN'T CARE ABOUT HOW CORRUPT HIS DAD IS. OR HOW MUCH OF A JERK HE IS.
I'M NOT EVERYONE.

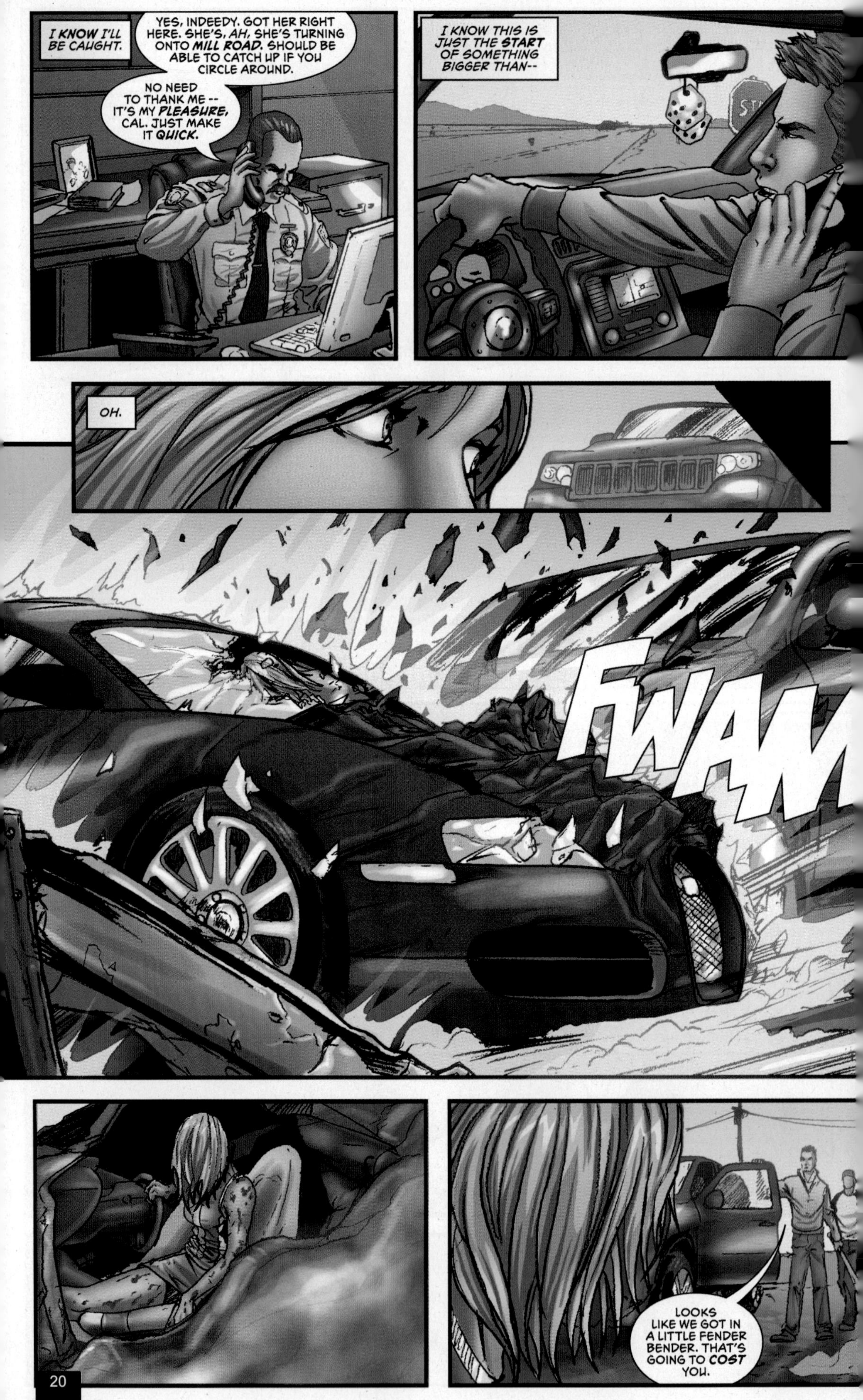
I KNOW I'LL BE CAUGHT.
YES, INDEEDY. GOT HER RIGHT HERE. SHE'S, AH, SHE'S TURNING ONTO MILL ROAD. SHOULD BE ABLE TO CATCH UP IF YOU CIRCLE AROUND.
NO NEED TO THANK ME -- IT'S MY PLEASURE, CAL. JUST MAKE IT QUICK.
I KNOW THIS IS JUST THE START OF SOMETHING BIGGER THAN--
OH.
FWAM
LOOKS LIKE WE GOT IN A LITTLE FENDER BENDER. THAT'S GOING TO COST YOU.

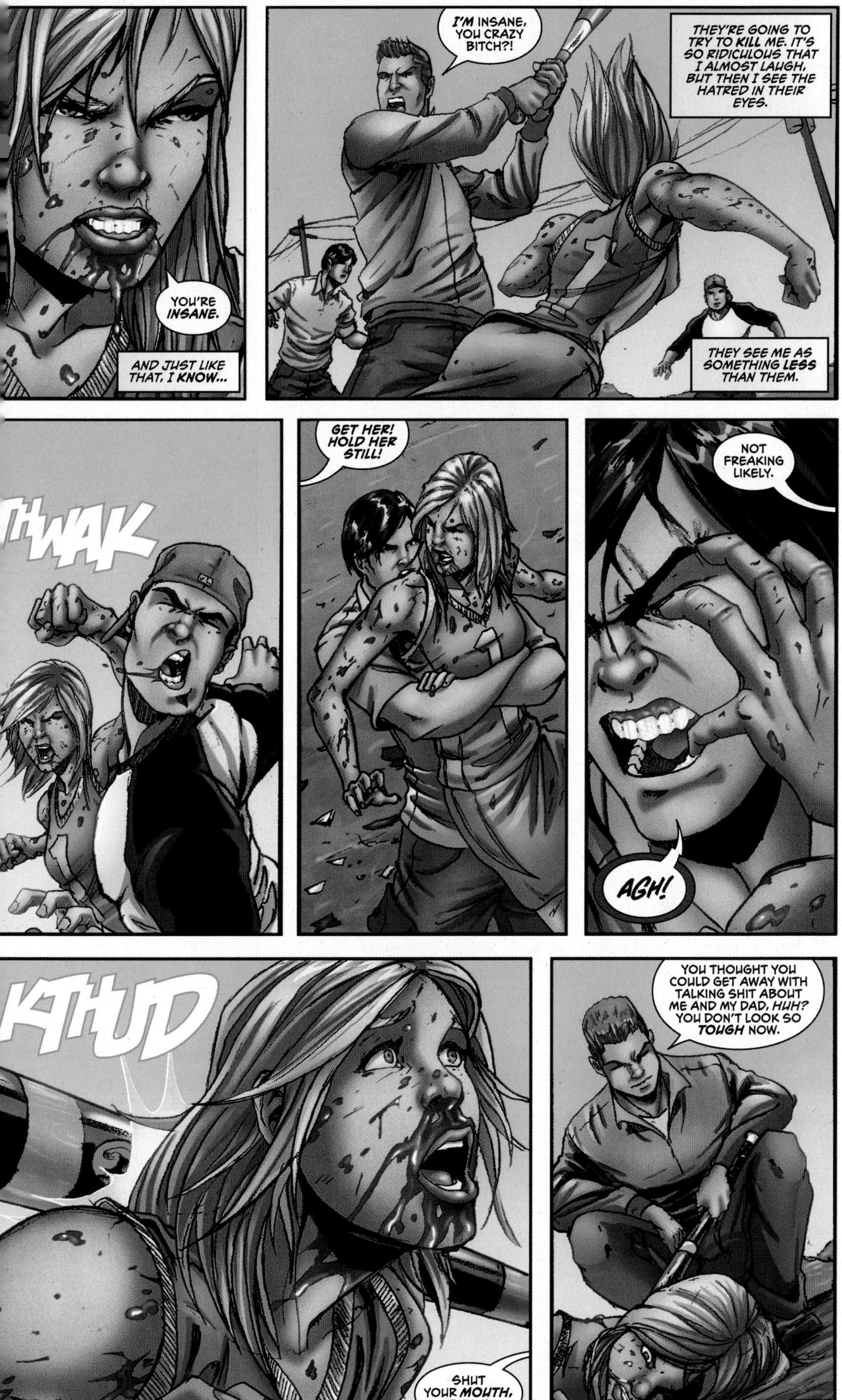
YOU'RE INSANE.
AND JUST LIKE THAT, I KNOW...
I'M INSANE, YOU CRAZY BITCH?!
THEY'RE GOING TO TRY TO KILL ME. IT'S SO RIDICULOUS THAT I ALMOST LAUGH, BUT THEN I SEE THE HATRED IN THEIR EYES.
THEY SEE ME AS SOMETHING LESS THAN THEM.
THWAK
GET HER! HOLD HER STILL!
NOT FREAKING LIKELY.
AGH!
KTHUD
SHUT YOUR MOUTH, BITCH!
YOU THOUGHT YOU COULD GET AWAY WITH TALKING SHIT ABOUT ME AND MY DAD, HUH? YOU DON'T LOOK SO TOUGH NOW.

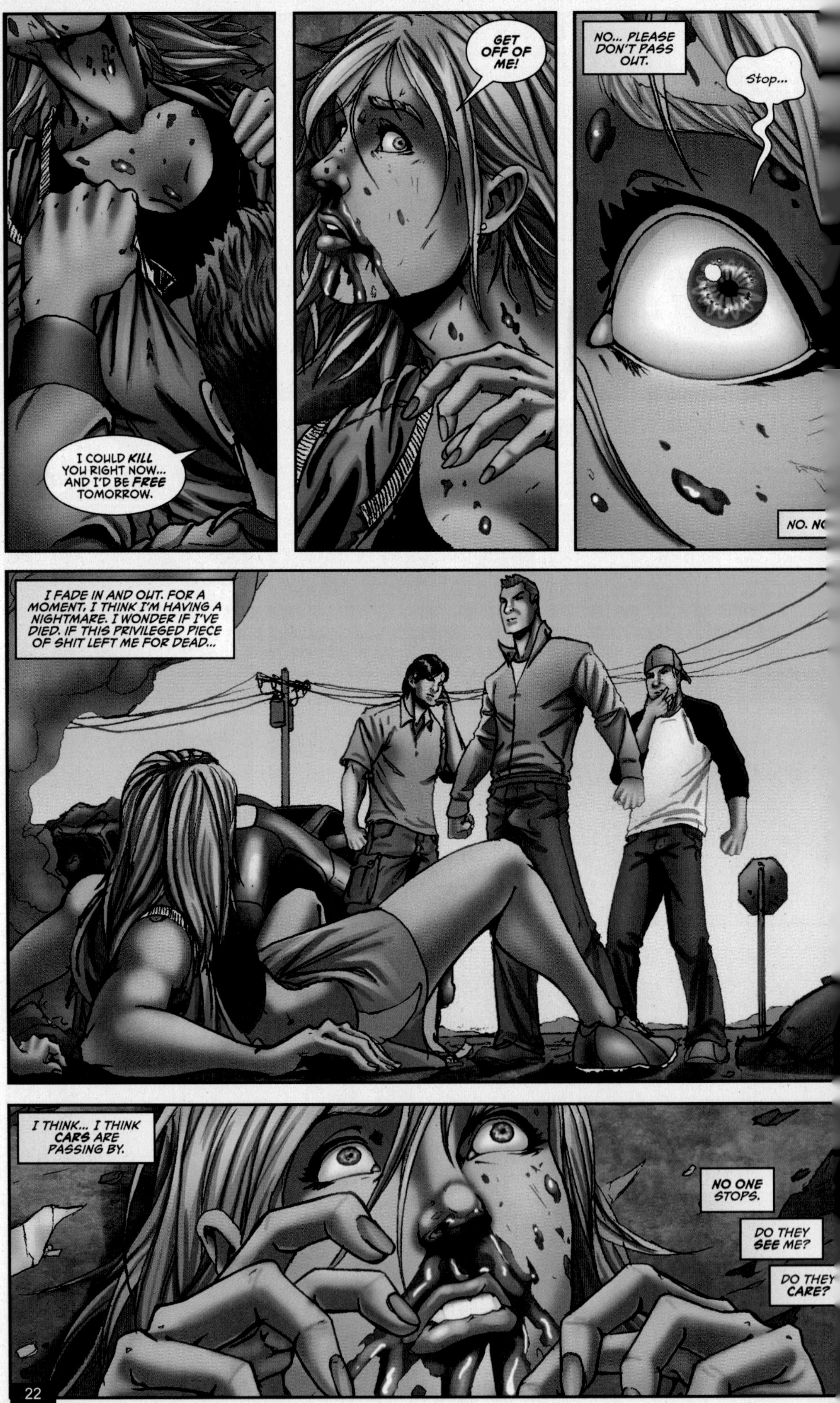
I COULD KILL YOU RIGHT NOW... AND I'D BE FREE TOMORROW.
GET OFF OF ME!
NO... PLEASE DON'T PASS OUT.
Stop...
NO. NO
I FADE IN AND OUT. FOR A MOMENT, I THINK I'M HAVING A NIGHTMARE. I WONDER IF I'VE DIED. IF THIS PRIVILEGED PIECE OF SHIT LEFT ME FOR DEAD...
I THINK... I THINK CARS ARE PASSING BY.
NO ONE STOPS.
DO THEY SEE ME?
DO THEY CARE?

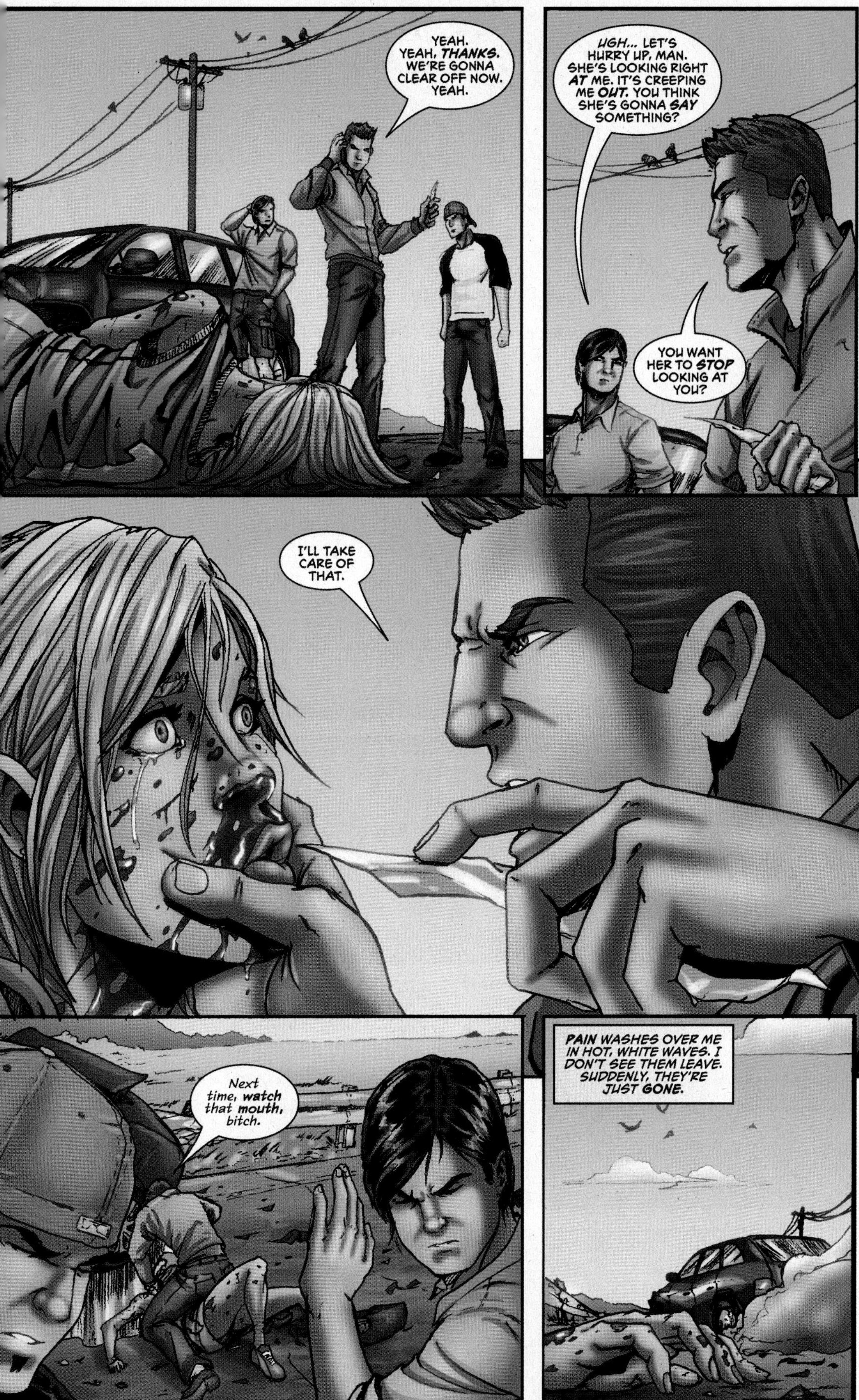
YEAH. YEAH, THANKS. WE'RE GONNA CLEAR OFF NOW. YEAH.
UGH... LET'S HURRY UP, MAN. SHE'S LOOKING RIGHT AT ME. IT'S CREEPING ME OUT. YOU THINK SHE'S GONNA SAY SOMETHING?
YOU WANT HER TO STOP LOOKING AT YOU?
I'LL TAKE CARE OF THAT.
Next time, watch that mouth, bitch.
PAIN WASHES OVER ME IN HOT, WHITE WAVES. I DON'T SEE THEM LEAVE. SUDDENLY, THEY'RE JUST GONE.
I FEEL LIKE A GHOST.

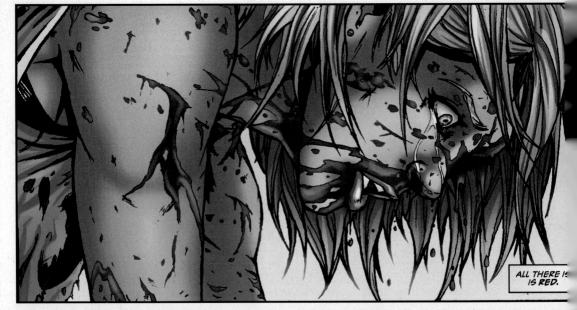

ALL THERE IS IS RED.

MISS? MISS, ARE YOU OKAY?

QUIET, MAN. YOU *KNOW* WHO DID THIS.

JESUS. *LOOK* AT HER, DELTON. THIS WASN'T AN *ACCIDENT.*

THEY THINK CAN'T HEAR THEM.

THIS ISN'T *RIGHT.* I CAN'T--

I *KNOW* IT AIN'T *RIGHT,* MAN. BUT DO YOU WANT TO GET *FIRED?*

MY SON JUST GOT *BRACES* PUT IN -- YOU KNOW HOW MUCH BRACES *COST?*

HOW DO YOU THINK THINGS ARE GONNA BE WITH *GRACE* IF YOU LOSE YOUR *JOB?* THERE AIN'T NO WAY *AROUND* THIS.

I--I GUESS YOU'RE RIGHT. IT'S JUST... POOR GIRL.

I KNOW. I *KNOW.*

THEY'RE WRONG.

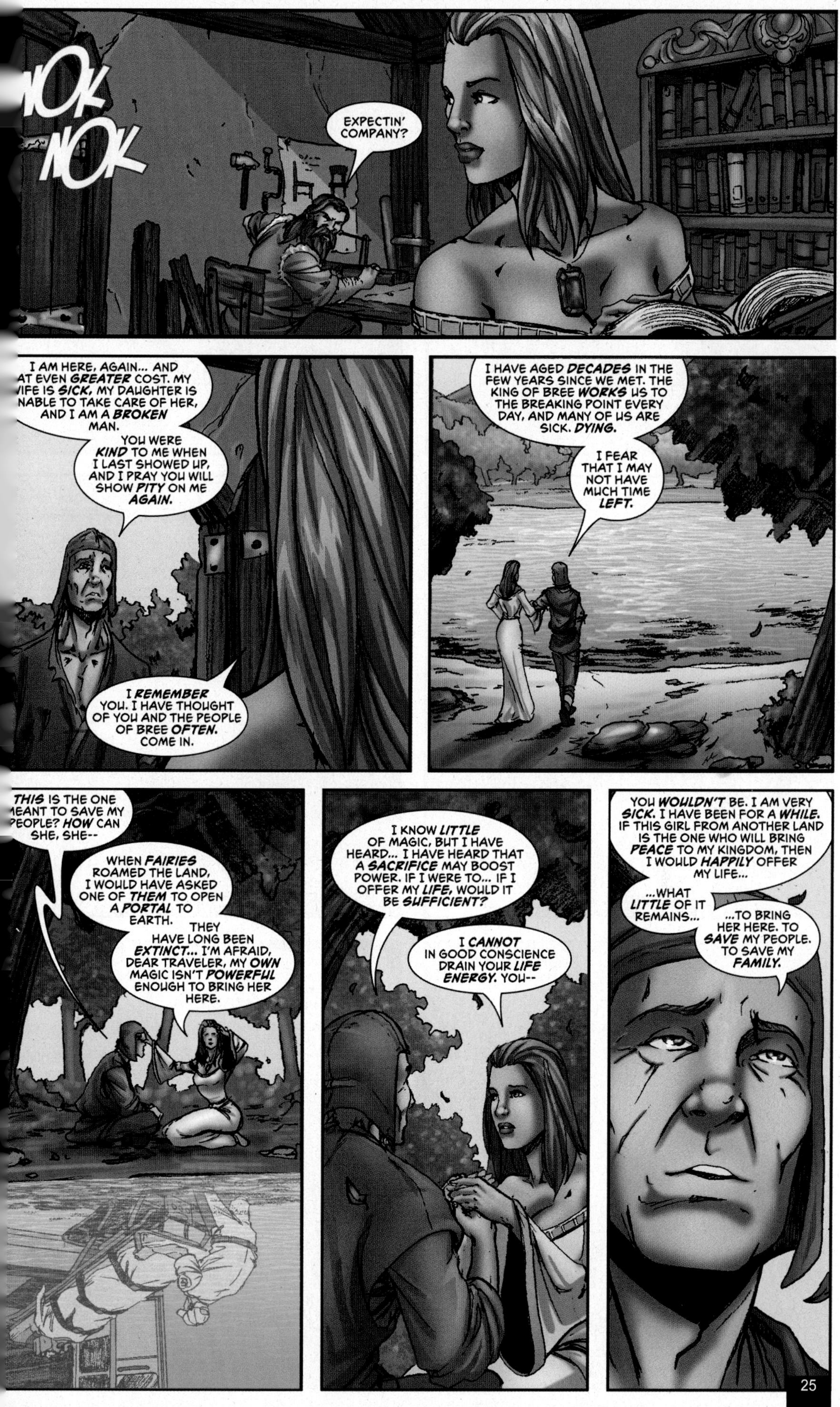
NOK NOK
EXPECTIN' COMPANY?
I AM HERE, AGAIN... AND AT EVEN GREATER COST. MY WIFE IS SICK, MY DAUGHTER IS NABLE TO TAKE CARE OF HER, AND I AM A BROKEN MAN.
YOU WERE KIND TO ME WHEN I LAST SHOWED UP, AND I PRAY YOU WILL SHOW PITY ON ME AGAIN.
I REMEMBER YOU. I HAVE THOUGHT OF YOU AND THE PEOPLE OF BREE OFTEN. COME IN.
I HAVE AGED DECADES IN THE FEW YEARS SINCE WE MET. THE KING OF BREE WORKS US TO THE BREAKING POINT EVERY DAY, AND MANY OF US ARE SICK. DYING.
I FEAR THAT I MAY NOT HAVE MUCH TIME LEFT.
THIS IS THE ONE MEANT TO SAVE MY PEOPLE? HOW CAN SHE, SHE--
WHEN FAIRIES ROAMED THE LAND, I WOULD HAVE ASKED ONE OF THEM TO OPEN A PORTAL TO EARTH.
THEY HAVE LONG BEEN EXTINCT... I'M AFRAID, DEAR TRAVELER, MY OWN MAGIC ISN'T POWERFUL ENOUGH TO BRING HER HERE.
I KNOW LITTLE OF MAGIC, BUT I HAVE HEARD... I HAVE HEARD THAT A SACRIFICE MAY BOOST POWER. IF I WERE TO... IF I OFFER MY LIFE, WOULD IT BE SUFFICIENT?
I CANNOT IN GOOD CONSCIENCE DRAIN YOUR LIFE ENERGY. YOU--
YOU WOULDN'T BE. I AM VERY SICK. I HAVE BEEN FOR A WHILE. IF THIS GIRL FROM ANOTHER LAND IS THE ONE WHO WILL BRING PEACE TO MY KINGDOM, THEN I WOULD HAPPILY OFFER MY LIFE...
...WHAT LITTLE OF IT REMAINS...
...TO BRING HER HERE. TO SAVE MY PEOPLE. TO SAVE MY FAMILY.

YOU ARE VERY *BRAVE,* AND YOUR LOVE IS *INSPIRING.* HERE. CLOSE YOUR EYES.

YOU HAVE WORKED VERY HARD.

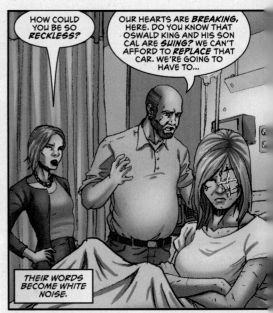

HOW COULD YOU BE SO *RECKLESS?*

OUR HEARTS ARE *BREAKING,* HERE. DO YOU KNOW THAT OSWALD KING AND HIS SON CAL ARE *SUING?* WE CAN'T AFFORD TO *REPLACE* THAT CAR. WE'RE GOING TO HAVE TO...

THEIR WORDS BECOME WHITE NOISE.

IT IS TIME TO *REST.*

THEY'RE SAYING THINGS ABOUT ME. WEAVING THEIR LITTLE *STORIES.*

I TAKE IT ALL IN. REMEMBER IT ALL.

I HAVEN'T SAID A *WORD* SINCE IT HAPPENED.

SECOND TIME IN MY LIFE WORDS HAVE *FAILED* ME.

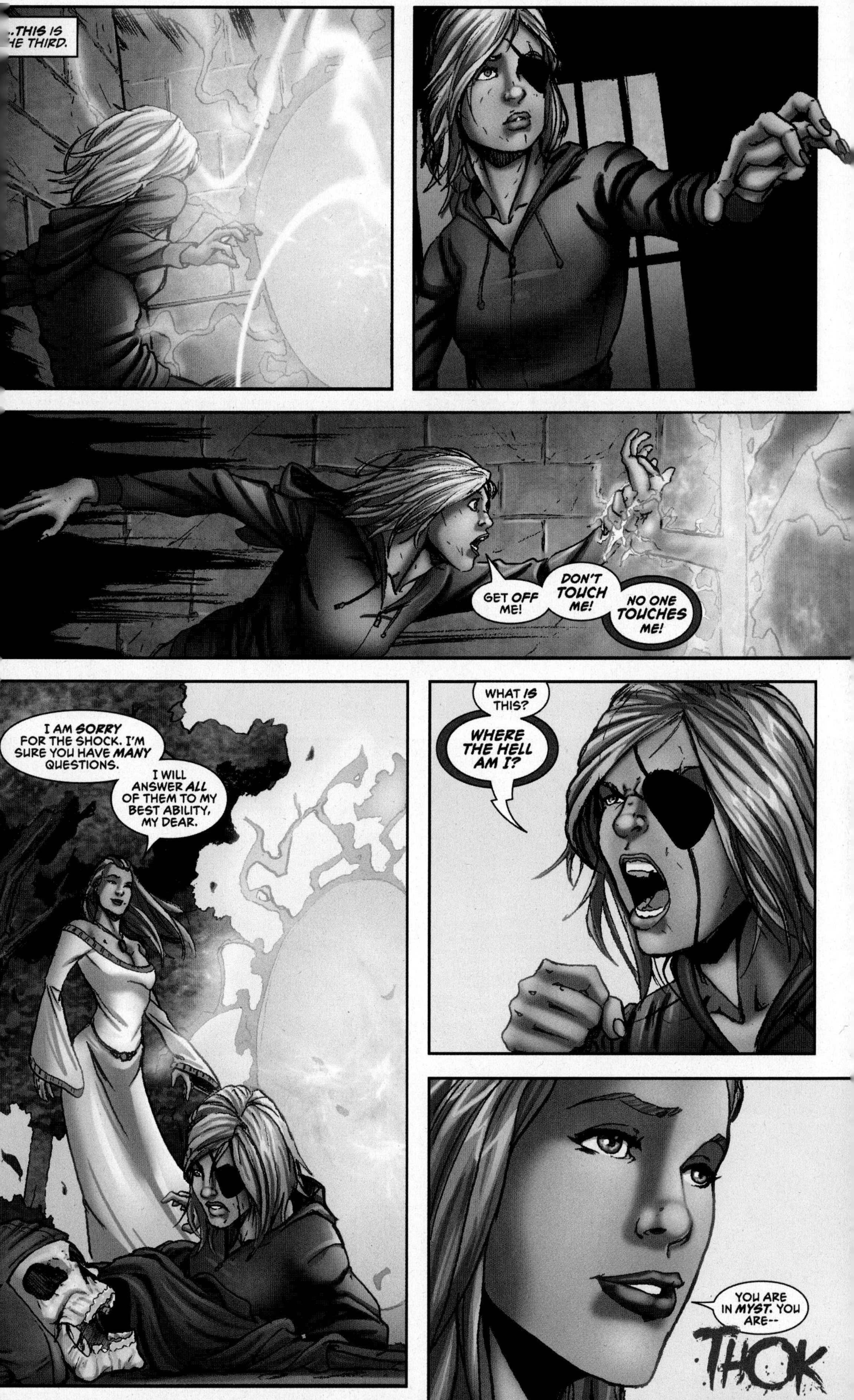

...THIS IS
THE THIRD.
GET OFF ME!
DON'T TOUCH ME!
NO ONE TOUCHES ME!
I AM SORRY FOR THE SHOCK. I'M SURE YOU HAVE MANY QUESTIONS.
I WILL ANSWER ALL OF THEM TO MY BEST ABILITY, MY DEAR.
WHAT IS THIS?
WHERE THE HELL AM I?
YOU ARE IN MYST. YOU ARE--
THOK

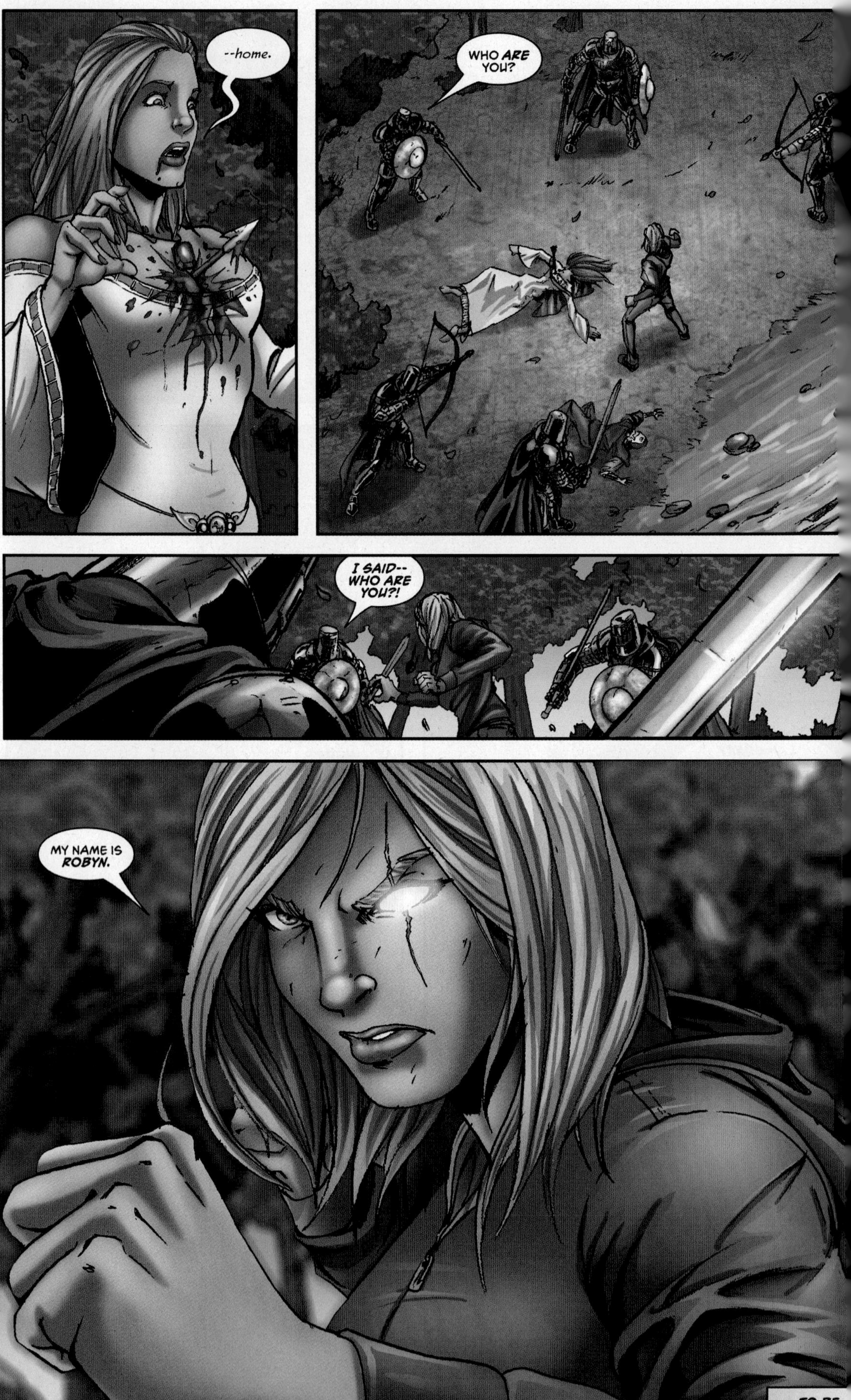
--home.
WHO *ARE* YOU?
I SAID-- WHO ARE YOU?!
MY NAME IS *ROBYN.*
TO BE CONTINUE

# Grimm Fairy Tales presents:

# ROBYN HOOD

## ORIGIN

# CHAPTER TWO

*Writer* Pat Shand
*Artwork* Larry Watts
*Colors* Andrew Elder
*Letters* Jim Campbell

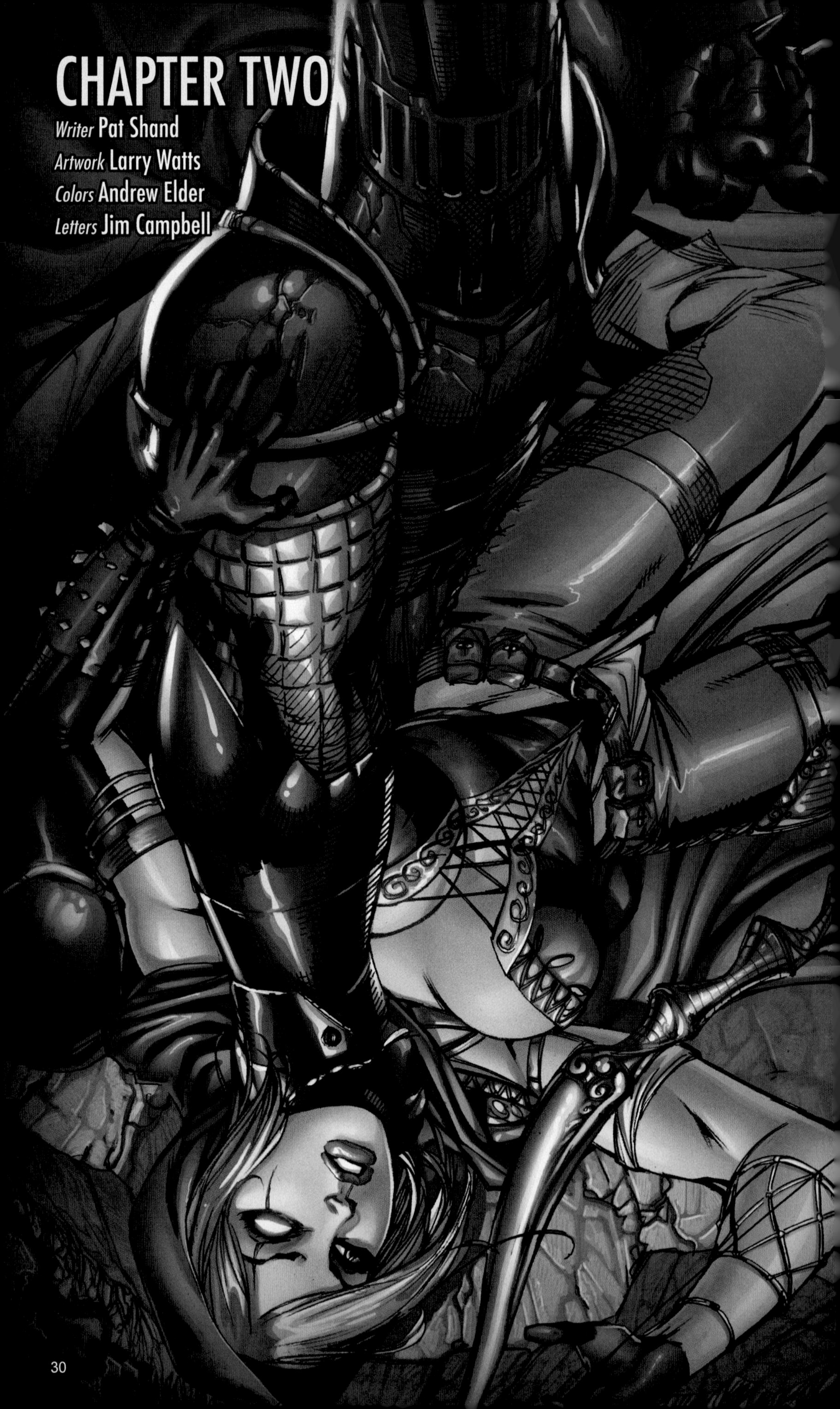

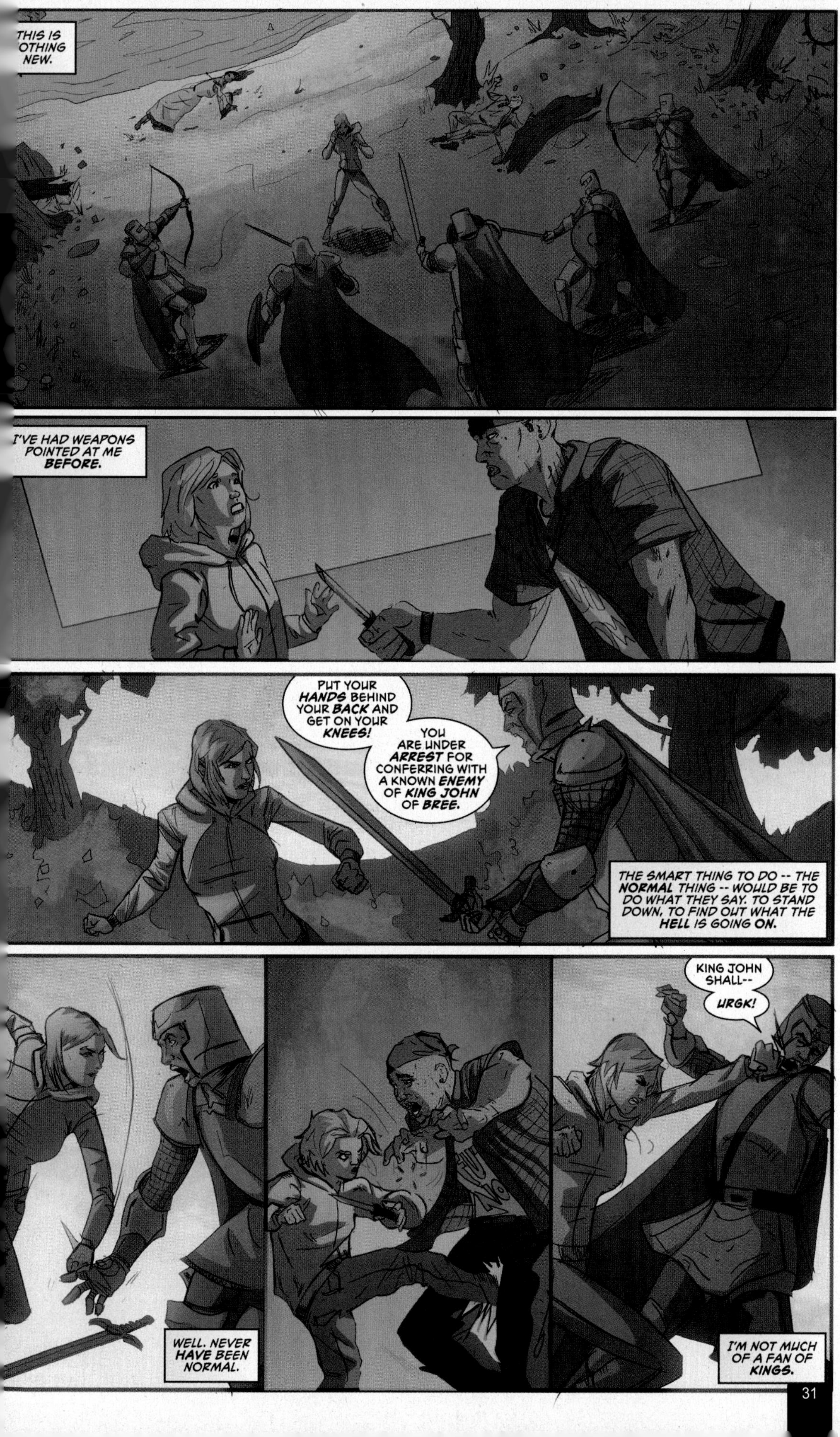

THIS IS NOTHING NEW.
I'VE HAD WEAPONS POINTED AT ME BEFORE.
PUT YOUR HANDS BEHIND YOUR BACK AND GET ON YOUR KNEES!
YOU ARE UNDER ARREST FOR CONFERRING WITH A KNOWN ENEMY OF KING JOHN OF BREE.
THE SMART THING TO DO -- THE NORMAL THING -- WOULD BE TO DO WHAT THEY SAY. TO STAND DOWN, TO FIND OUT WHAT THE HELL IS GOING ON.
WELL. NEVER HAVE BEEN NORMAL.
KING JOHN SHALL--
URGK!
I'M NOT MUCH OF A FAN OF KINGS.

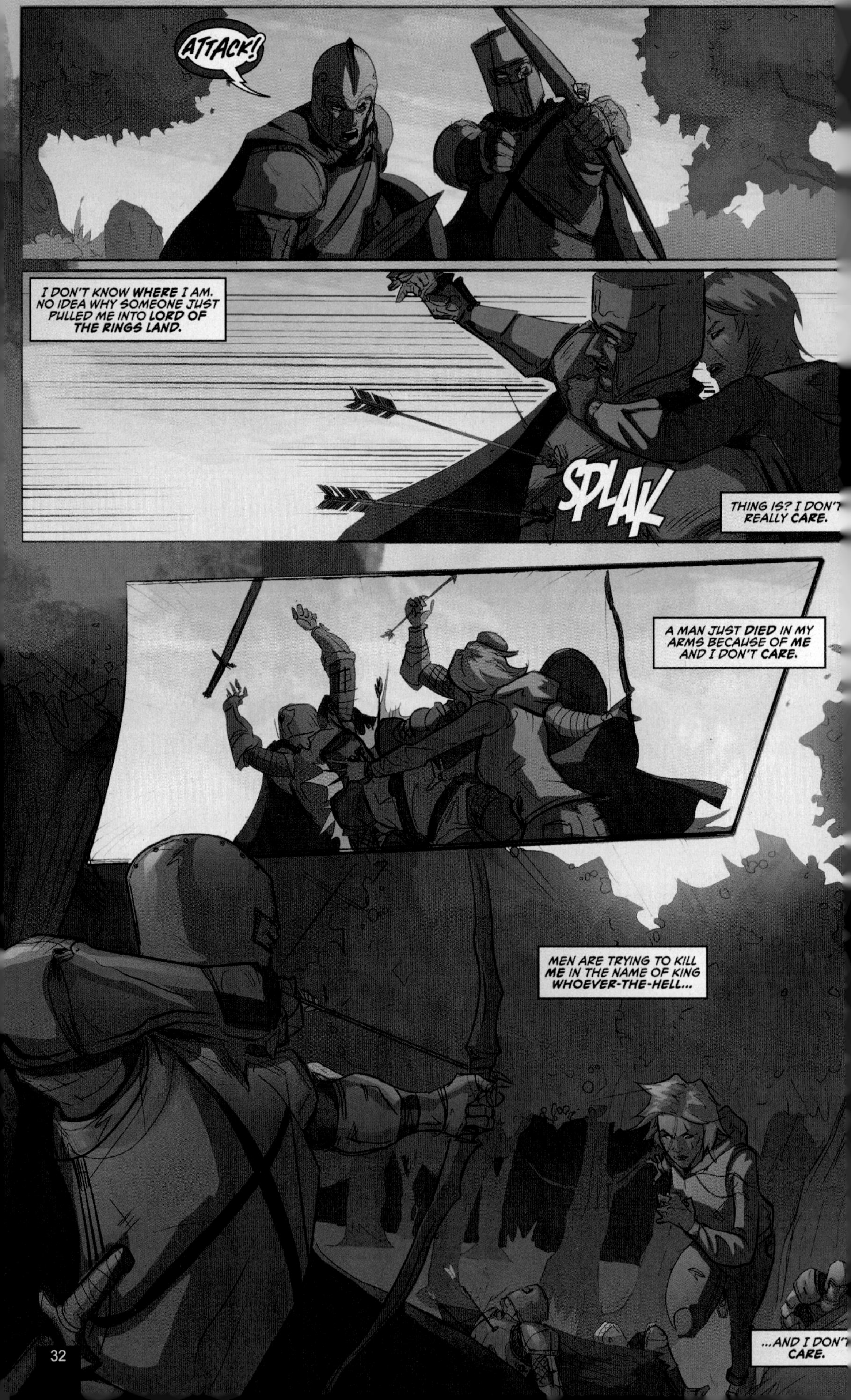

ATTACK!
I DON'T KNOW WHERE I AM. NO IDEA WHY SOMEONE JUST PULLED ME INTO LORD OF THE RINGS LAND.
SPLAK
THING IS? I DON'T REALLY CARE.
A MAN JUST DIED IN MY ARMS BECAUSE OF ME AND I DON'T CARE.
MEN ARE TRYING TO KILL ME IN THE NAME OF KING WHOEVER-THE-HELL...
...AND I DON'T CARE.

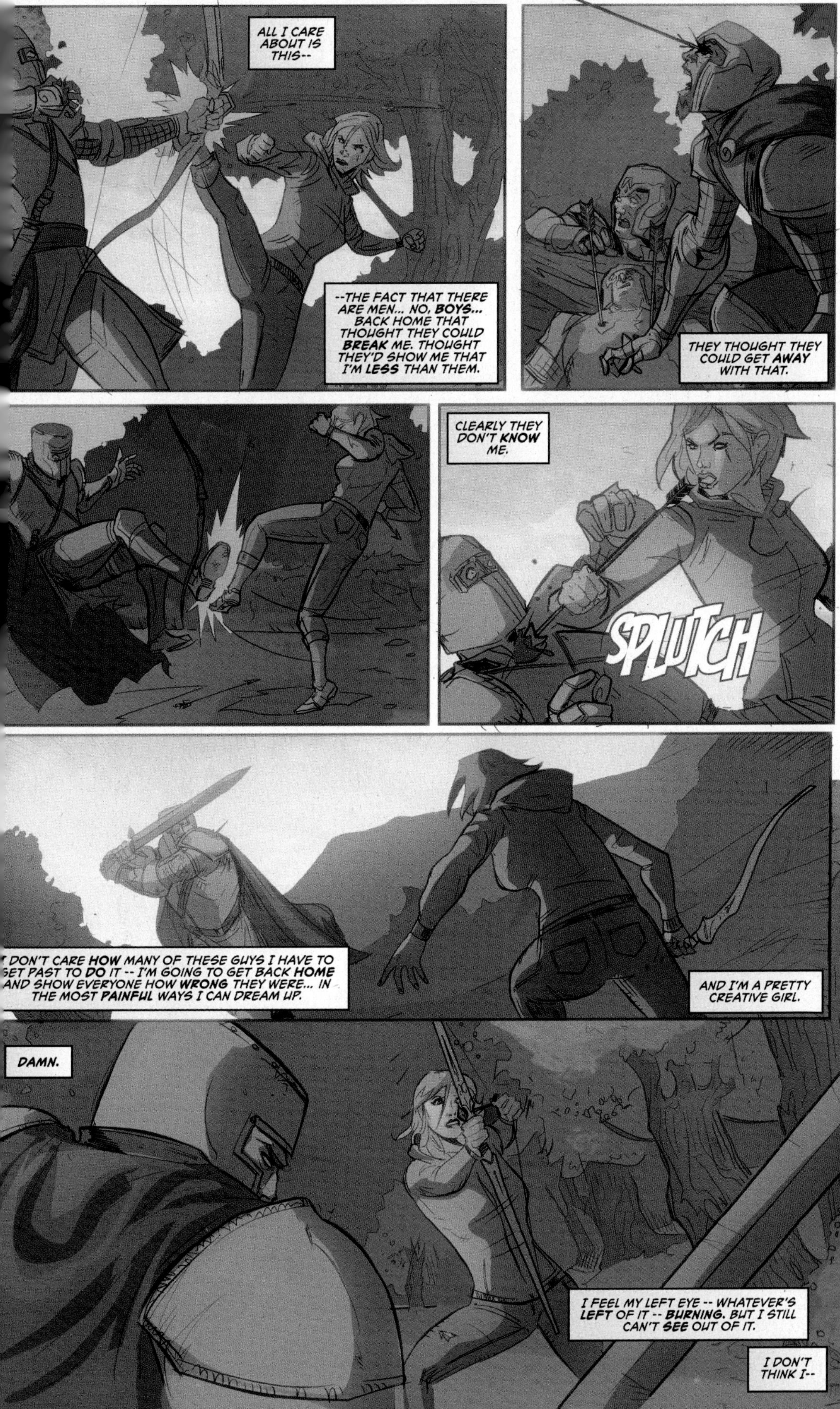
ALL I CARE ABOUT IS THIS--
--THE FACT THAT THERE ARE MEN... NO, BOYS... BACK HOME THAT THOUGHT THEY COULD BREAK ME. THOUGHT THEY'D SHOW ME THAT I'M LESS THAN THEM.
THEY THOUGHT THEY COULD GET AWAY WITH THAT.
CLEARLY THEY DON'T KNOW ME.
SPLUTCH
I DON'T CARE HOW MANY OF THESE GUYS I HAVE TO GET PAST TO DO IT -- I'M GOING TO GET BACK HOME AND SHOW EVERYONE HOW WRONG THEY WERE... IN THE MOST PAINFUL WAYS I CAN DREAM UP.
AND I'M A PRETTY CREATIVE GIRL.
DAMN.
I FEEL MY LEFT EYE -- WHATEVER'S LEFT OF IT -- BURNING. BUT I STILL CAN'T SEE OUT OF IT.
I DON'T THINK I--

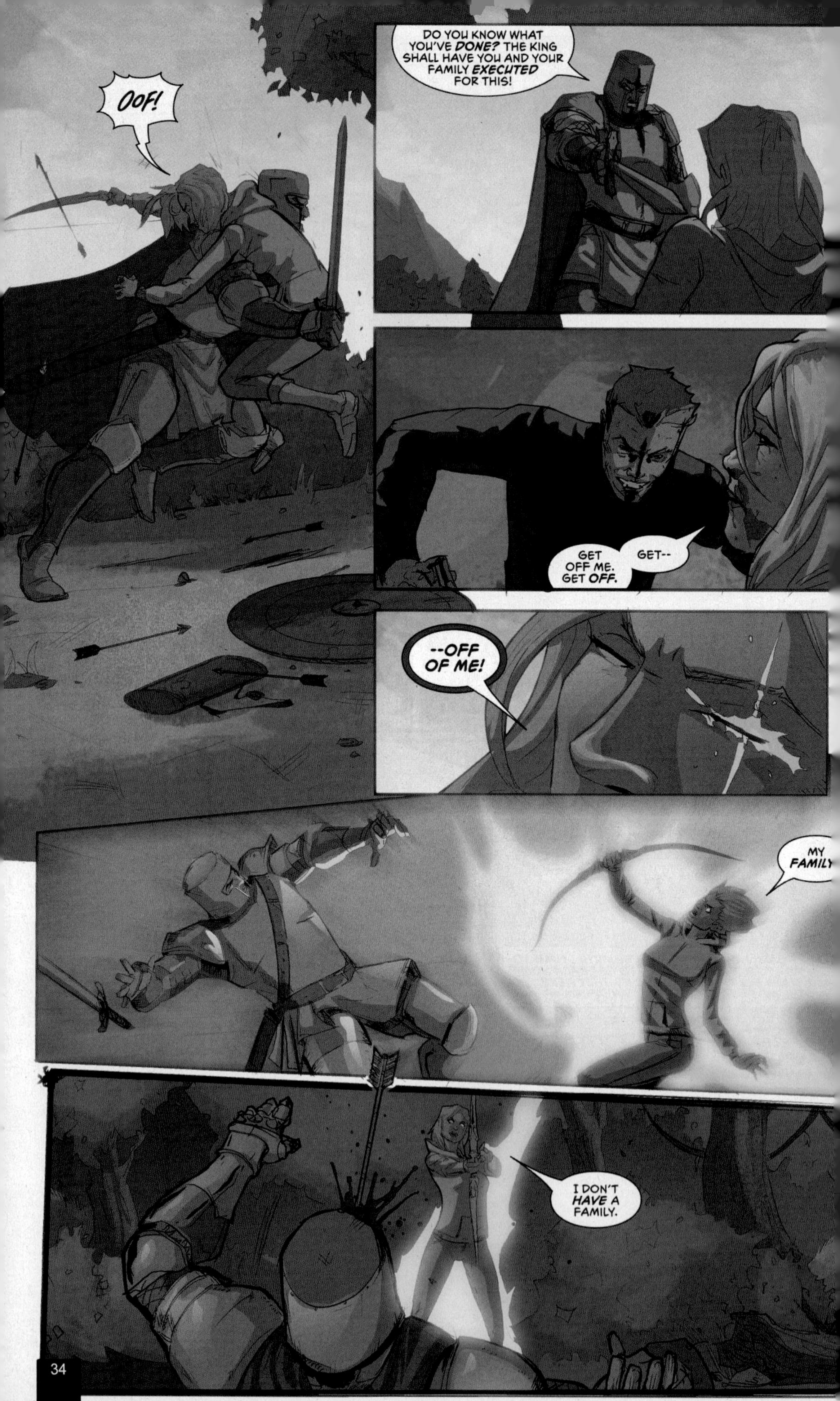
OOF!
DO YOU KNOW WHAT YOU'VE DONE? THE KING SHALL HAVE YOU AND YOUR FAMILY EXECUTED FOR THIS!
GET--
GET OFF ME. GET OFF.
--OFF OF ME!
MY FAMILY
I DON'T HAVE A FAMILY.

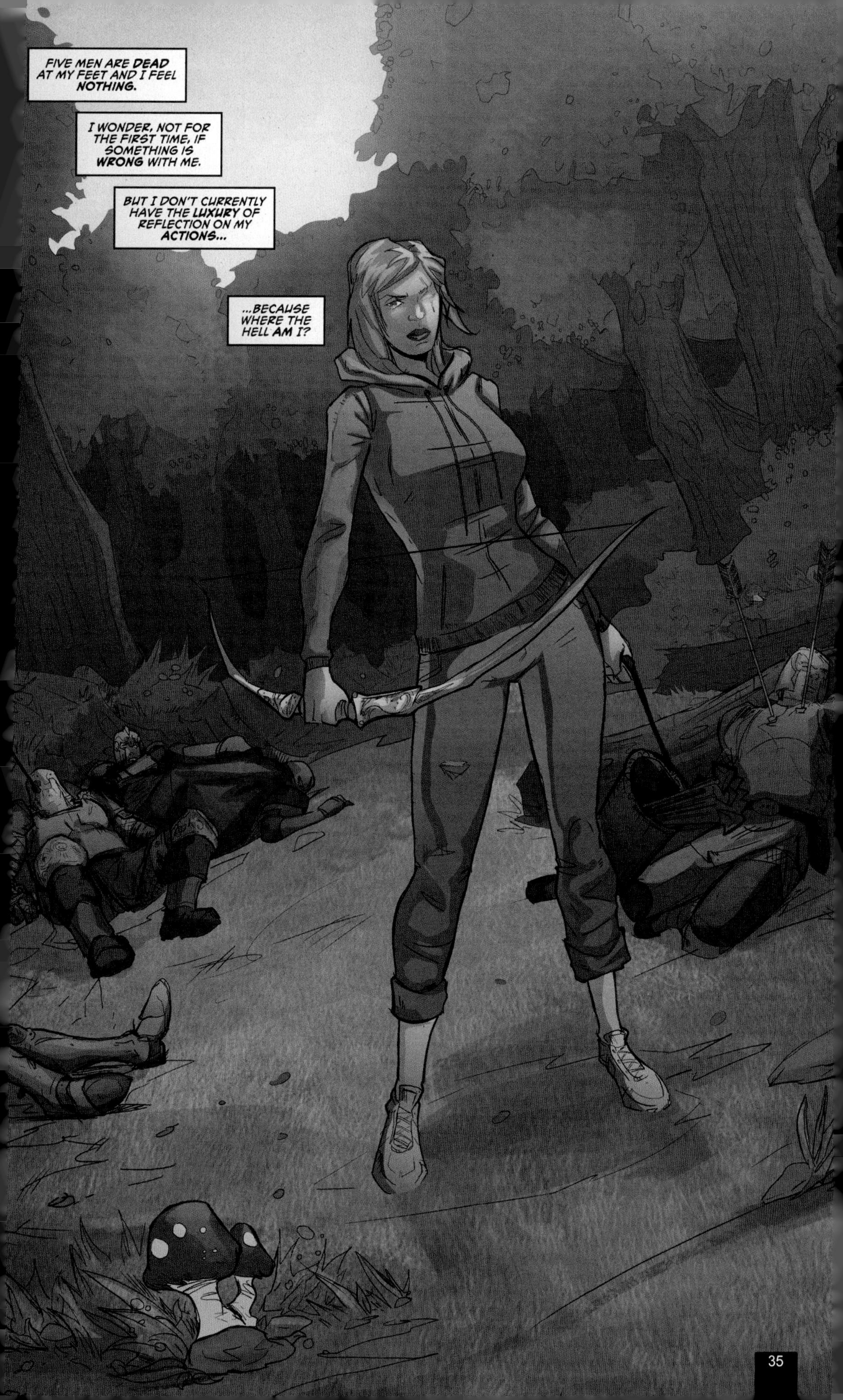
FIVE MEN ARE DEAD AT MY FEET AND I FEEL NOTHING.
I WONDER, NOT FOR THE FIRST TIME, IF SOMETHING IS WRONG WITH ME.
BUT I DON'T CURRENTLY HAVE THE LUXURY OF REFLECTION ON MY ACTIONS...
...BECAUSE WHERE THE HELL AM I?

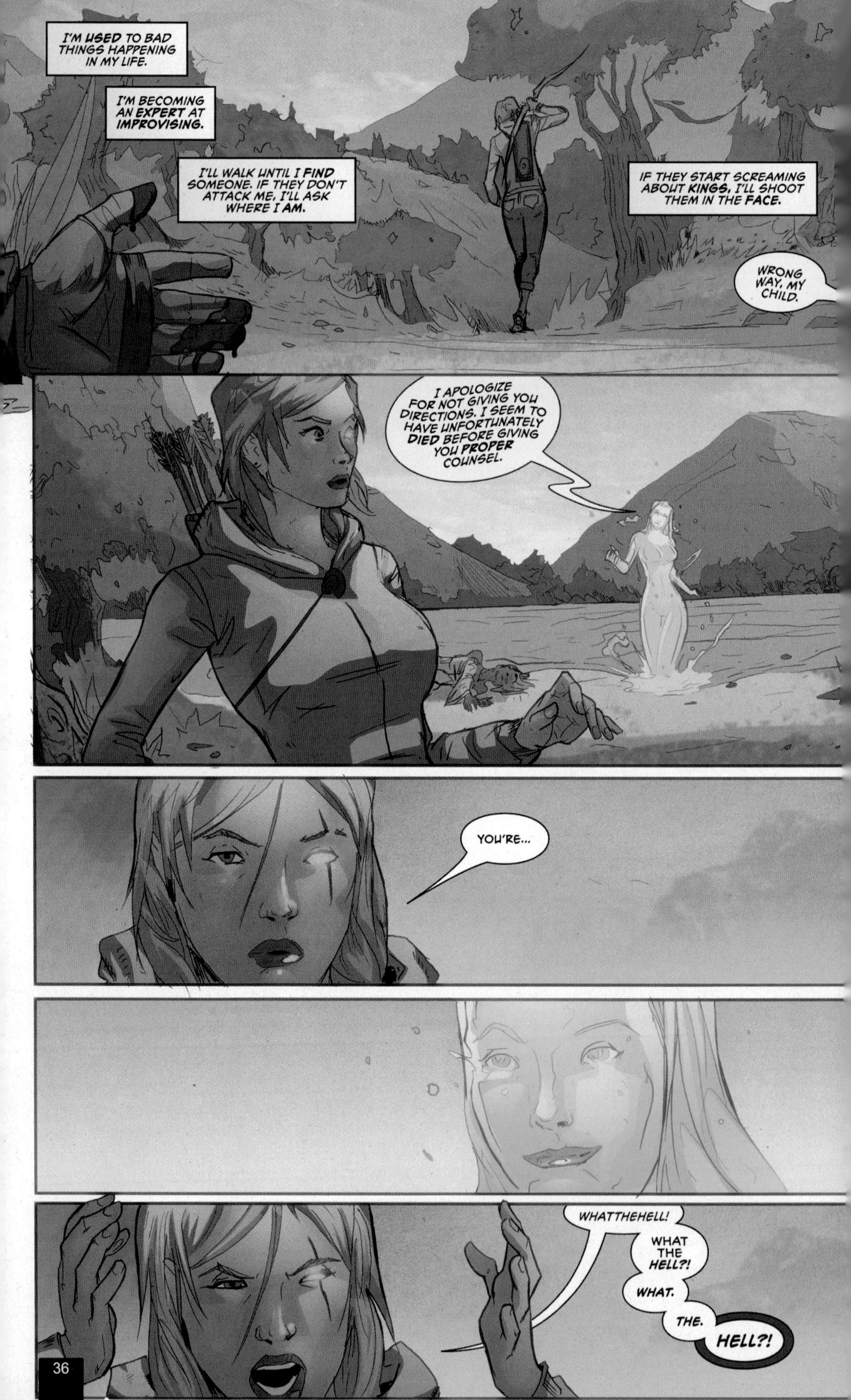

I'M USED TO BAD THINGS HAPPENING IN MY LIFE.
I'M BECOMING AN EXPERT AT IMPROVISING.
I'LL WALK UNTIL I FIND SOMEONE. IF THEY DON'T ATTACK ME, I'LL ASK WHERE I AM.
IF THEY START SCREAMING ABOUT KINGS, I'LL SHOOT THEM IN THE FACE.
WRONG WAY, MY CHILD.
I APOLOGIZE FOR NOT GIVING YOU DIRECTIONS. I SEEM TO HAVE UNFORTUNATELY DIED BEFORE GIVING YOU PROPER COUNSEL.
YOU'RE...
WHATTHEHELL!
WHAT THE HELL?!
WHAT.
THE.
HELL?!

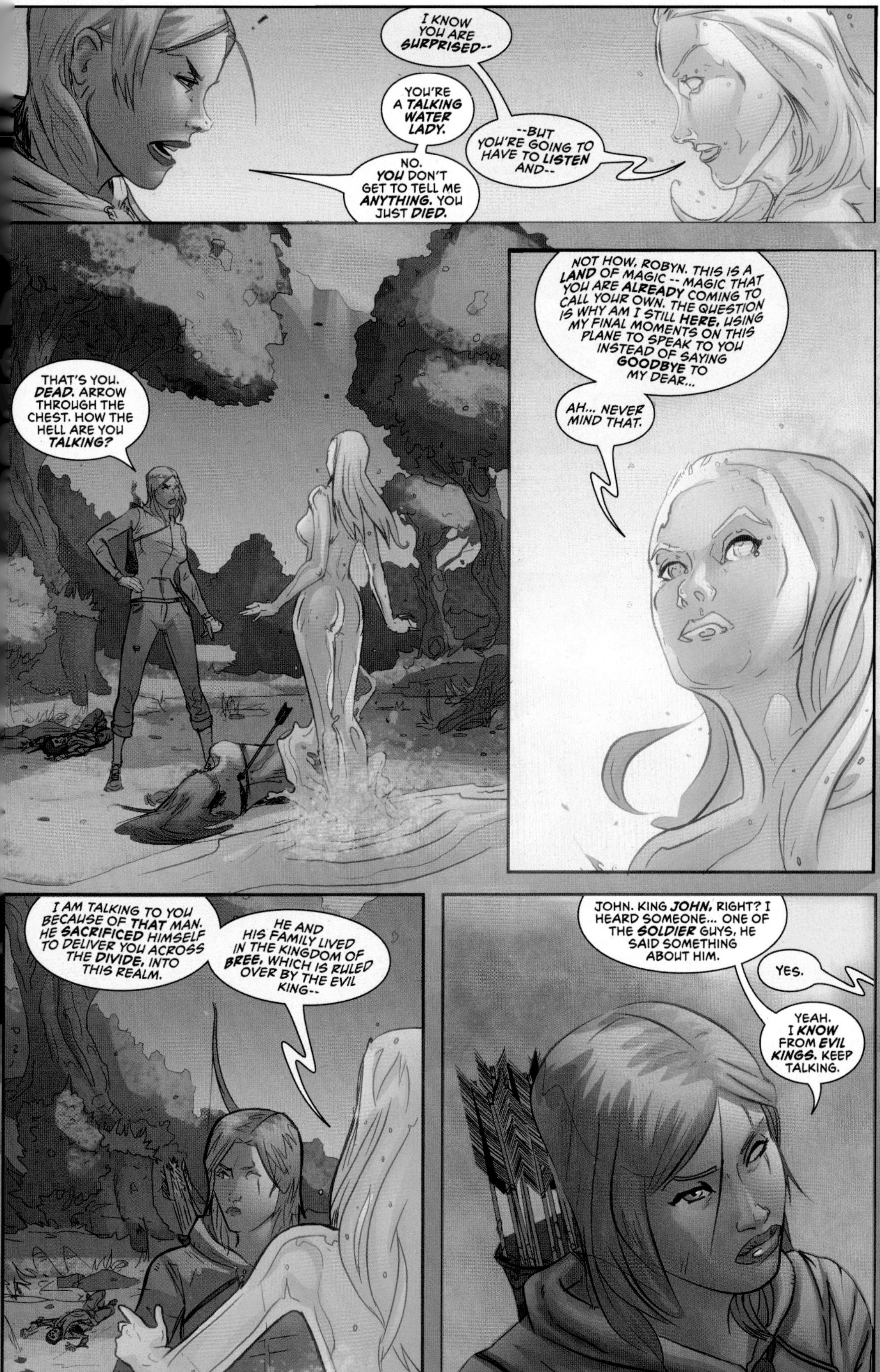

I KNOW YOU ARE SURPRISED--
YOU'RE A TALKING WATER LADY.
--BUT YOU'RE GOING TO HAVE TO LISTEN AND--
NO. YOU DON'T GET TO TELL ME ANYTHING. YOU JUST DIED.
THAT'S YOU. DEAD. ARROW THROUGH THE CHEST. HOW THE HELL ARE YOU TALKING?
NOT HOW, ROBYN. THIS IS A LAND OF MAGIC -- MAGIC THAT YOU ARE ALREADY COMING TO CALL YOUR OWN. THE QUESTION IS WHY AM I STILL HERE, USING MY FINAL MOMENTS ON THIS PLANE TO SPEAK TO YOU INSTEAD OF SAYING GOODBYE TO MY DEAR...
AH... NEVER MIND THAT.
I AM TALKING TO YOU BECAUSE OF THAT MAN. HE SACRIFICED HIMSELF TO DELIVER YOU ACROSS THE DIVIDE, INTO THIS REALM.
HE AND HIS FAMILY LIVED IN THE KINGDOM OF BREE, WHICH IS RULED OVER BY THE EVIL KING--
JOHN. KING JOHN, RIGHT? I HEARD SOMEONE... ONE OF THE SOLDIER GUYS, HE SAID SOMETHING ABOUT HIM.
YES.
YEAH. I KNOW FROM EVIL KINGS. KEEP TALKING.

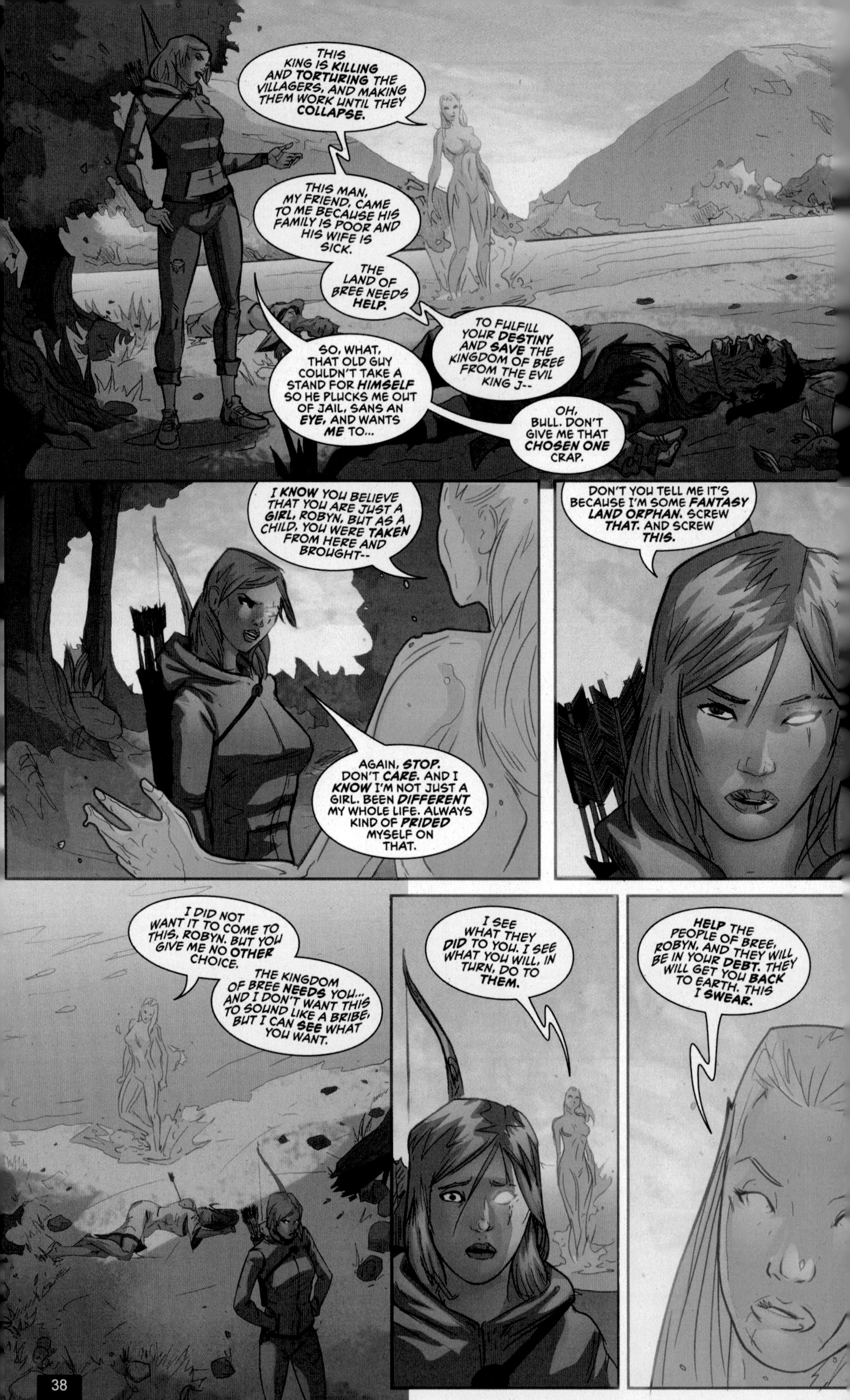
THIS KING IS KILLING AND TORTURING THE VILLAGERS, AND MAKING THEM WORK UNTIL THEY COLLAPSE.
THIS MAN, MY FRIEND, CAME TO ME BECAUSE HIS FAMILY IS POOR AND HIS WIFE IS SICK.
THE LAND OF BREE NEEDS HELP.
TO FULFILL YOUR DESTINY AND SAVE THE KINGDOM OF BREE FROM THE EVIL KING J--
SO, WHAT, THAT OLD GUY COULDN'T TAKE A STAND FOR HIMSELF SO HE PLUCKS ME OUT OF JAIL, SANS AN EYE, AND WANTS ME TO...
OH, BULL. DON'T GIVE ME THAT CHOSEN ONE CRAP.
I KNOW YOU BELIEVE THAT YOU ARE JUST A GIRL, ROBYN, BUT AS A CHILD, YOU WERE TAKEN FROM HERE AND BROUGHT--
AGAIN, STOP. DON'T CARE. AND I KNOW I'M NOT JUST A GIRL. BEEN DIFFERENT MY WHOLE LIFE. ALWAYS KIND OF PRIDED MYSELF ON THAT.
DON'T YOU TELL ME IT'S BECAUSE I'M SOME FANTASY LAND ORPHAN. SCREW THAT. AND SCREW THIS.
I DID NOT WANT IT TO COME TO THIS, ROBYN. BUT YOU GIVE ME NO OTHER CHOICE.
THE KINGDOM OF BREE NEEDS YOU... AND I DON'T WANT THIS TO SOUND LIKE A BRIBE, BUT I CAN SEE WHAT YOU WANT.
I SEE WHAT THEY DID TO YOU. I SEE WHAT YOU WILL, IN TURN, DO TO THEM.
HELP THE PEOPLE OF BREE, ROBYN, AND THEY WILL BE IN YOUR DEBT. THEY WILL GET YOU BACK TO EARTH. THIS I SWEAR.

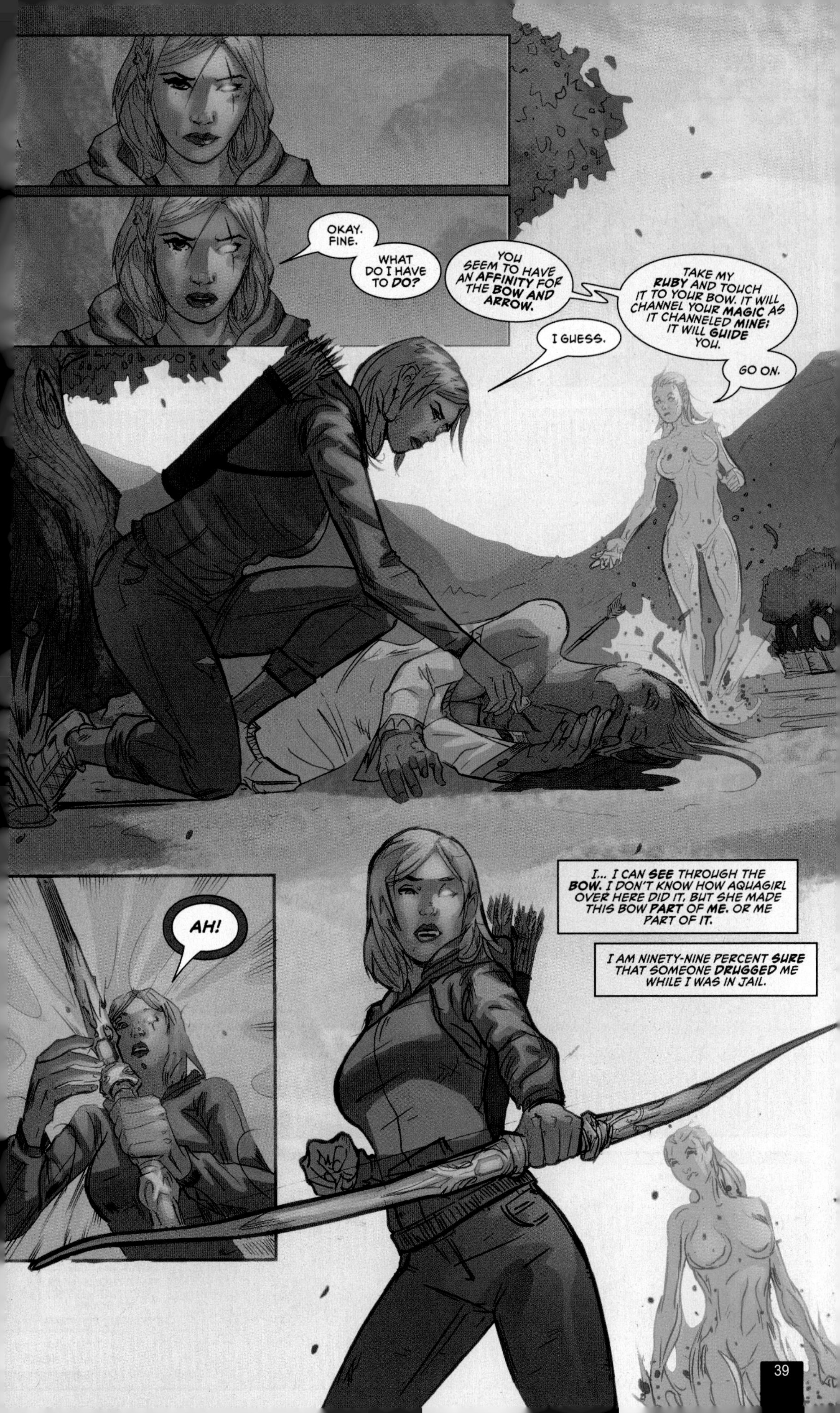
OKAY. FINE.
WHAT DO I HAVE TO DO?
YOU SEEM TO HAVE AN AFFINITY FOR THE BOW AND ARROW.
I GUESS.
TAKE MY RUBY AND TOUCH IT TO YOUR BOW. IT WILL CHANNEL YOUR MAGIC AS IT CHANNELED MINE: IT WILL GUIDE YOU.
GO ON.
AH!
I... I CAN SEE THROUGH THE BOW. I DON'T KNOW HOW AQUAGIRL OVER HERE DID IT, BUT SHE MADE THIS BOW PART OF ME. OR ME PART OF IT.
I AM NINETY-NINE PERCENT SURE THAT SOMEONE DRUGGED ME WHILE I WAS IN JAIL.

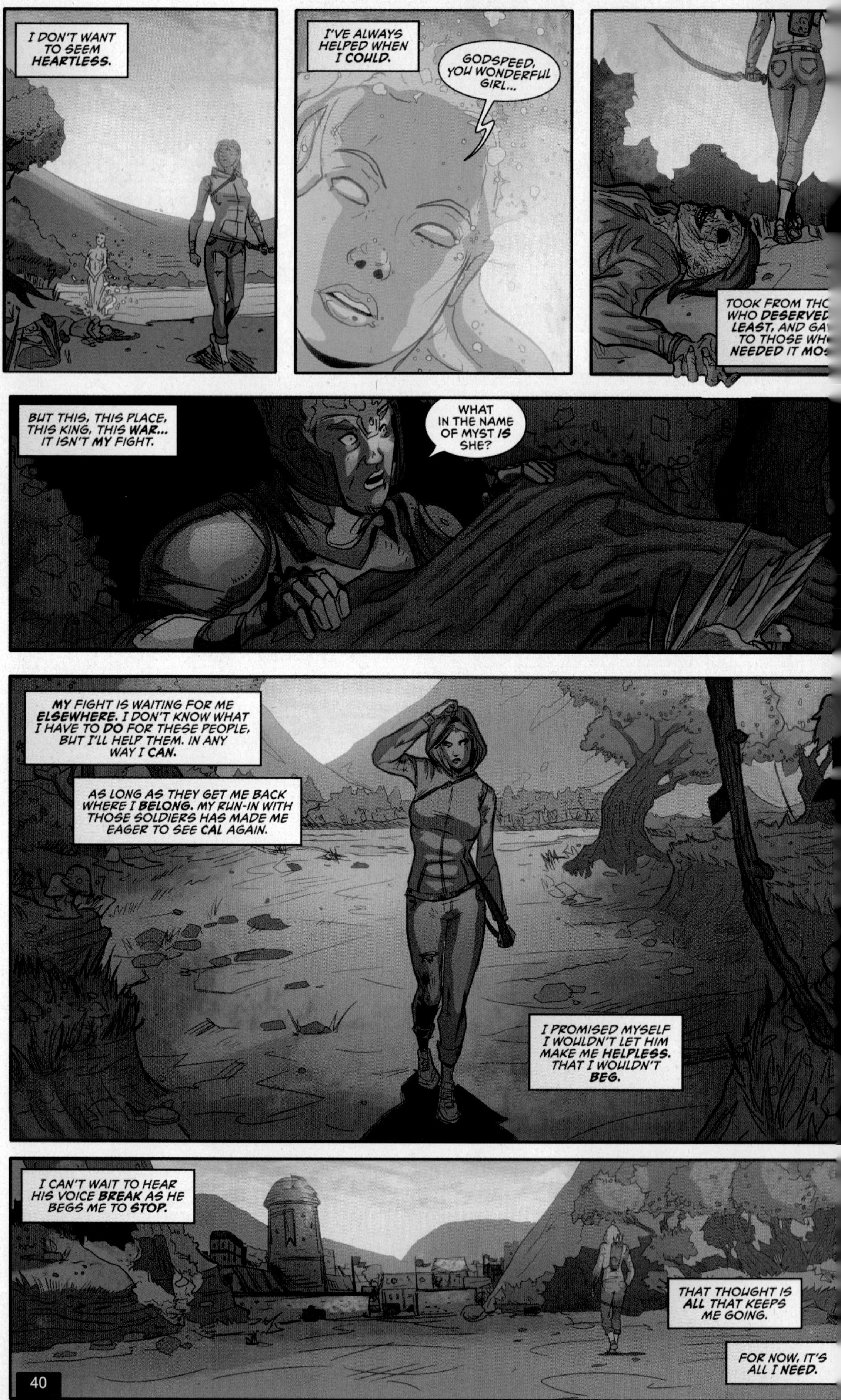
I DON'T WANT TO SEEM HEARTLESS.
I'VE ALWAYS HELPED WHEN I COULD.
GODSPEED, YOU WONDERFUL GIRL...
TOOK FROM THO WHO DESERVED LEAST, AND GA TO THOSE WH NEEDED IT MOS
BUT THIS, THIS PLACE, THIS KING, THIS WAR... IT ISN'T MY FIGHT.
WHAT IN THE NAME OF MYST IS SHE?
MY FIGHT IS WAITING FOR ME ELSEWHERE. I DON'T KNOW WHAT I HAVE TO DO FOR THESE PEOPLE, BUT I'LL HELP THEM. IN ANY WAY I CAN.
AS LONG AS THEY GET ME BACK WHERE I BELONG. MY RUN-IN WITH THOSE SOLDIERS HAS MADE ME EAGER TO SEE CAL AGAIN.
I PROMISED MYSELF I WOULDN'T LET HIM MAKE ME HELPLESS. THAT I WOULDN'T BEG.
I CAN'T WAIT TO HEAR HIS VOICE BREAK AS HE BEGS ME TO STOP.
THAT THOUGHT IS ALL THAT KEEPS ME GOING.
FOR NOW, IT'S ALL I NEED.

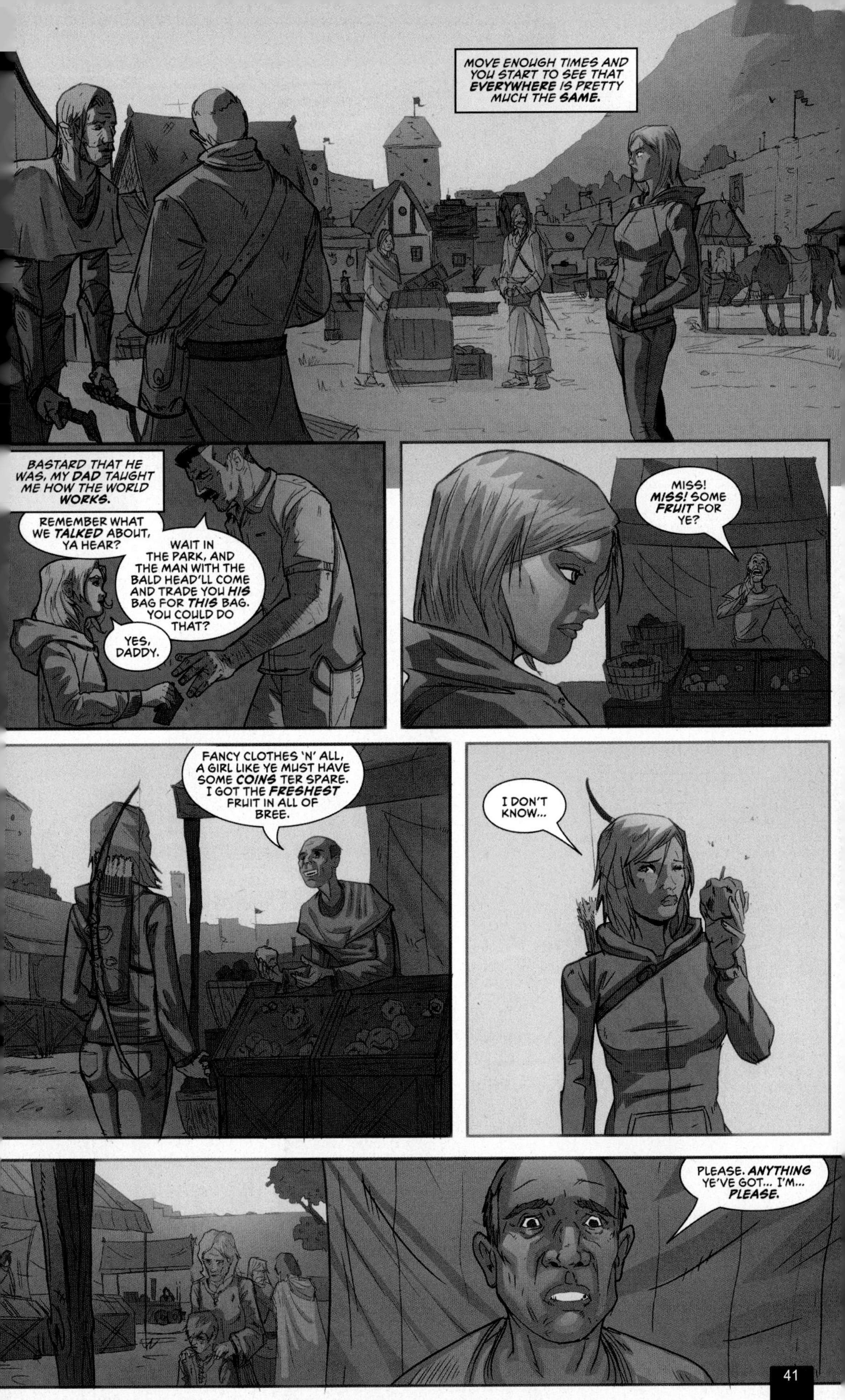
MOVE ENOUGH TIMES AND YOU START TO SEE THAT EVERYWHERE IS PRETTY MUCH THE SAME.
BASTARD THAT HE WAS, MY DAD TAUGHT ME HOW THE WORLD WORKS.
REMEMBER WHAT WE TALKED ABOUT, YA HEAR?
WAIT IN THE PARK, AND THE MAN WITH THE BALD HEAD'LL COME AND TRADE YOU HIS BAG FOR THIS BAG. YOU COULD DO THAT?
YES, DADDY.
MISS! MISS! SOME FRUIT FOR YE?
FANCY CLOTHES 'N' ALL, A GIRL LIKE YE MUST HAVE SOME COINS TER SPARE. I GOT THE FRESHEST FRUIT IN ALL OF BREE.
I DON'T KNOW...
PLEASE. ANYTHING YE'VE GOT... I'M... PLEASE.

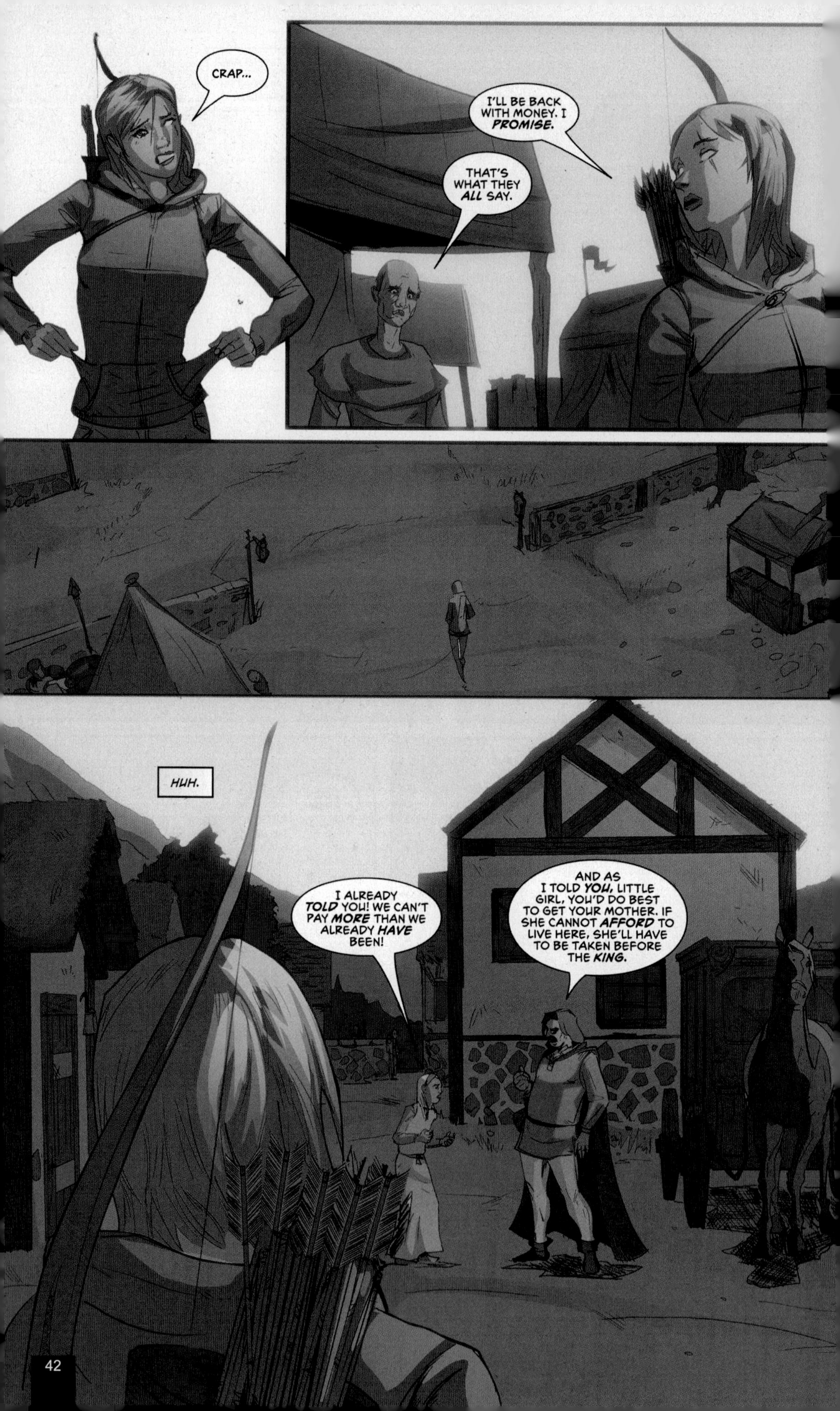
CRAP...
I'LL BE BACK WITH MONEY. I PROMISE.
THAT'S WHAT THEY ALL SAY.
HUH.
I ALREADY TOLD YOU! WE CAN'T PAY MORE THAN WE ALREADY HAVE BEEN!
AND AS I TOLD YOU, LITTLE GIRL, YOU'D DO BEST TO GET YOUR MOTHER. IF SHE CANNOT AFFORD TO LIVE HERE, SHE'LL HAVE TO BE TAKEN BEFORE THE KING.

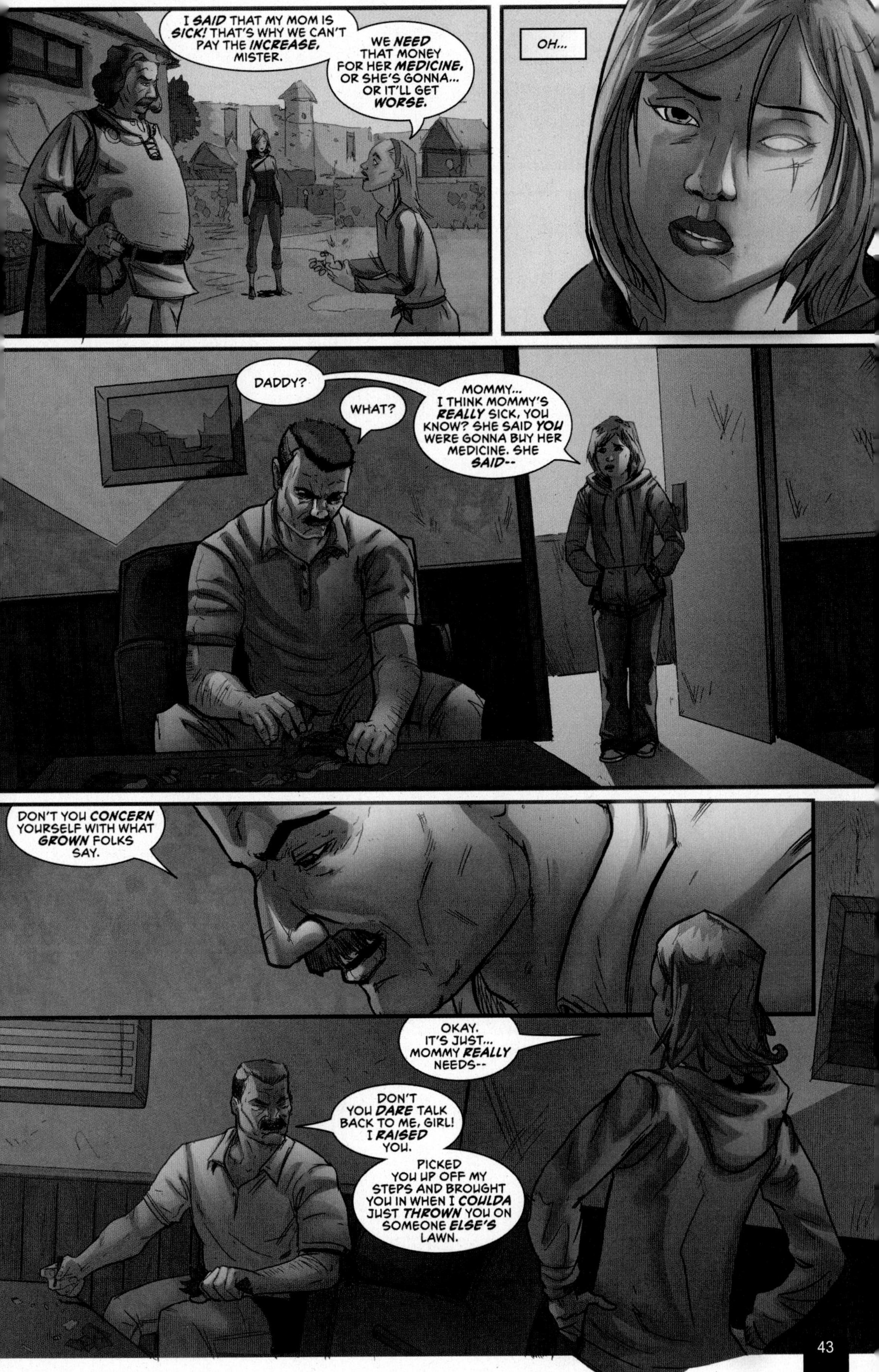
I SAID THAT MY MOM IS SICK! THAT'S WHY WE CAN'T PAY THE INCREASE, MISTER.
WE NEED THAT MONEY FOR HER MEDICINE, OR SHE'S GONNA... OR IT'LL GET WORSE.
OH...
DADDY?
WHAT?
MOMMY... I THINK MOMMY'S REALLY SICK, YOU KNOW? SHE SAID YOU WERE GONNA BUY HER MEDICINE. SHE SAID--
DON'T YOU CONCERN YOURSELF WITH WHAT GROWN FOLKS SAY.
OKAY. IT'S JUST... MOMMY REALLY NEEDS--
DON'T YOU DARE TALK BACK TO ME, GIRL! I RAISED YOU.
PICKED YOU UP OFF MY STEPS AND BROUGHT YOU IN WHEN I COULDA JUST THROWN YOU ON SOMEONE ELSE'S LAWN.

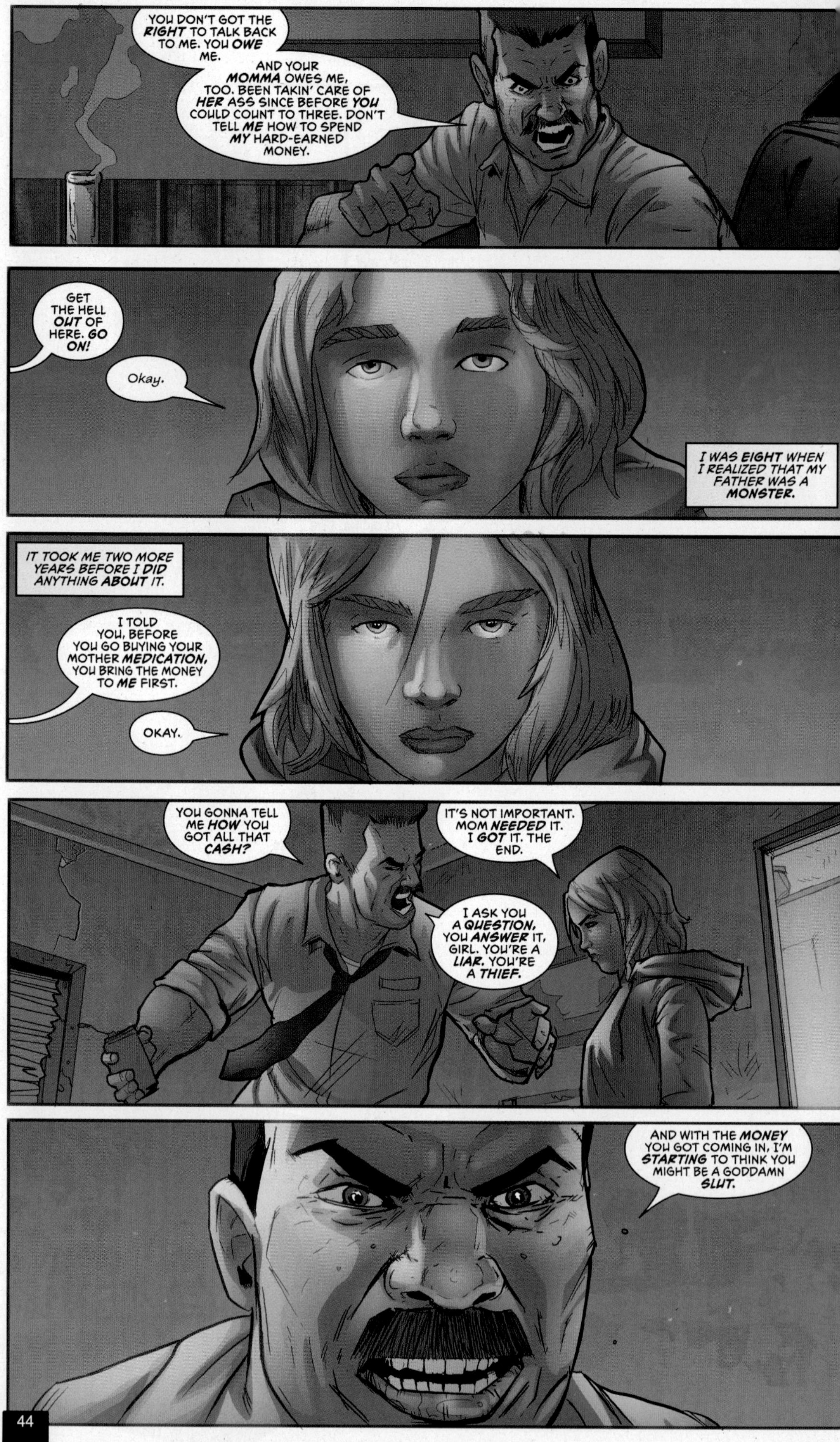
YOU DON'T GOT THE RIGHT TO TALK BACK TO ME. YOU OWE ME.
AND YOUR MOMMA OWES ME, TOO. BEEN TAKIN' CARE OF HER ASS SINCE BEFORE YOU COULD COUNT TO THREE. DON'T TELL ME HOW TO SPEND MY HARD-EARNED MONEY.
GET THE HELL OUT OF HERE. GO ON!
Okay.
I WAS EIGHT WHEN I REALIZED THAT MY FATHER WAS A MONSTER.
IT TOOK ME TWO MORE YEARS BEFORE I DID ANYTHING ABOUT IT.
I TOLD YOU, BEFORE YOU GO BUYING YOUR MOTHER MEDICATION, YOU BRING THE MONEY TO ME FIRST.
OKAY.
YOU GONNA TELL ME HOW YOU GOT ALL THAT CASH?
IT'S NOT IMPORTANT. MOM NEEDED IT. I GOT IT. THE END.
I ASK YOU A QUESTION, YOU ANSWER IT, GIRL. YOU'RE A LIAR. YOU'RE A THIEF.
AND WITH THE MONEY YOU GOT COMING IN, I'M STARTING TO THINK YOU MIGHT BE A GODDAMN SLUT.

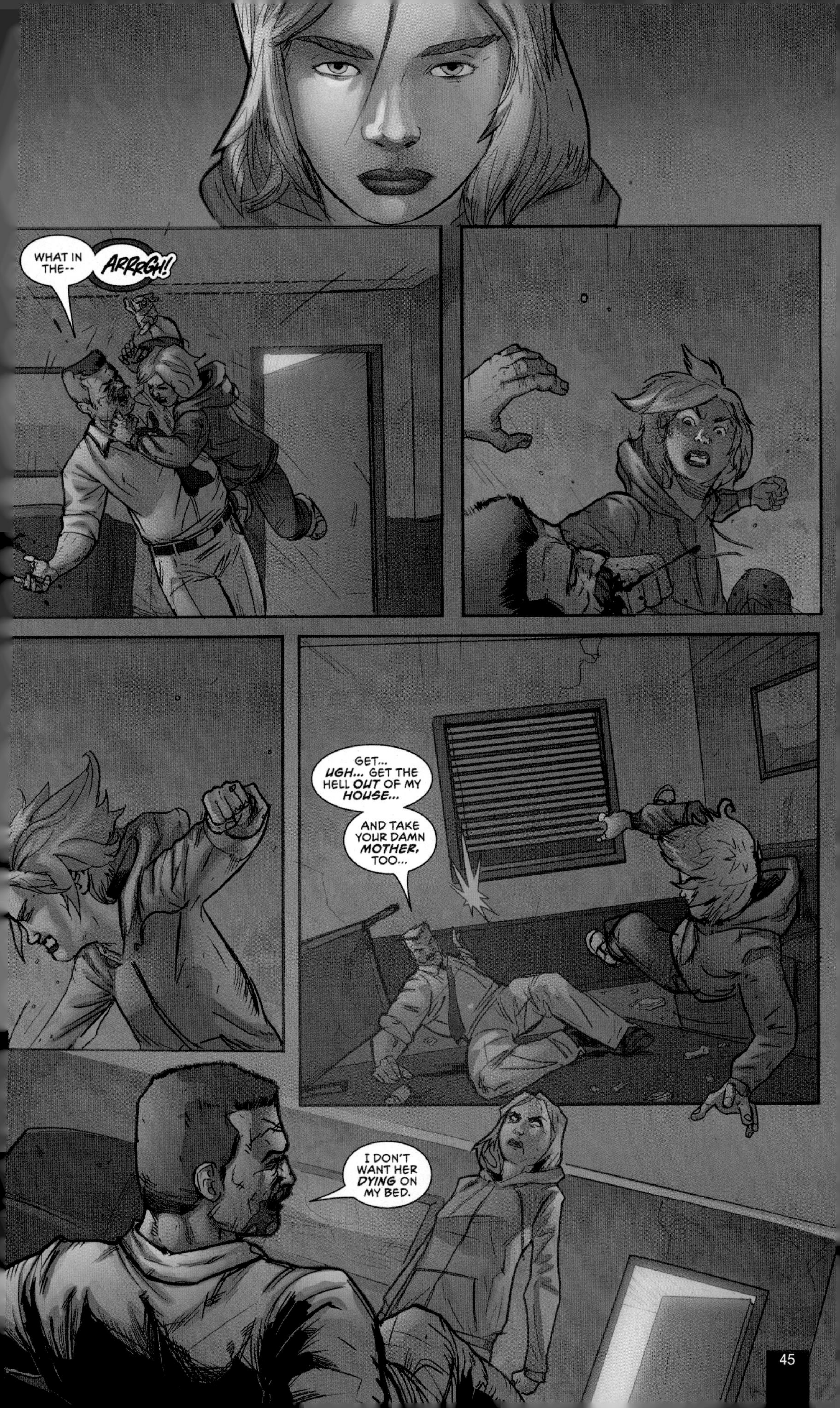
WHAT IN THE--
ARRRGH!
GET... UGH... GET THE HELL OUT OF MY HOUSE...
AND TAKE YOUR DAMN MOTHER, TOO...
I DON'T WANT HER DYING ON MY BED.

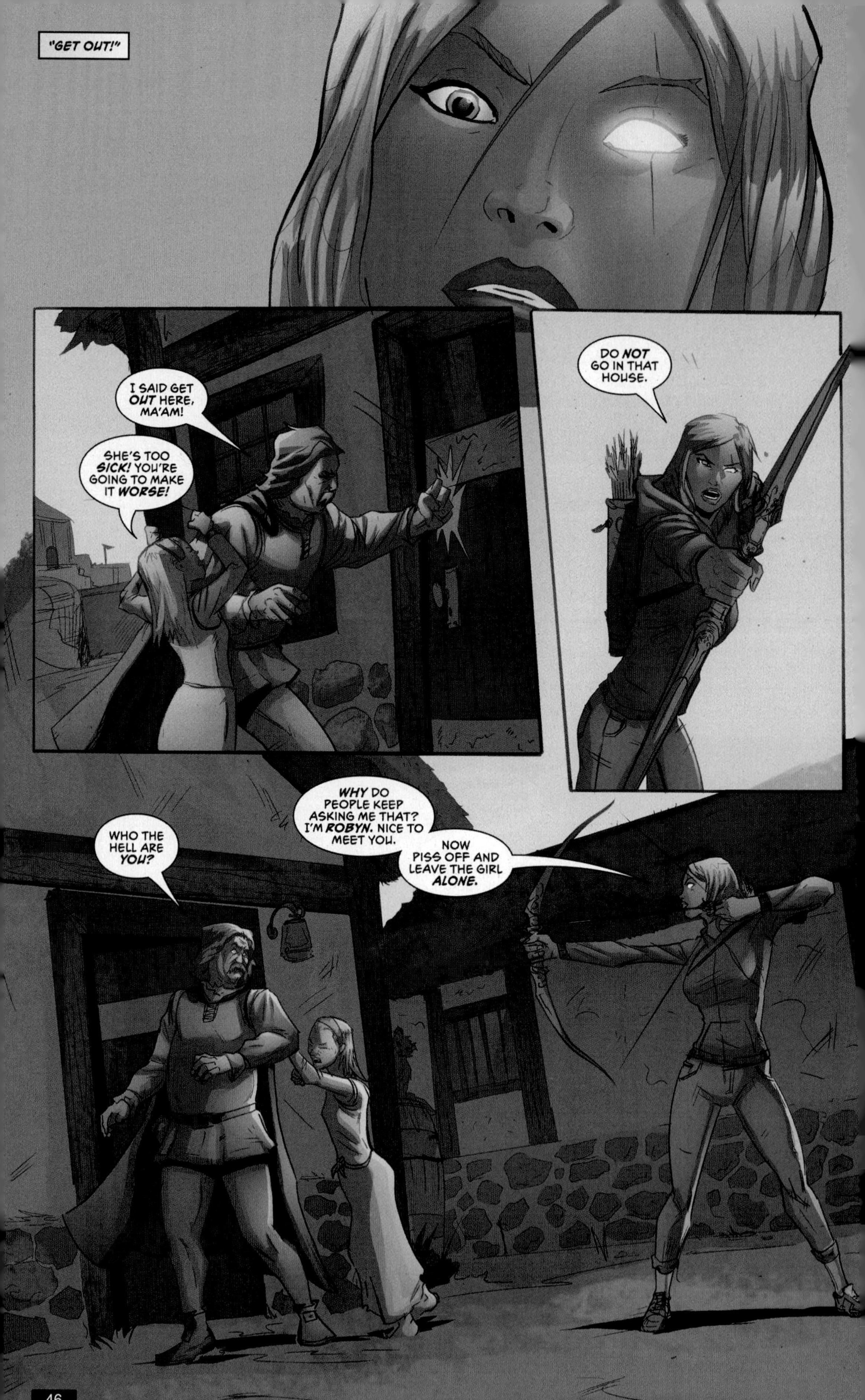
"GET OUT!"
I SAID GET OUT HERE, MA'AM!
SHE'S TOO SICK! YOU'RE GOING TO MAKE IT WORSE!
DO NOT GO IN THAT HOUSE.
WHO THE HELL ARE YOU?
WHY DO PEOPLE KEEP ASKING ME THAT? I'M ROBYN. NICE TO MEET YOU.
NOW PISS OFF AND LEAVE THE GIRL ALONE.

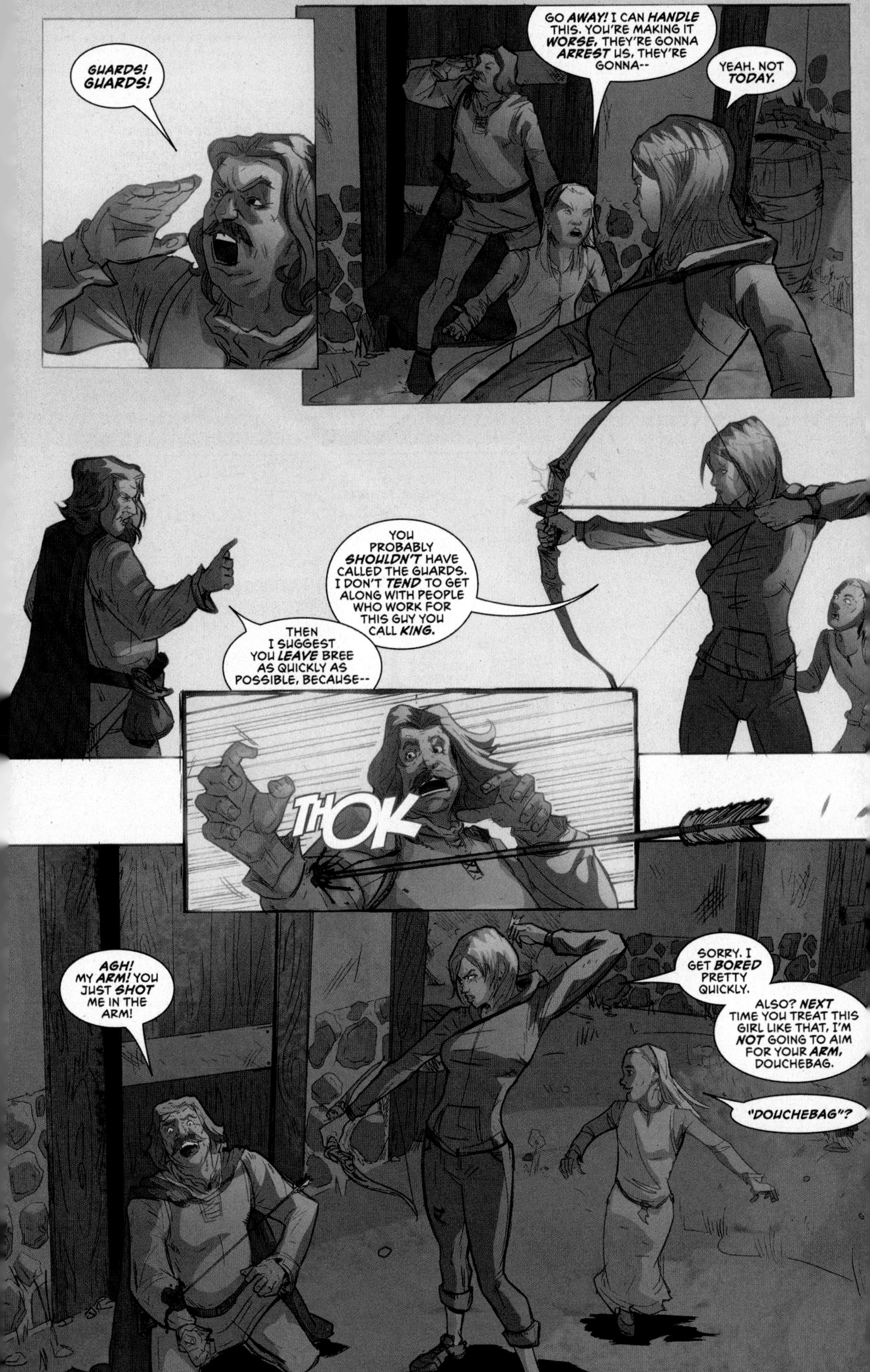
GUARDS! GUARDS!
GO AWAY! I CAN HANDLE THIS. YOU'RE MAKING IT WORSE, THEY'RE GONNA ARREST US, THEY'RE GONNA--
YEAH. NOT TODAY.
YOU PROBABLY SHOULDN'T HAVE CALLED THE GUARDS. I DON'T TEND TO GET ALONG WITH PEOPLE WHO WORK FOR THIS GUY YOU CALL KING.
THEN I SUGGEST YOU LEAVE BREE AS QUICKLY AS POSSIBLE, BECAUSE--
THOK
AGH! MY ARM! YOU JUST SHOT ME IN THE ARM!
SORRY. I GET BORED PRETTY QUICKLY.
ALSO? NEXT TIME YOU TREAT THIS GIRL LIKE THAT, I'M NOT GOING TO AIM FOR YOUR ARM, DOUCHEBAG.
"DOUCHEBAG"?

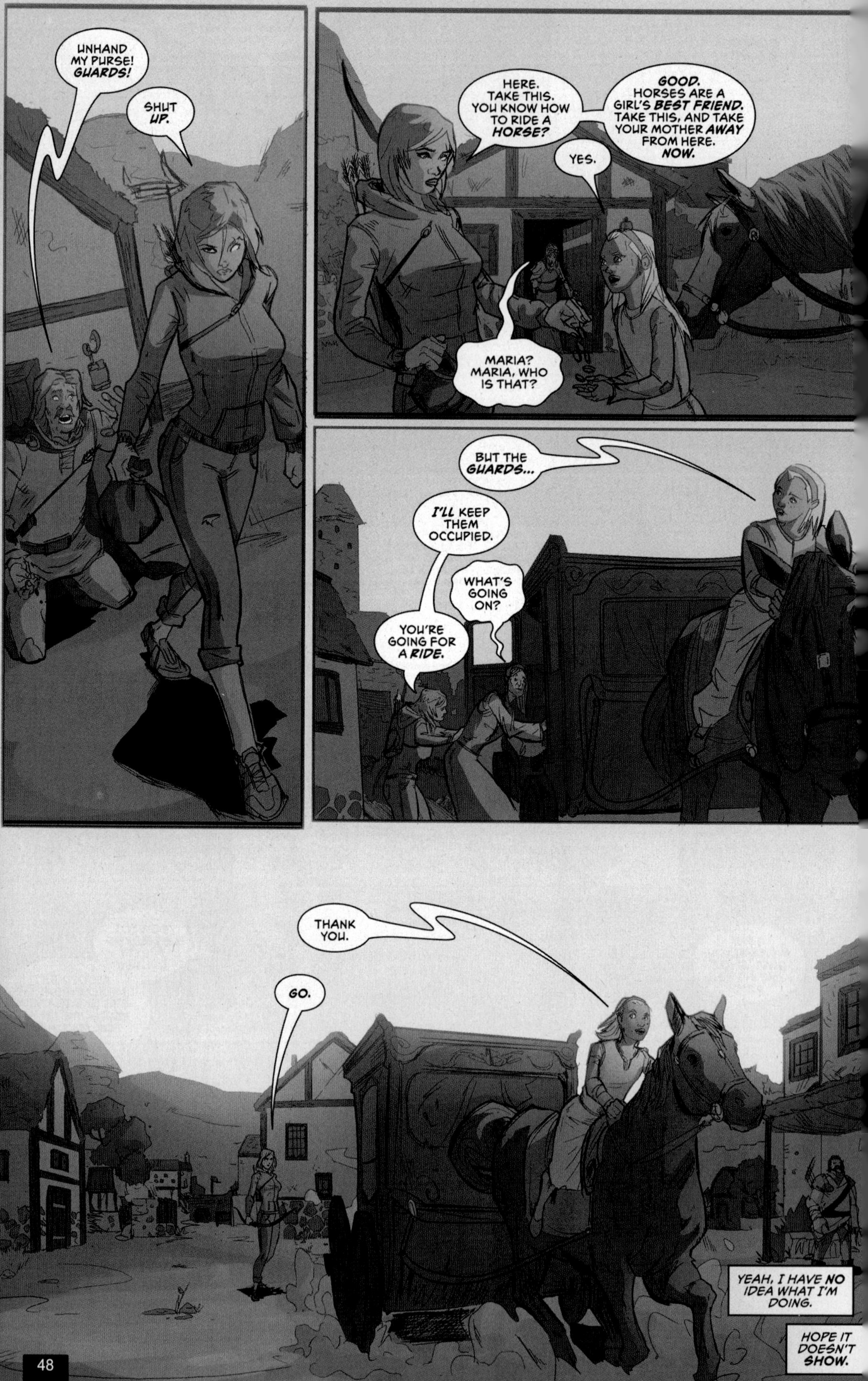
UNHAND MY PURSE! GUARDS!
SHUT UP.
HERE. TAKE THIS. YOU KNOW HOW TO RIDE A HORSE?
YES.
GOOD. HORSES ARE A GIRL'S BEST FRIEND. TAKE THIS, AND TAKE YOUR MOTHER AWAY FROM HERE. NOW.
MARIA? MARIA, WHO IS THAT?
BUT THE GUARDS...
I'LL KEEP THEM OCCUPIED.
WHAT'S GOING ON?
YOU'RE GOING FOR A RIDE.
THANK YOU.
GO.
YEAH, I HAVE NO IDEA WHAT I'M DOING.
HOPE IT DOESN'T SHOW.

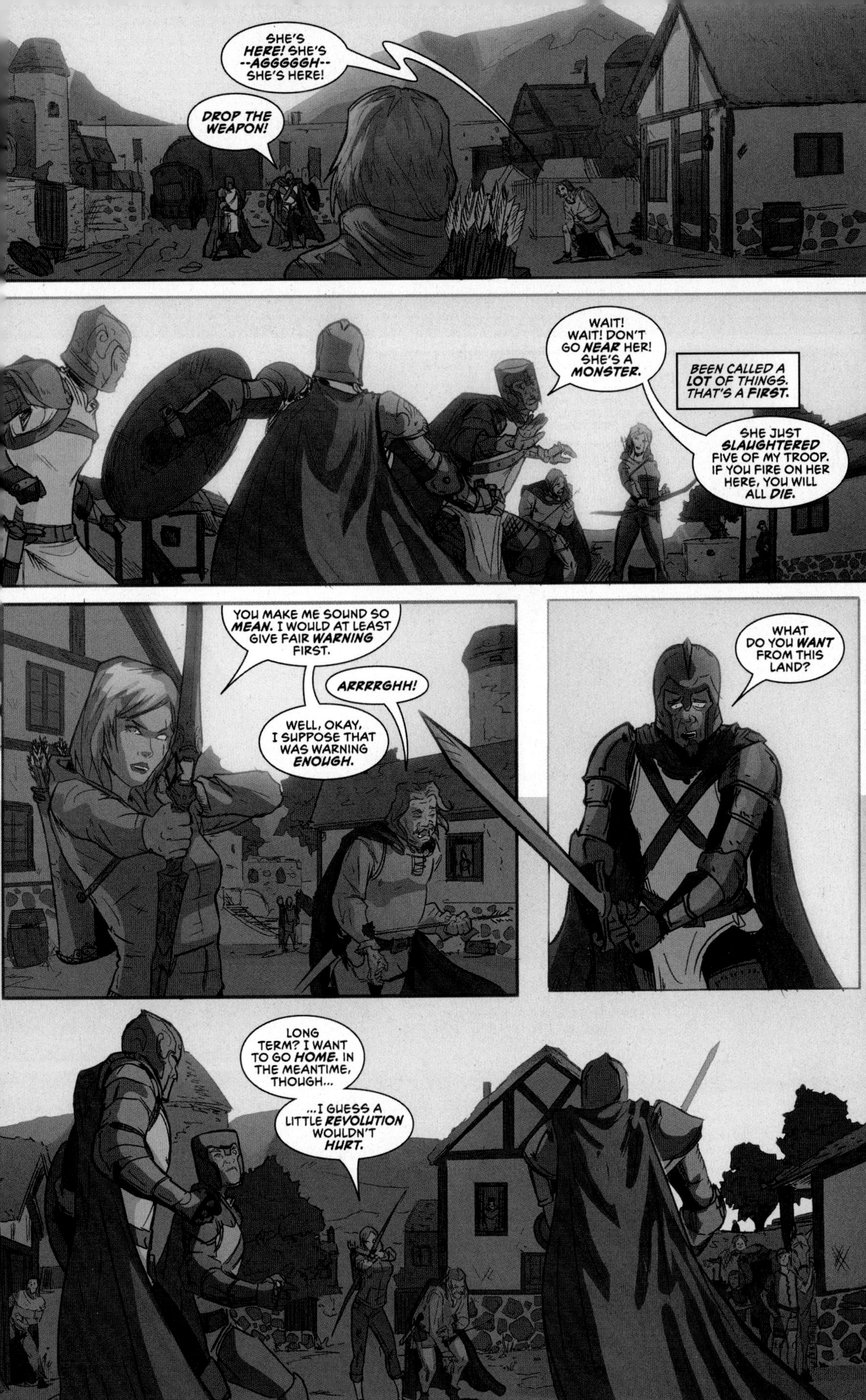
SHE'S HERE! SHE'S --AGGGGGH-- SHE'S HERE!
DROP THE WEAPON!
WAIT! WAIT! DON'T GO NEAR HER! SHE'S A MONSTER.
BEEN CALLED A LOT OF THINGS. THAT'S A FIRST.
SHE JUST SLAUGHTERED FIVE OF MY TROOP. IF YOU FIRE ON HER HERE, YOU WILL ALL DIE.
YOU MAKE ME SOUND SO MEAN. I WOULD AT LEAST GIVE FAIR WARNING FIRST.
ARRRRGHH!
WELL, OKAY, I SUPPOSE THAT WAS WARNING ENOUGH.
WHAT DO YOU WANT FROM THIS LAND?
LONG TERM? I WANT TO GO HOME. IN THE MEANTIME, THOUGH...
...I GUESS A LITTLE REVOLUTION WOULDN'T HURT.

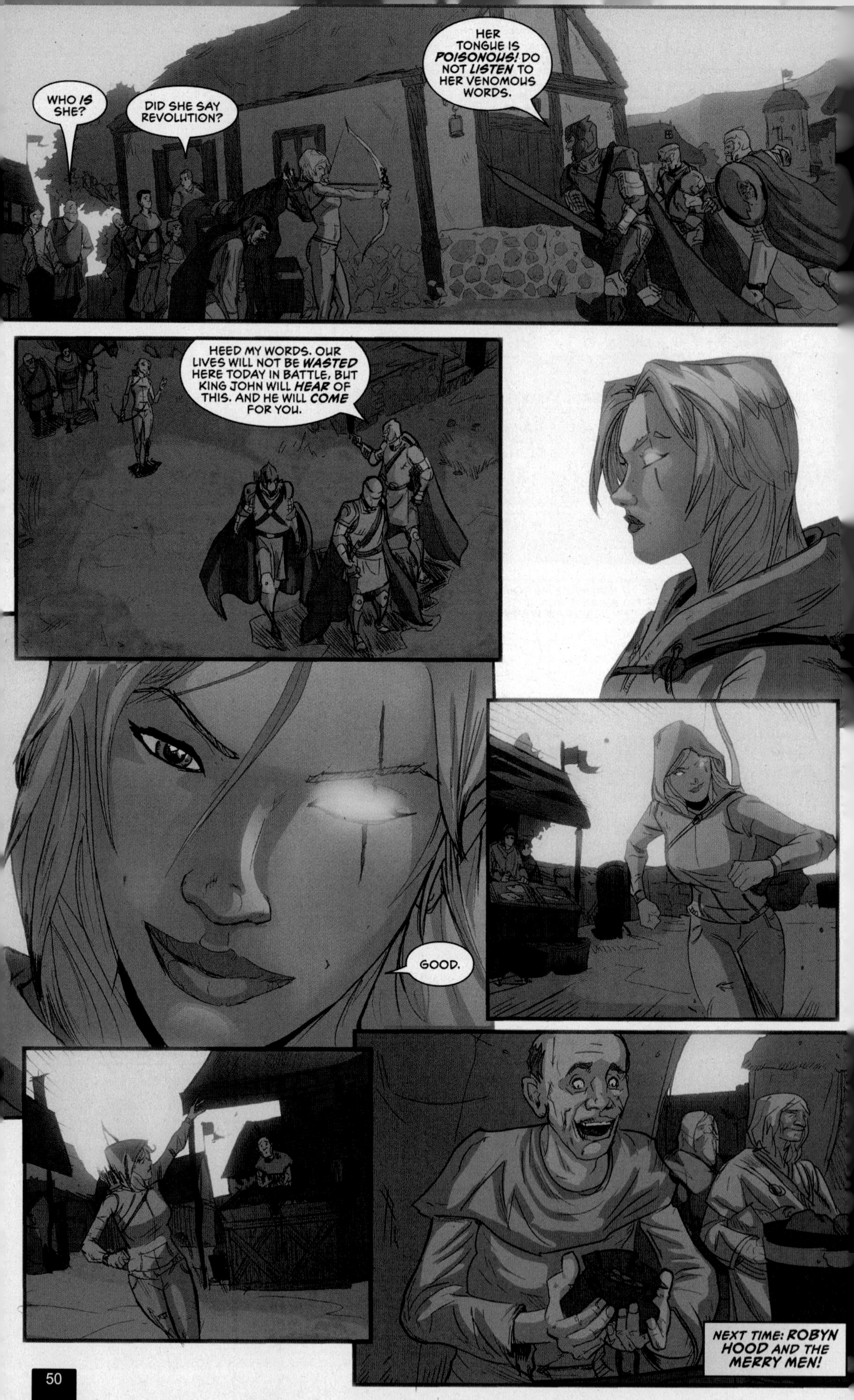
WHO IS SHE?
DID SHE SAY REVOLUTION?
HER TONGUE IS POISONOUS! DO NOT LISTEN TO HER VENOMOUS WORDS.
HEED MY WORDS. OUR LIVES WILL NOT BE WASTED HERE TODAY IN BATTLE, BUT KING JOHN WILL HEAR OF THIS. AND HE WILL COME FOR YOU.
GOOD.
NEXT TIME: ROBYN HOOD AND THE MERRY MEN!

# Grimm Fairy Tales

presents:

# ROBYN HOOD

# ORIGIN

# CHAPTER THREE

*Writer* Pat Shand
*Artwork* Rob Dumo
*Colors* Adam Metcalfe
*Letters* Jim Campbell

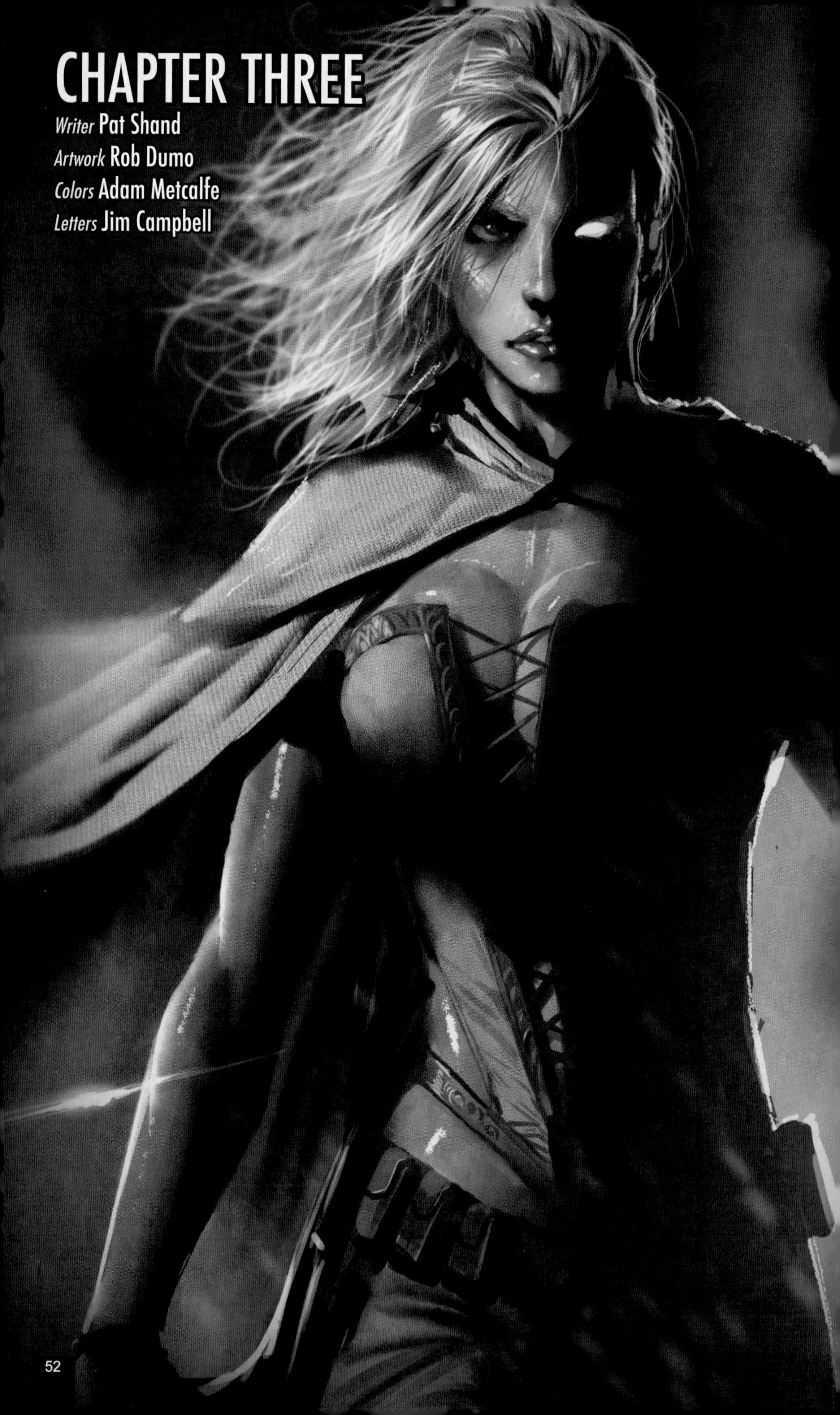

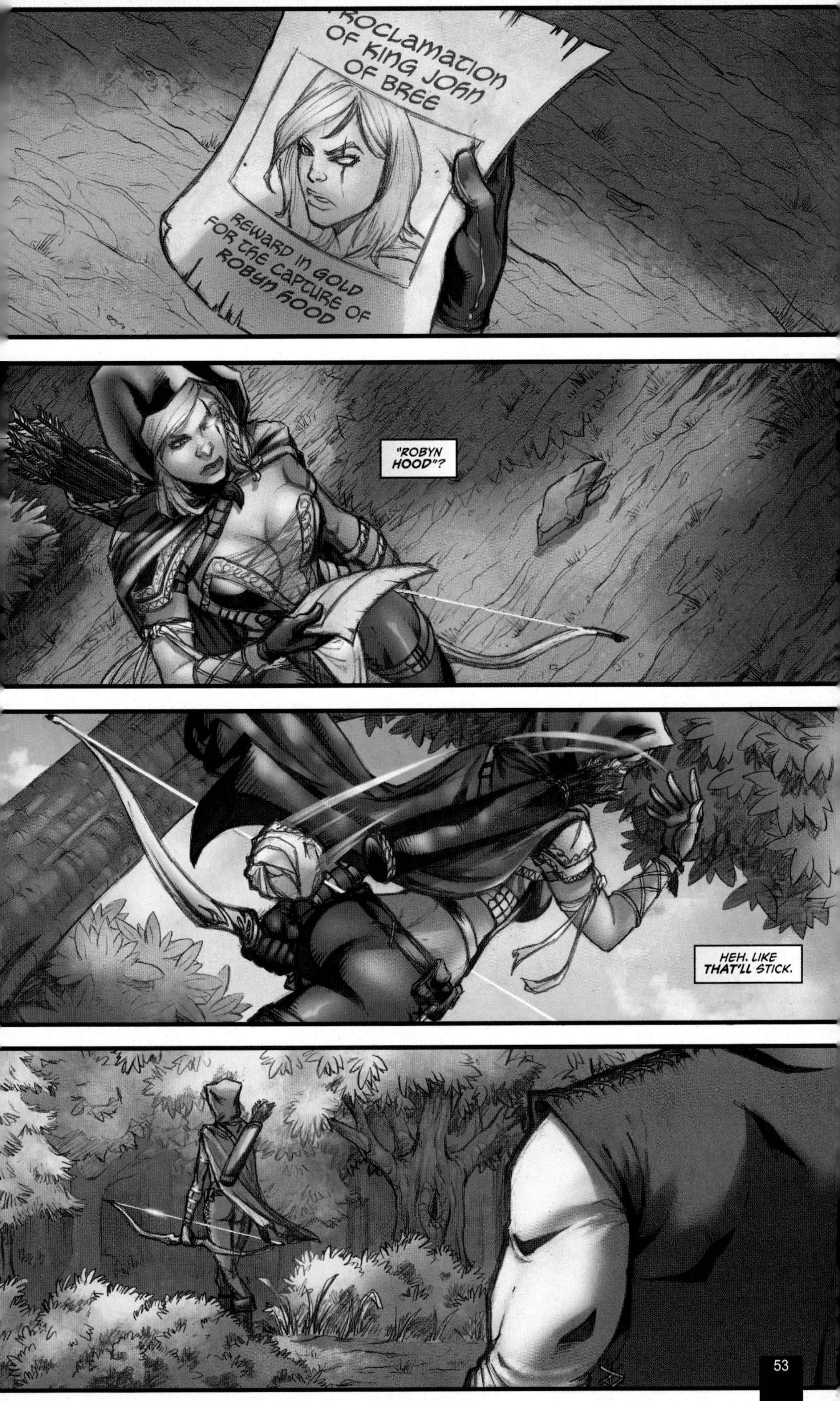
ROCLAMATION OF KING JOHN OF BREE
REWARD IN GOLD FOR THE CAPTURE OF ROBYN HOOD
"ROBYN HOOD"?
HEH. LIKE THAT'LL STICK.

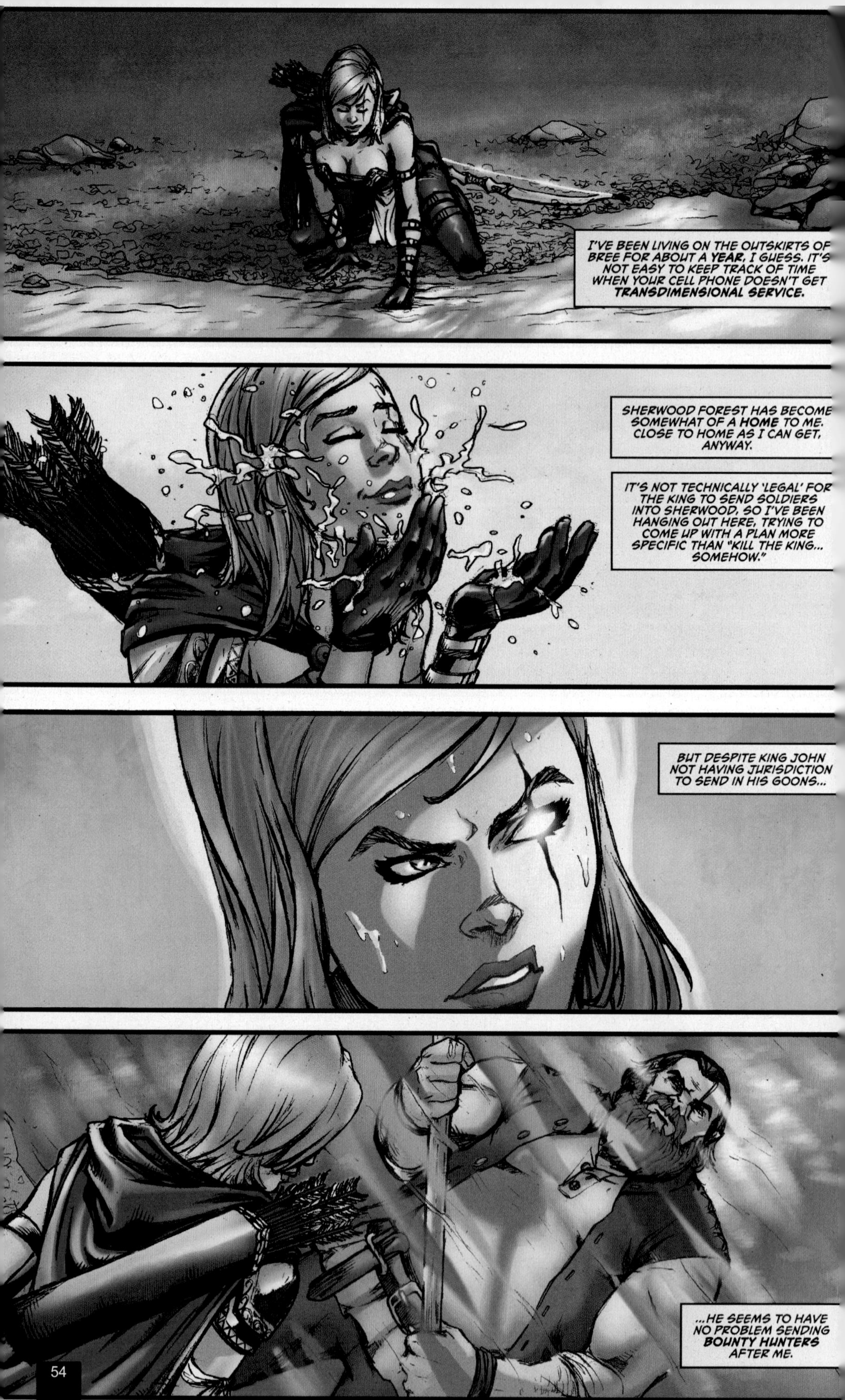
I'VE BEEN LIVING ON THE OUTSKIRTS OF BREE FOR ABOUT A **YEAR**, I GUESS. IT'S NOT EASY TO KEEP TRACK OF TIME WHEN YOUR CELL PHONE DOESN'T GET **TRANSDIMENSIONAL SERVICE**.
SHERWOOD FOREST HAS BECOME SOMEWHAT OF A **HOME** TO ME. CLOSE TO HOME AS I CAN GET, ANYWAY.
IT'S NOT TECHNICALLY 'LEGAL' FOR THE KING TO SEND SOLDIERS INTO SHERWOOD, SO I'VE BEEN HANGING OUT HERE, TRYING TO COME UP WITH A PLAN MORE SPECIFIC THAN "KILL THE KING... SOMEHOW."
BUT DESPITE KING JOHN NOT HAVING JURISDICTION TO SEND IN HIS GOONS...
...HE SEEMS TO HAVE NO PROBLEM SENDING **BOUNTY HUNTERS** AFTER ME.

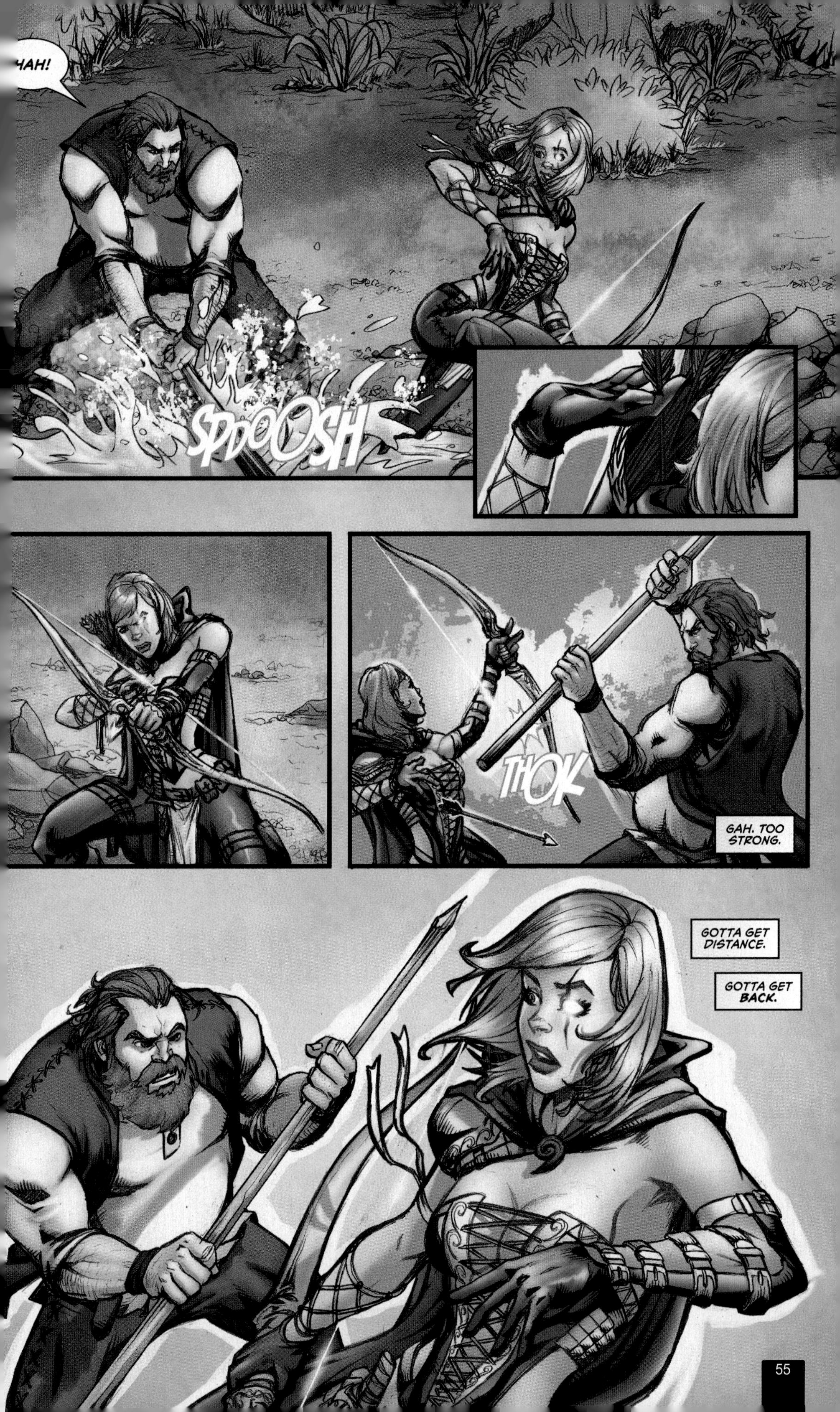
HAH!
SPDOOSH
THOK
GAH. TOO STRONG.
GOTTA GET DISTANCE.
GOTTA GET BACK.

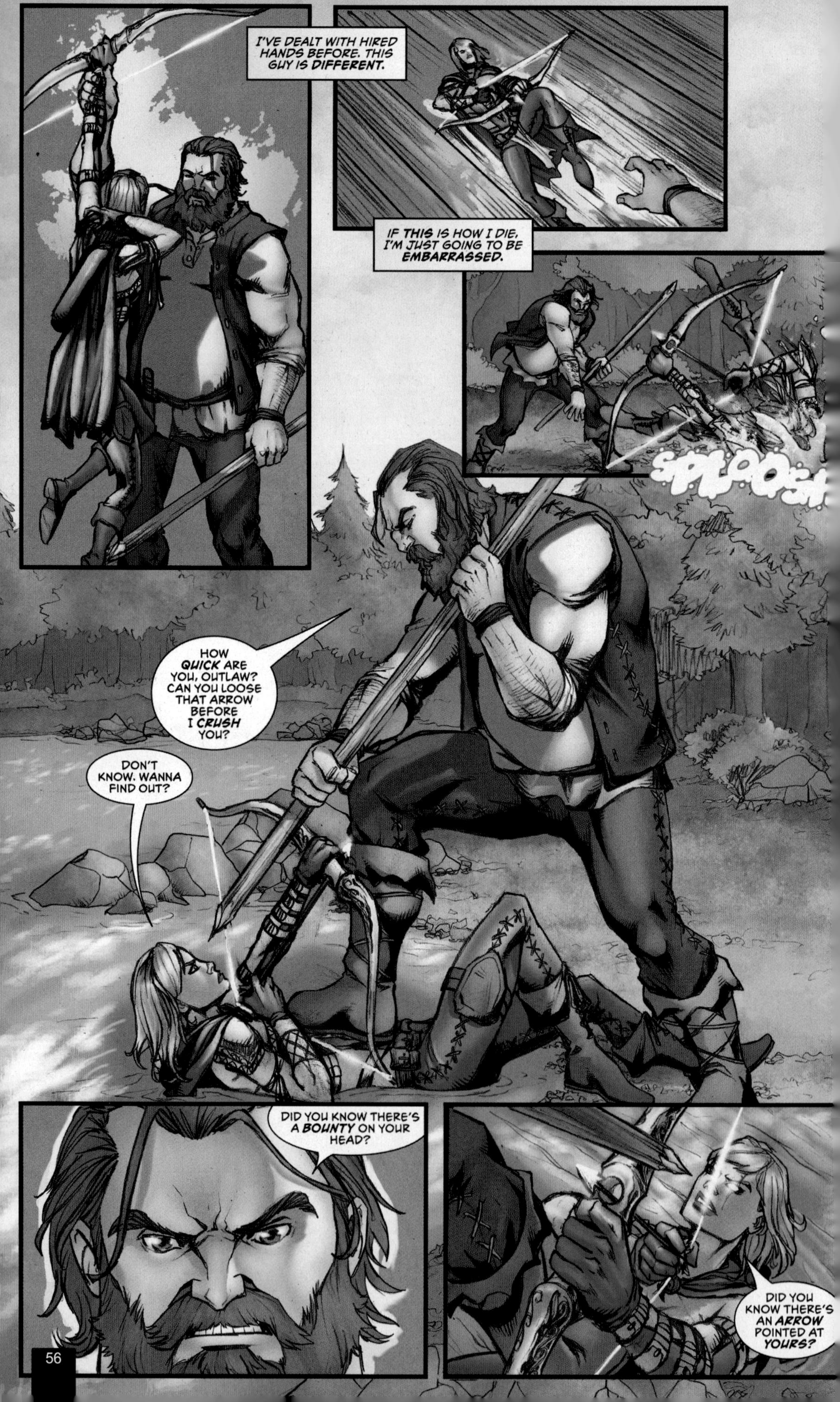

I'VE DEALT WITH HIRED HANDS BEFORE. THIS GUY IS DIFFERENT.
IF THIS IS HOW I DIE, I'M JUST GOING TO BE EMBARRASSED.
SPLOOSH
HOW QUICK ARE YOU, OUTLAW? CAN YOU LOOSE THAT ARROW BEFORE I CRUSH YOU?
DON'T KNOW. WANNA FIND OUT?
DID YOU KNOW THERE'S A BOUNTY ON YOUR HEAD?
DID YOU KNOW THERE'S AN ARROW POINTED AT YOURS?

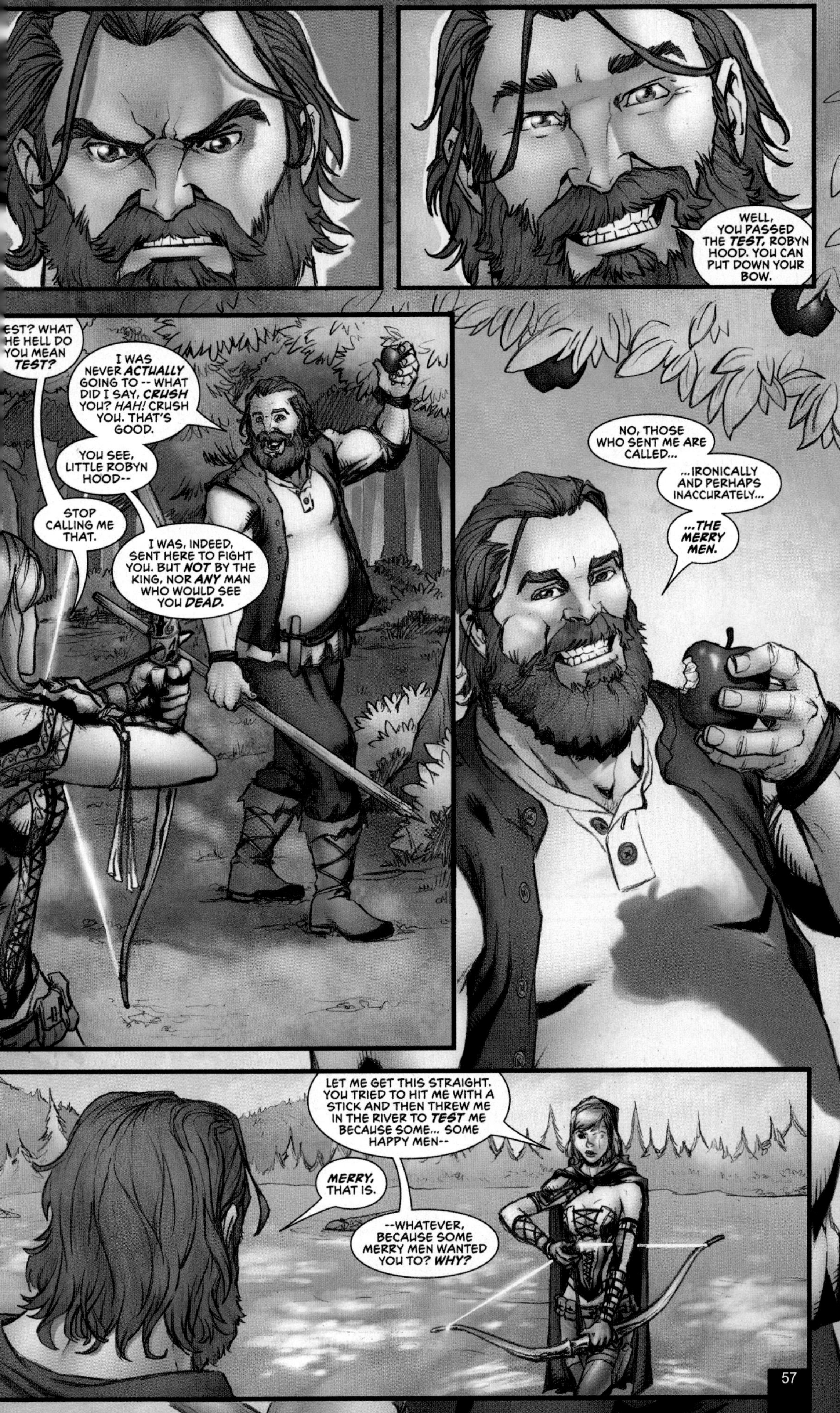
WELL, YOU PASSED THE TEST, ROBYN HOOD. YOU CAN PUT DOWN YOUR BOW.
EST? WHAT HE HELL DO YOU MEAN TEST?
I WAS NEVER ACTUALLY GOING TO -- WHAT DID I SAY, CRUSH YOU? HAH! CRUSH YOU. THAT'S GOOD.
YOU SEE, LITTLE ROBYN HOOD--
STOP CALLING ME THAT.
I WAS, INDEED, SENT HERE TO FIGHT YOU. BUT NOT BY THE KING, NOR ANY MAN WHO WOULD SEE YOU DEAD.
NO, THOSE WHO SENT ME ARE CALLED...
...IRONICALLY AND PERHAPS INACCURATELY...
...THE MERRY MEN.
LET ME GET THIS STRAIGHT. YOU TRIED TO HIT ME WITH A STICK AND THEN THREW ME IN THE RIVER TO TEST ME BECAUSE SOME... SOME HAPPY MEN--
MERRY, THAT IS.
--WHATEVER, BECAUSE SOME MERRY MEN WANTED YOU TO? WHY?

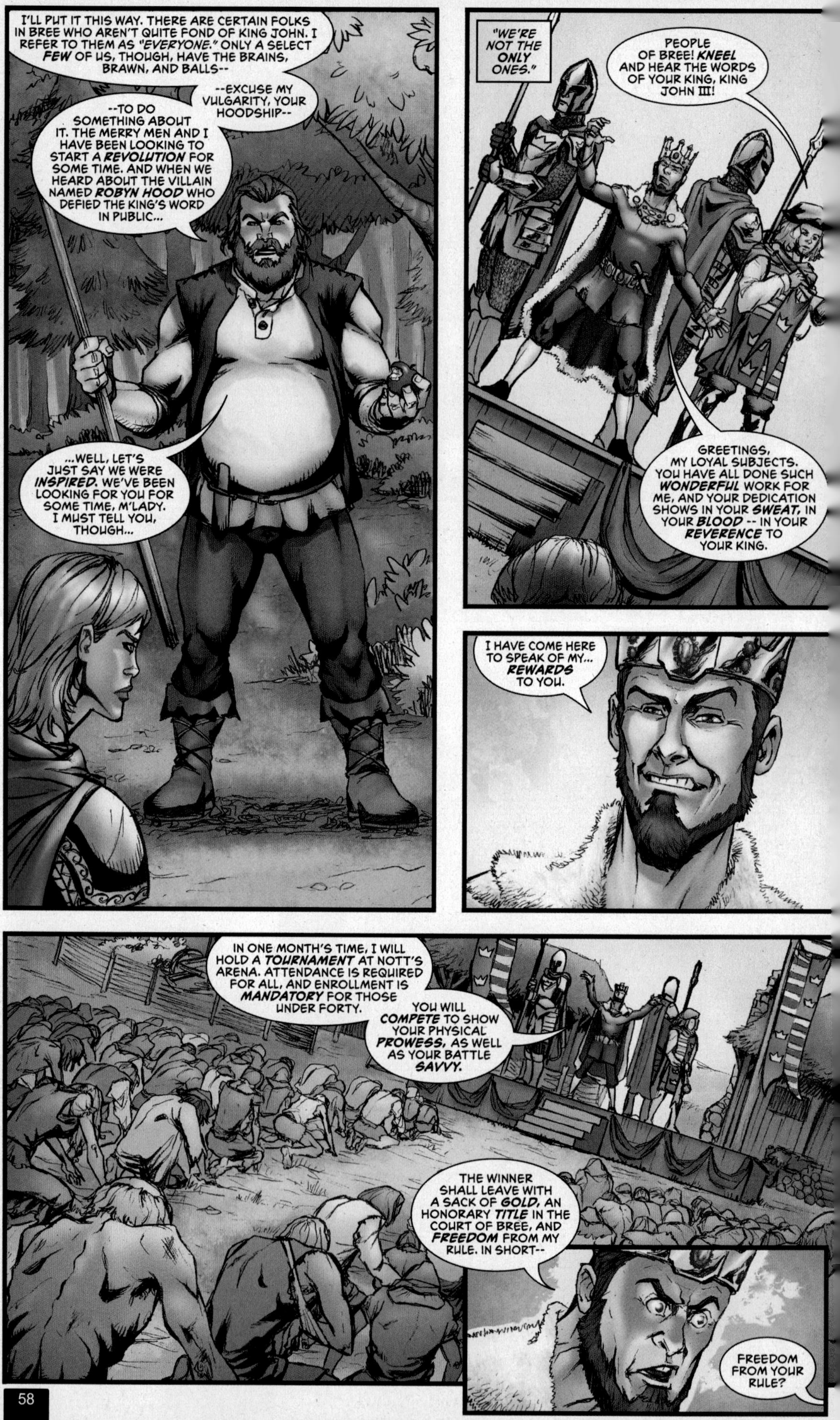
I'LL PUT IT THIS WAY. THERE ARE CERTAIN FOLKS IN BREE WHO AREN'T QUITE FOND OF KING JOHN. I REFER TO THEM AS "EVERYONE." ONLY A SELECT FEW OF US, THOUGH, HAVE THE BRAINS, BRAWN, AND BALLS--
--EXCUSE MY VULGARITY, YOUR HOODSHIP--
--TO DO SOMETHING ABOUT IT. THE MERRY MEN AND I HAVE BEEN LOOKING TO START A REVOLUTION FOR SOME TIME. AND WHEN WE HEARD ABOUT THE VILLAIN NAMED ROBYN HOOD WHO DEFIED THE KING'S WORD IN PUBLIC...
...WELL, LET'S JUST SAY WE WERE INSPIRED. WE'VE BEEN LOOKING FOR YOU FOR SOME TIME, M'LADY. I MUST TELL YOU, THOUGH...
"WE'RE NOT THE ONLY ONES."
PEOPLE OF BREE! KNEEL AND HEAR THE WORDS OF YOUR KING, KING JOHN III!
GREETINGS, MY LOYAL SUBJECTS. YOU HAVE ALL DONE SUCH WONDERFUL WORK FOR ME, AND YOUR DEDICATION SHOWS IN YOUR SWEAT, IN YOUR BLOOD -- IN YOUR REVERENCE TO YOUR KING.
I HAVE COME HERE TO SPEAK OF MY... REWARDS TO YOU.
IN ONE MONTH'S TIME, I WILL HOLD A TOURNAMENT AT NOTT'S ARENA. ATTENDANCE IS REQUIRED FOR ALL, AND ENROLLMENT IS MANDATORY FOR THOSE UNDER FORTY.
YOU WILL COMPETE TO SHOW YOUR PHYSICAL PROWESS, AS WELL AS YOUR BATTLE SAVVY.
THE WINNER SHALL LEAVE WITH A SACK OF GOLD, AN HONORARY TITLE IN THE COURT OF BREE, AND FREEDOM FROM MY RULE. IN SHORT--
FREEDOM FROM YOUR RULE?

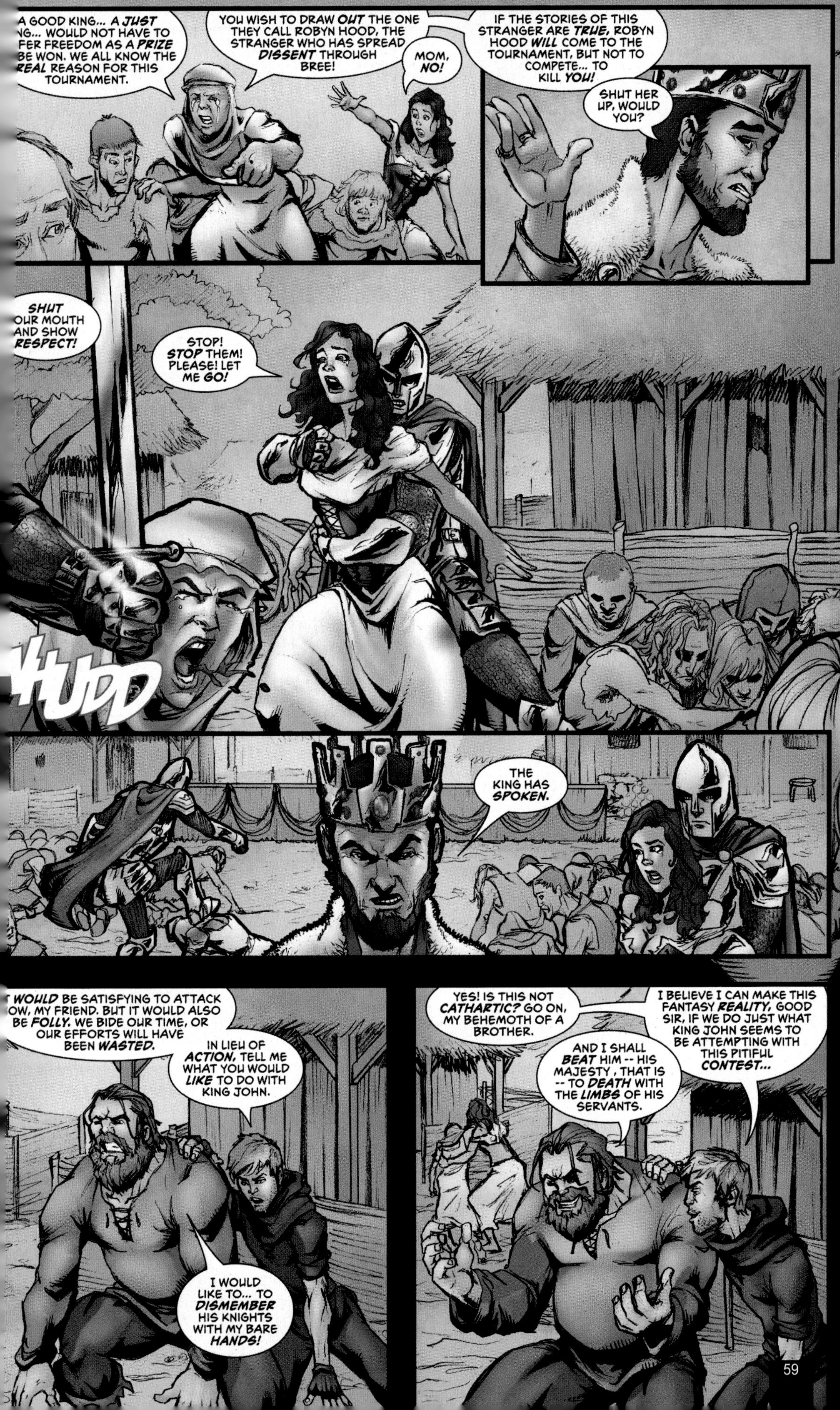

A GOOD KING... A JUST
NG... WOULD NOT HAVE TO
FER FREEDOM AS A PRIZE
BE WON. WE ALL KNOW THE
REAL REASON FOR THIS
TOURNAMENT.
YOU WISH TO DRAW OUT THE ONE THEY CALL ROBYN HOOD, THE STRANGER WHO HAS SPREAD DISSENT THROUGH BREE!
MOM, NO!
IF THE STORIES OF THIS STRANGER ARE TRUE, ROBYN HOOD WILL COME TO THE TOURNAMENT, BUT NOT TO COMPETE... TO KILL YOU!
SHUT HER UP, WOULD YOU?
SHUT
OUR MOUTH
AND SHOW
RESPECT!
STOP! STOP THEM! PLEASE! LET ME GO!
HUDD
THE KING HAS SPOKEN.
T WOULD BE SATISFYING TO ATTACK
OW, MY FRIEND. BUT IT WOULD ALSO
BE FOLLY. WE BIDE OUR TIME, OR
OUR EFFORTS WILL HAVE
BEEN WASTED.
IN LIEU OF ACTION, TELL ME WHAT YOU WOULD LIKE TO DO WITH KING JOHN.
I WOULD LIKE TO... TO DISMEMBER HIS KNIGHTS WITH MY BARE HANDS!
YES! IS THIS NOT CATHARTIC? GO ON, MY BEHEMOTH OF A BROTHER.
AND I SHALL BEAT HIM -- HIS MAJESTY, THAT IS -- TO DEATH WITH THE LIMBS OF HIS SERVANTS.
I BELIEVE I CAN MAKE THIS FANTASY REALITY, GOOD SIR, IF WE DO JUST WHAT KING JOHN SEEMS TO BE ATTEMPTING WITH THIS PITIFUL CONTEST...

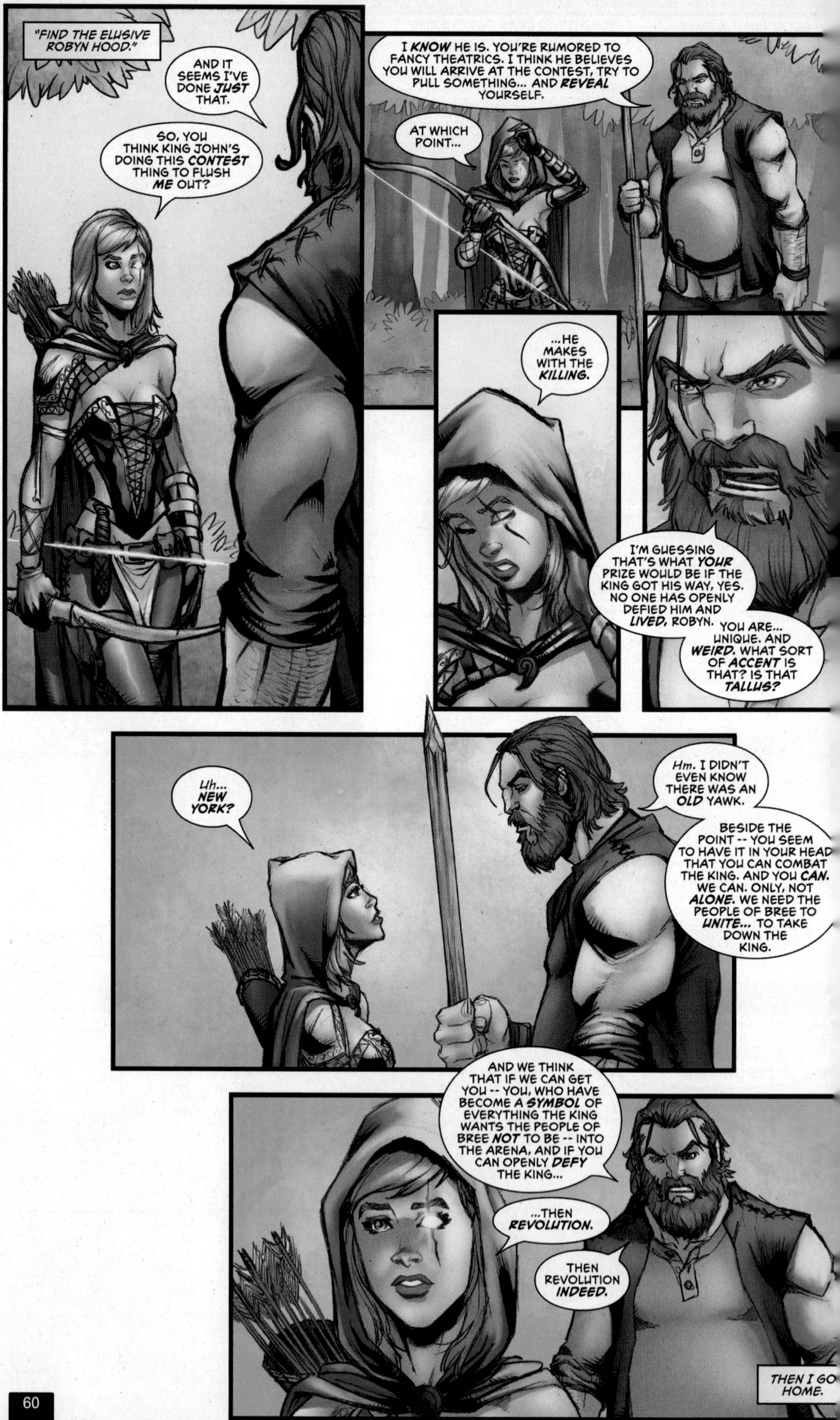
"FIND THE ELUSIVE ROBYN HOOD."
AND IT SEEMS I'VE DONE JUST THAT.
SO, YOU THINK KING JOHN'S DOING THIS CONTEST THING TO FLUSH ME OUT?
I KNOW HE IS. YOU'RE RUMORED TO FANCY THEATRICS. I THINK HE BELIEVES YOU WILL ARRIVE AT THE CONTEST, TRY TO PULL SOMETHING... AND REVEAL YOURSELF.
AT WHICH POINT...
...HE MAKES WITH THE KILLING.
I'M GUESSING THAT'S WHAT YOUR PRIZE WOULD BE IF THE KING GOT HIS WAY, YES. NO ONE HAS OPENLY DEFIED HIM AND LIVED, ROBYN.
YOU ARE... UNIQUE. AND WEIRD. WHAT SORT OF ACCENT IS THAT? IS THAT TALLUS?
Uh... NEW YORK?
Hm. I DIDN'T EVEN KNOW THERE WAS AN OLD YAWK.
BESIDE THE POINT -- YOU SEEM TO HAVE IT IN YOUR HEAD THAT YOU CAN COMBAT THE KING. AND YOU CAN. WE CAN. ONLY, NOT ALONE. WE NEED THE PEOPLE OF BREE TO UNITE... TO TAKE DOWN THE KING.
AND WE THINK THAT IF WE CAN GET YOU -- YOU, WHO HAVE BECOME A SYMBOL OF EVERYTHING THE KING WANTS THE PEOPLE OF BREE NOT TO BE -- INTO THE ARENA, AND IF YOU CAN OPENLY DEFY THE KING...
...THEN REVOLUTION.
THEN REVOLUTION INDEED.
THEN I GO HOME.

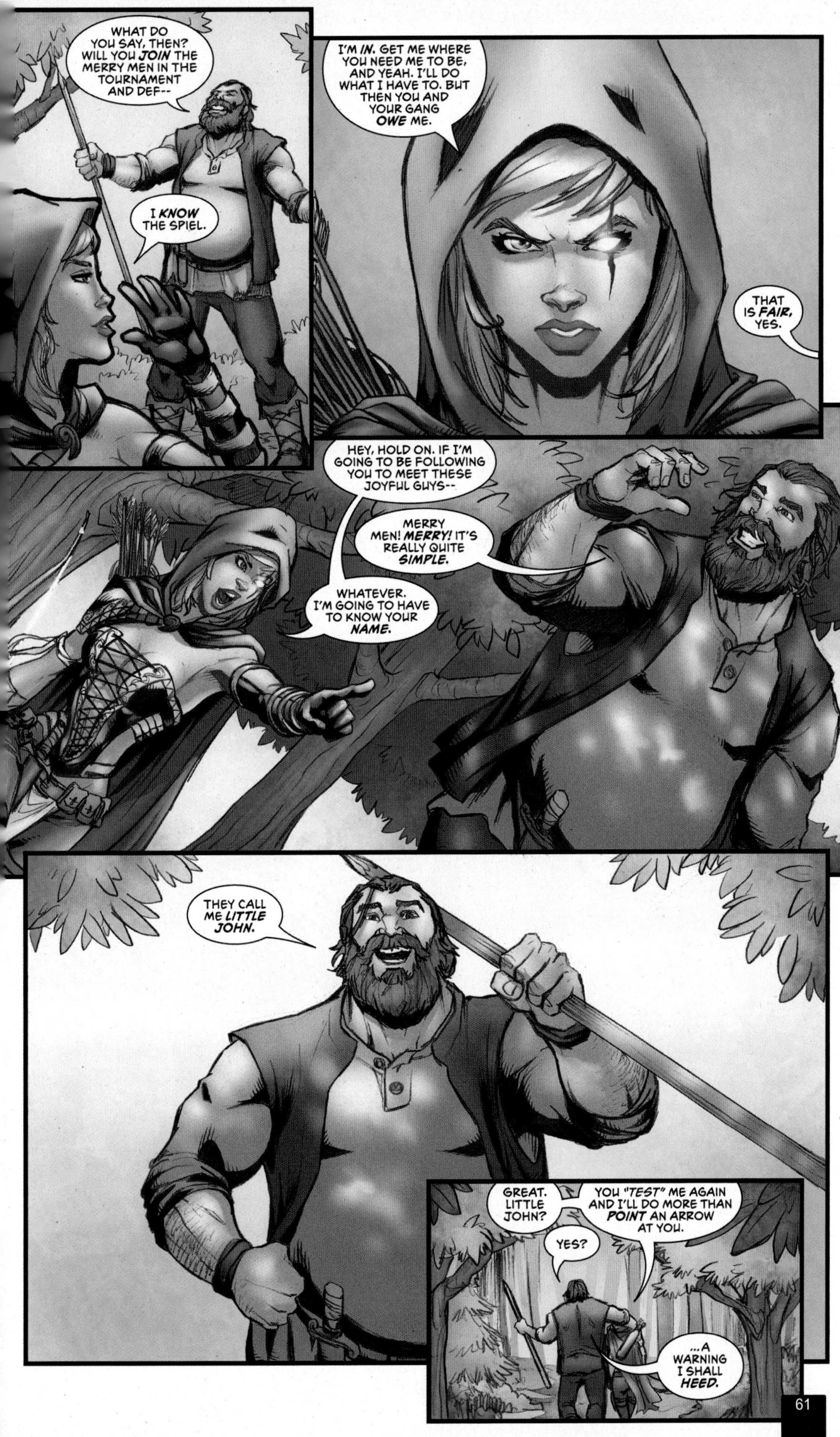
WHAT DO YOU SAY, THEN? WILL YOU JOIN THE MERRY MEN IN THE TOURNAMENT AND DEF--
I KNOW THE SPIEL.
I'M IN. GET ME WHERE YOU NEED ME TO BE, AND YEAH. I'LL DO WHAT I HAVE TO. BUT THEN YOU AND YOUR GANG OWE ME.
THAT IS FAIR, YES.
HEY, HOLD ON. IF I'M GOING TO BE FOLLOWING YOU TO MEET THESE JOYFUL GUYS--
MERRY MEN! MERRY! IT'S REALLY QUITE SIMPLE.
WHATEVER. I'M GOING TO HAVE TO KNOW YOUR NAME.
THEY CALL ME LITTLE JOHN.
GREAT. LITTLE JOHN?
YES?
YOU "TEST" ME AGAIN AND I'LL DO MORE THAN POINT AN ARROW AT YOU.
...A WARNING I SHALL HEED.

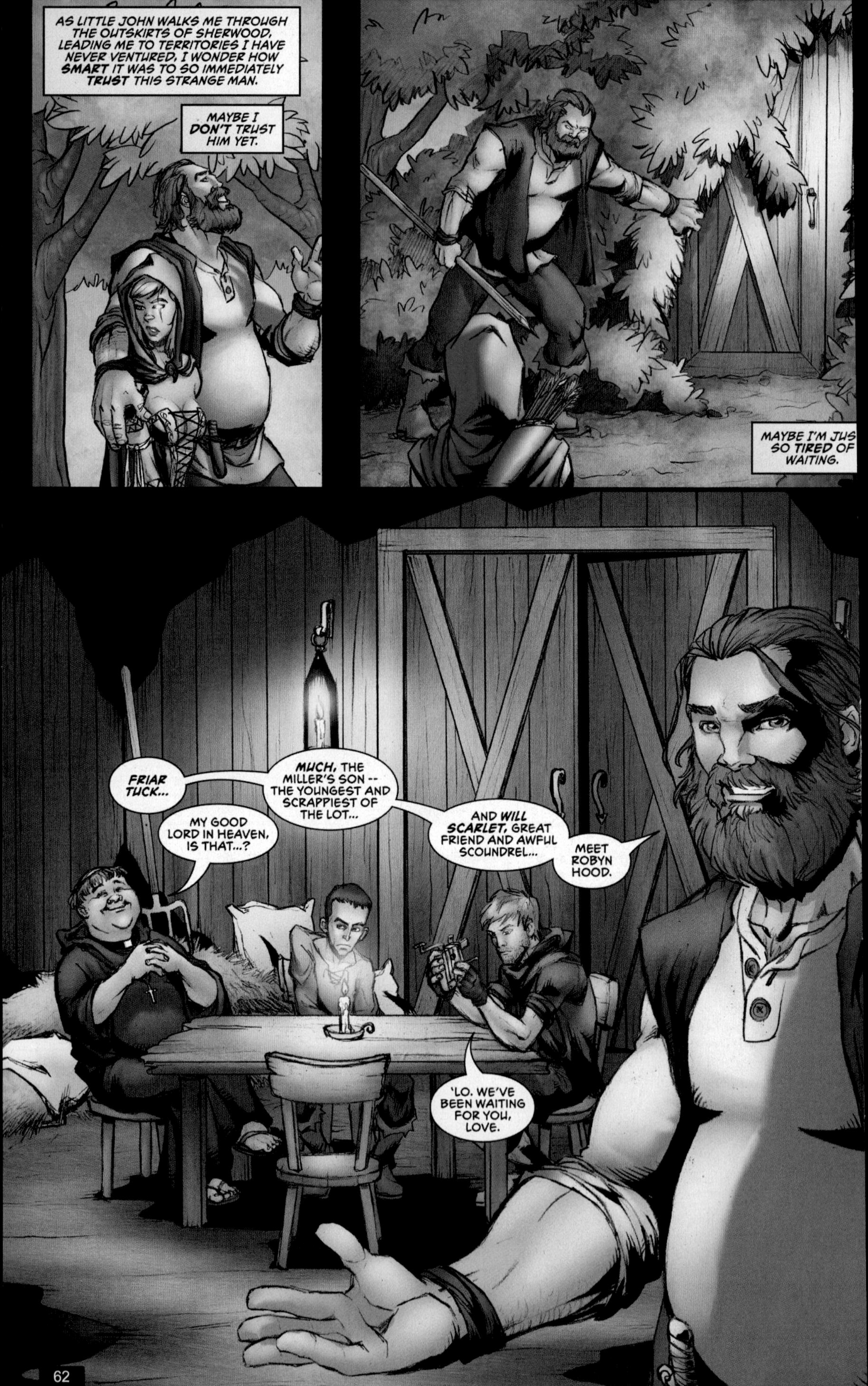
AS LITTLE JOHN WALKS ME THROUGH THE OUTSKIRTS OF SHERWOOD, LEADING ME TO TERRITORIES I HAVE NEVER VENTURED, I WONDER HOW SMART IT WAS TO SO IMMEDIATELY TRUST THIS STRANGE MAN.
MAYBE I DON'T TRUST HIM YET.
MAYBE I'M JUS SO TIRED OF WAITING.
FRIAR TUCK...
MUCH, THE MILLER'S SON -- THE YOUNGEST AND SCRAPPIEST OF THE LOT...
AND WILL SCARLET, GREAT FRIEND AND AWFUL SCOUNDREL...
MEET ROBYN HOOD.
MY GOOD LORD IN HEAVEN, IS THAT...?
'LO. WE'VE BEEN WAITING FOR YOU, LOVE.

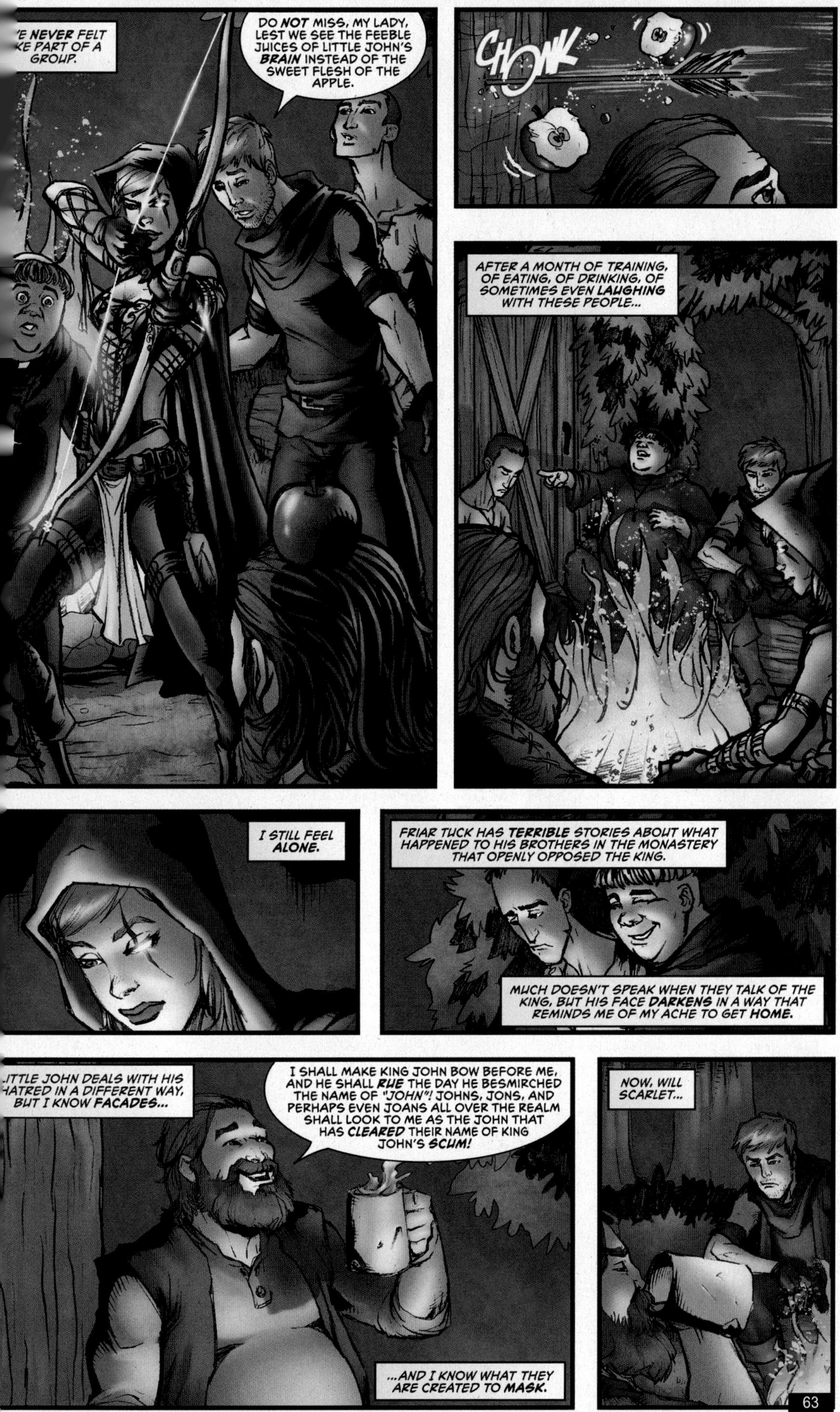
'VE NEVER FELT
KE PART OF A
GROUP.
DO NOT MISS, MY LADY, LEST WE SEE THE FEEBLE JUICES OF LITTLE JOHN'S BRAIN INSTEAD OF THE SWEET FLESH OF THE APPLE.
CHONK
AFTER A MONTH OF TRAINING, OF EATING, OF DRINKING, OF SOMETIMES EVEN LAUGHING WITH THESE PEOPLE...
I STILL FEEL ALONE.
FRIAR TUCK HAS TERRIBLE STORIES ABOUT WHAT HAPPENED TO HIS BROTHERS IN THE MONASTERY THAT OPENLY OPPOSED THE KING.
MUCH DOESN'T SPEAK WHEN THEY TALK OF THE KING, BUT HIS FACE DARKENS IN A WAY THAT REMINDS ME OF MY ACHE TO GET HOME.
LITTLE JOHN DEALS WITH HIS HATRED IN A DIFFERENT WAY, BUT I KNOW FACADES...
I SHALL MAKE KING JOHN BOW BEFORE ME, AND HE SHALL RUE THE DAY HE BESMIRCHED THE NAME OF "JOHN"! JOHNS, JONS, AND PERHAPS EVEN JOANS ALL OVER THE REALM SHALL LOOK TO ME AS THE JOHN THAT HAS CLEARED THEIR NAME OF KING JOHN'S SCUM!
...AND I KNOW WHAT THEY ARE CREATED TO MASK.
NOW, WILL SCARLET...

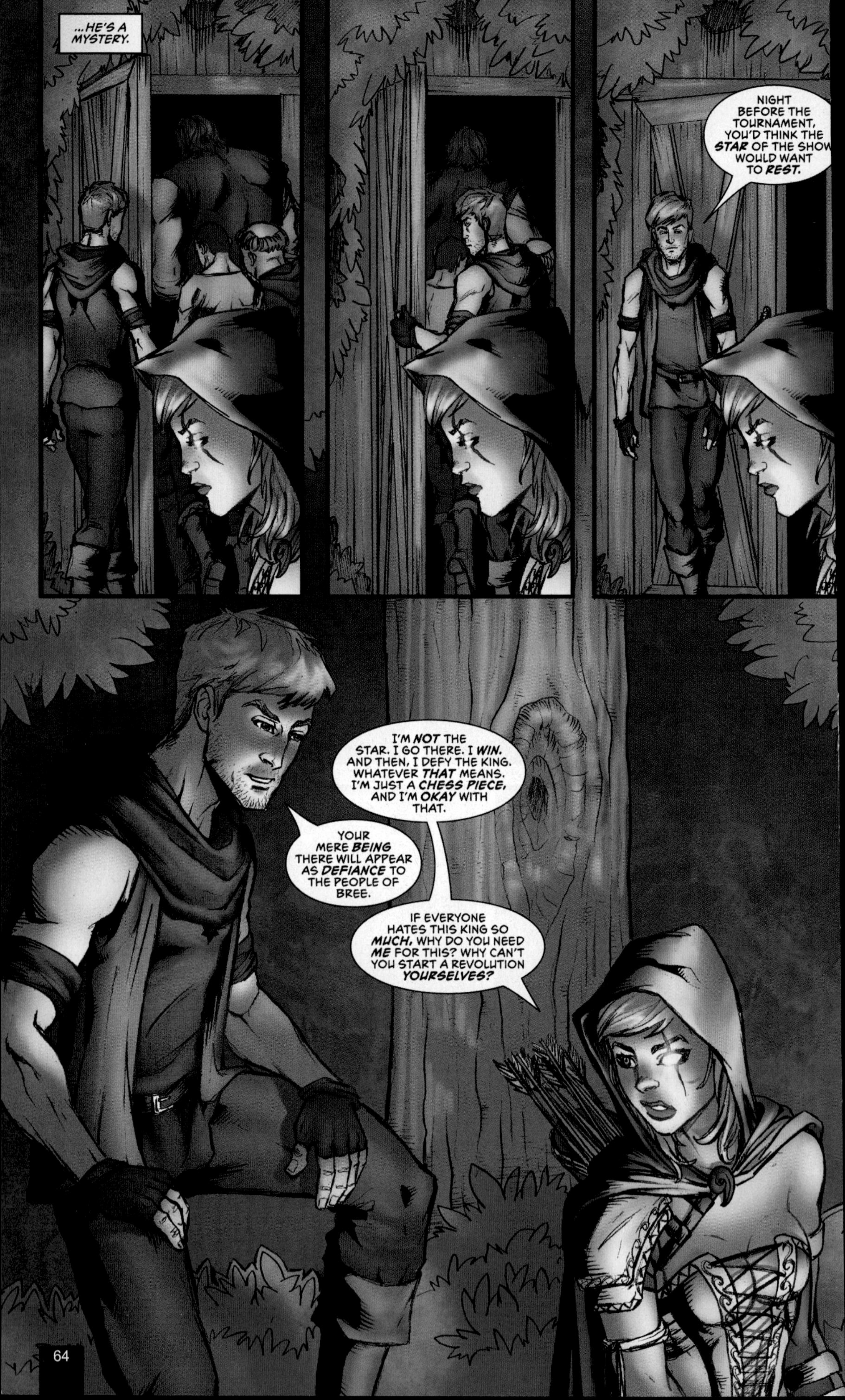
...HE'S A MYSTERY.
NIGHT BEFORE THE TOURNAMENT, YOU'D THINK THE STAR OF THE SHOW WOULD WANT TO REST.
I'M NOT THE STAR. I GO THERE. I WIN. AND THEN, I DEFY THE KING. WHATEVER THAT MEANS. I'M JUST A CHESS PIECE, AND I'M OKAY WITH THAT.
YOUR MERE BEING THERE WILL APPEAR AS DEFIANCE TO THE PEOPLE OF BREE.
IF EVERYONE HATES THIS KING SO MUCH, WHY DO YOU NEED ME FOR THIS? WHY CAN'T YOU START A REVOLUTION YOURSELVES?

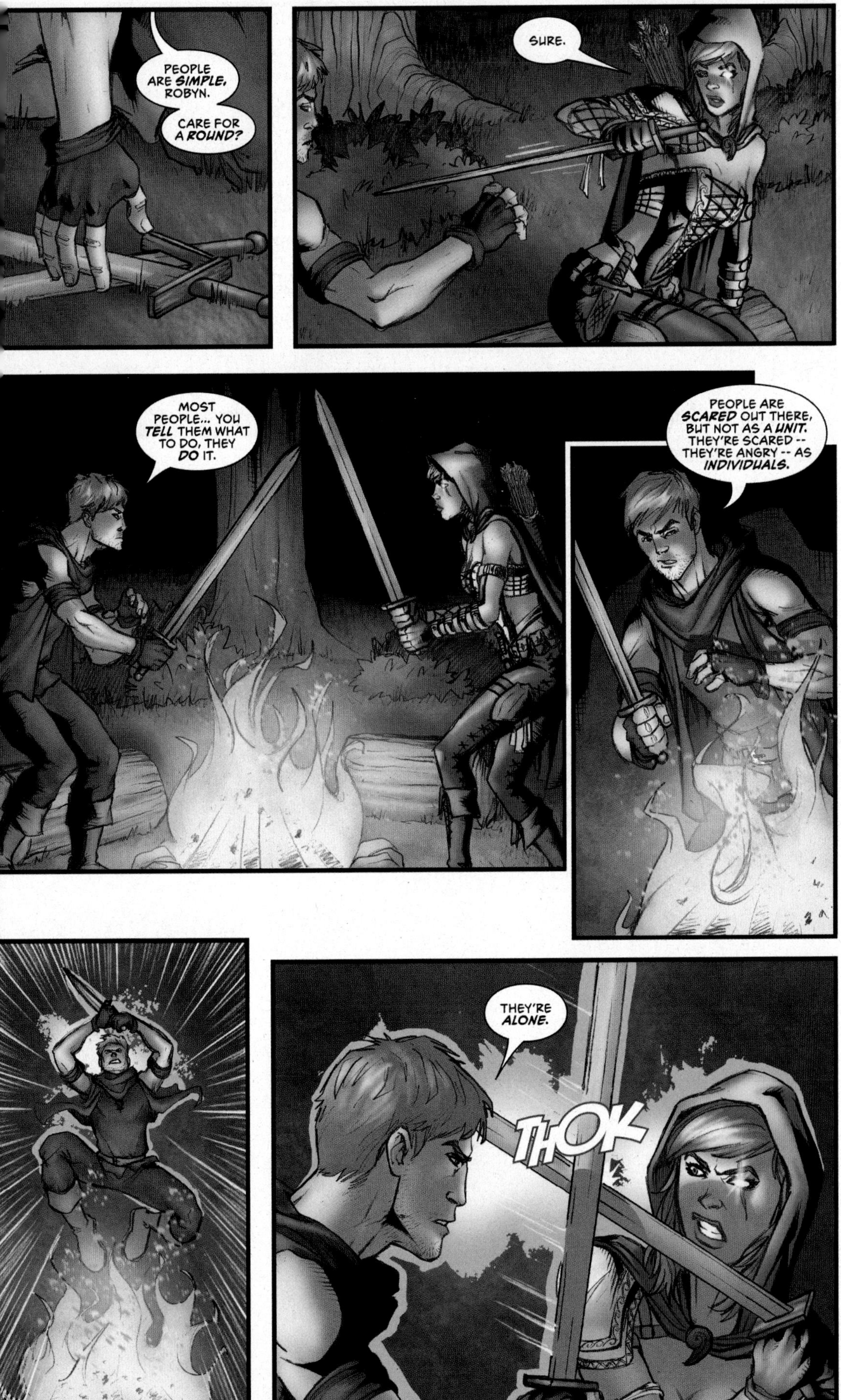
PEOPLE ARE SIMPLE, ROBYN.
CARE FOR A ROUND?
SURE.
MOST PEOPLE... YOU TELL THEM WHAT TO DO, THEY DO IT.
PEOPLE ARE SCARED OUT THERE, BUT NOT AS A UNIT. THEY'RE SCARED -- THEY'RE ANGRY -- AS INDIVIDUALS.
THEY'RE ALONE.
THOK

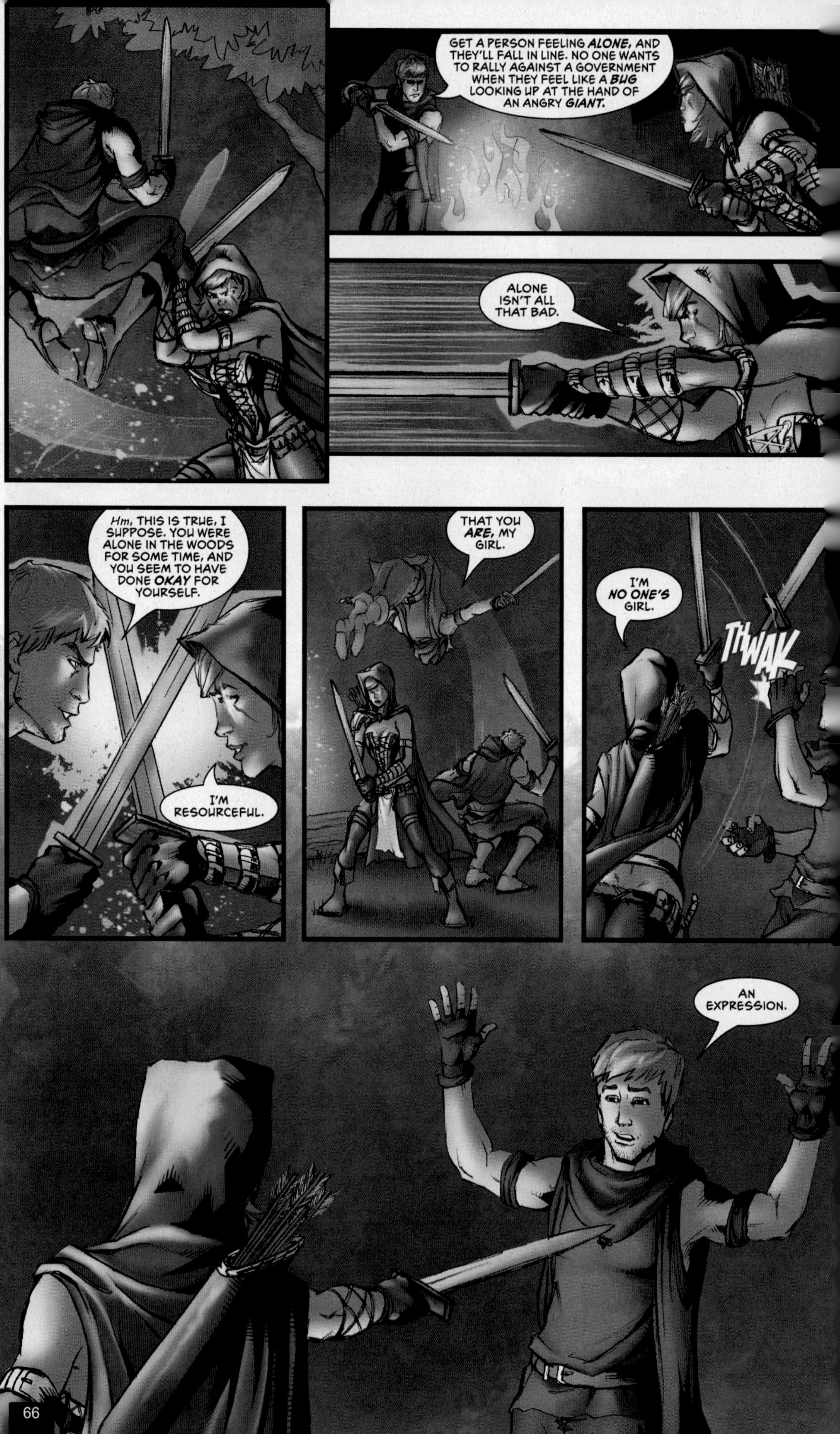
GET A PERSON FEELING ALONE, AND THEY'LL FALL IN LINE. NO ONE WANTS TO RALLY AGAINST A GOVERNMENT WHEN THEY FEEL LIKE A BUG LOOKING UP AT THE HAND OF AN ANGRY GIANT.
ALONE ISN'T ALL THAT BAD.
Hm, THIS IS TRUE, I SUPPOSE. YOU WERE ALONE IN THE WOODS FOR SOME TIME, AND YOU SEEM TO HAVE DONE OKAY FOR YOURSELF.
I'M RESOURCEFUL.
THAT YOU ARE, MY GIRL.
I'M NO ONE'S GIRL.
THWAK
AN EXPRESSION.

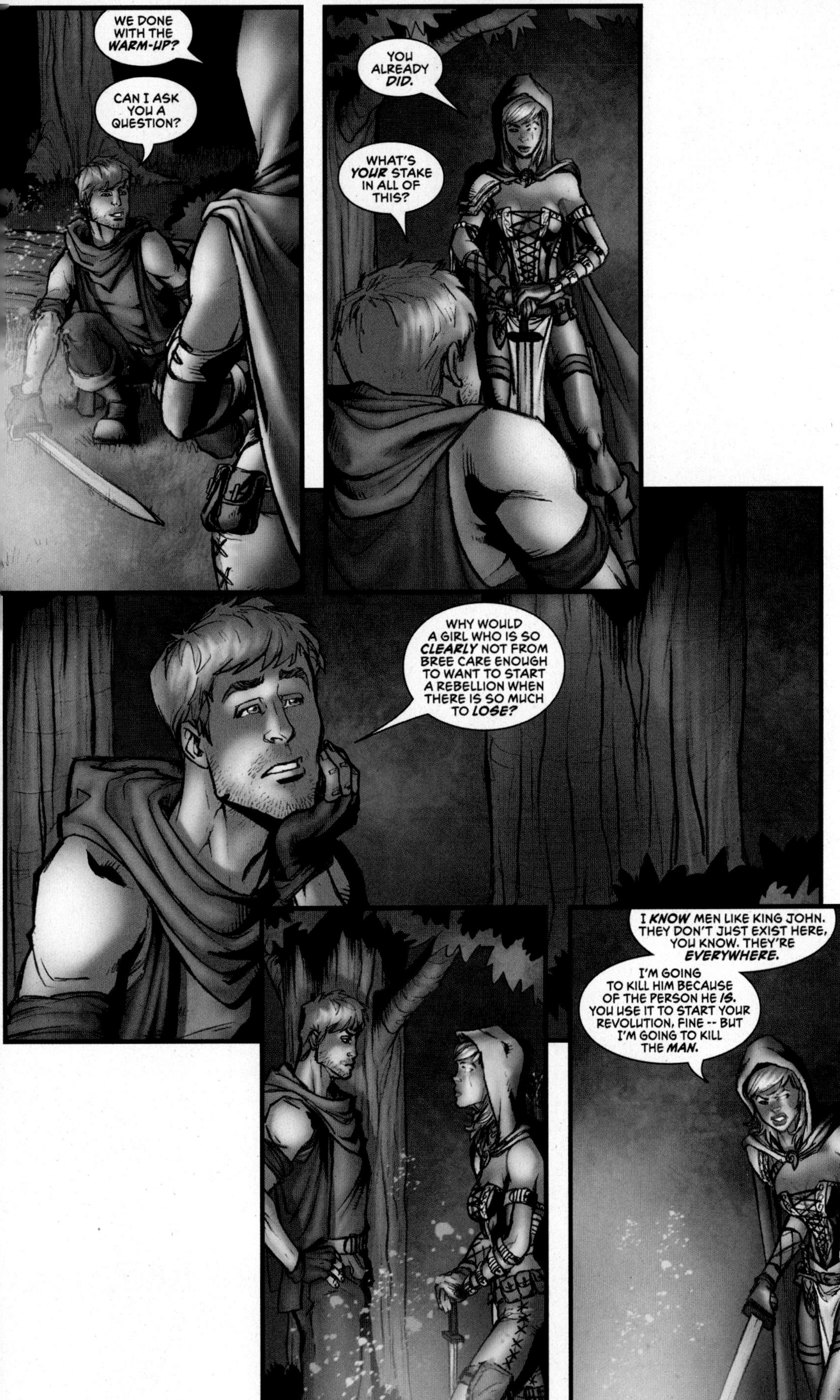
WE DONE WITH THE *WARM-UP?*
CAN I ASK YOU A QUESTION?
YOU ALREADY *DID.*
WHAT'S *YOUR* STAKE IN ALL OF THIS?
WHY WOULD A GIRL WHO IS SO *CLEARLY* NOT FROM BREE CARE ENOUGH TO WANT TO START A REBELLION WHEN THERE IS SO MUCH TO *LOSE?*
I *KNOW* MEN LIKE KING JOHN. THEY DON'T JUST EXIST HERE, YOU KNOW. THEY'RE *EVERYWHERE.*
I'M GOING TO KILL HIM BECAUSE OF THE PERSON HE *IS.* YOU USE IT TO START YOUR REVOLUTION, FINE -- BUT I'M GOING TO KILL THE *MAN.*

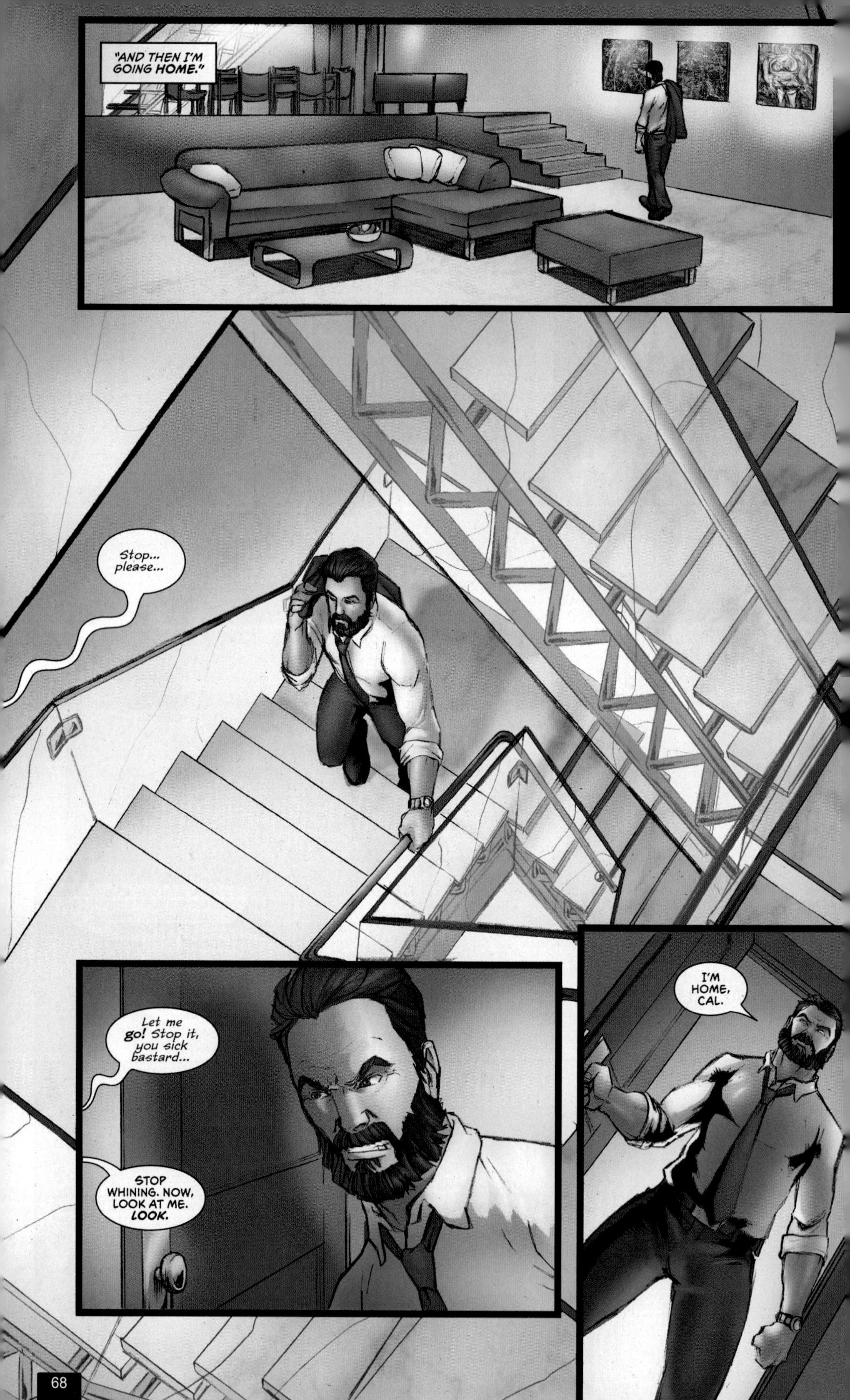
"AND THEN I'M GOING HOME."
Stop... please...
Let me go! Stop it, you sick bastard...
STOP WHINING. NOW, LOOK AT ME. LOOK.
I'M HOME, CAL.

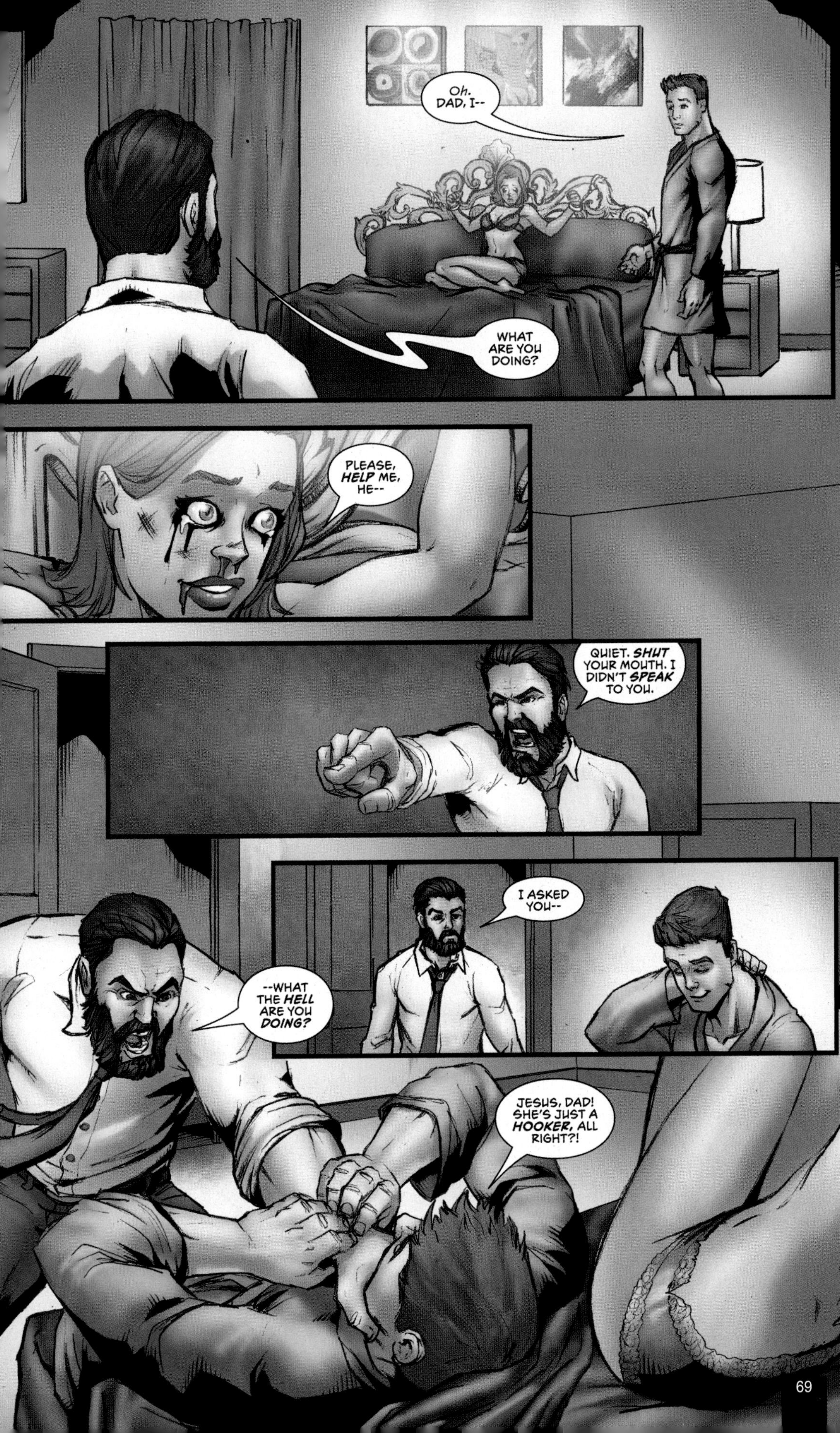
Oh. DAD, I--
WHAT ARE YOU DOING?
PLEASE, HELP ME, HE--
QUIET. SHUT YOUR MOUTH. I DIDN'T SPEAK TO YOU.
I ASKED YOU--
--WHAT THE HELL ARE YOU DOING?
JESUS, DAD! SHE'S JUST A HOOKER, ALL RIGHT?!

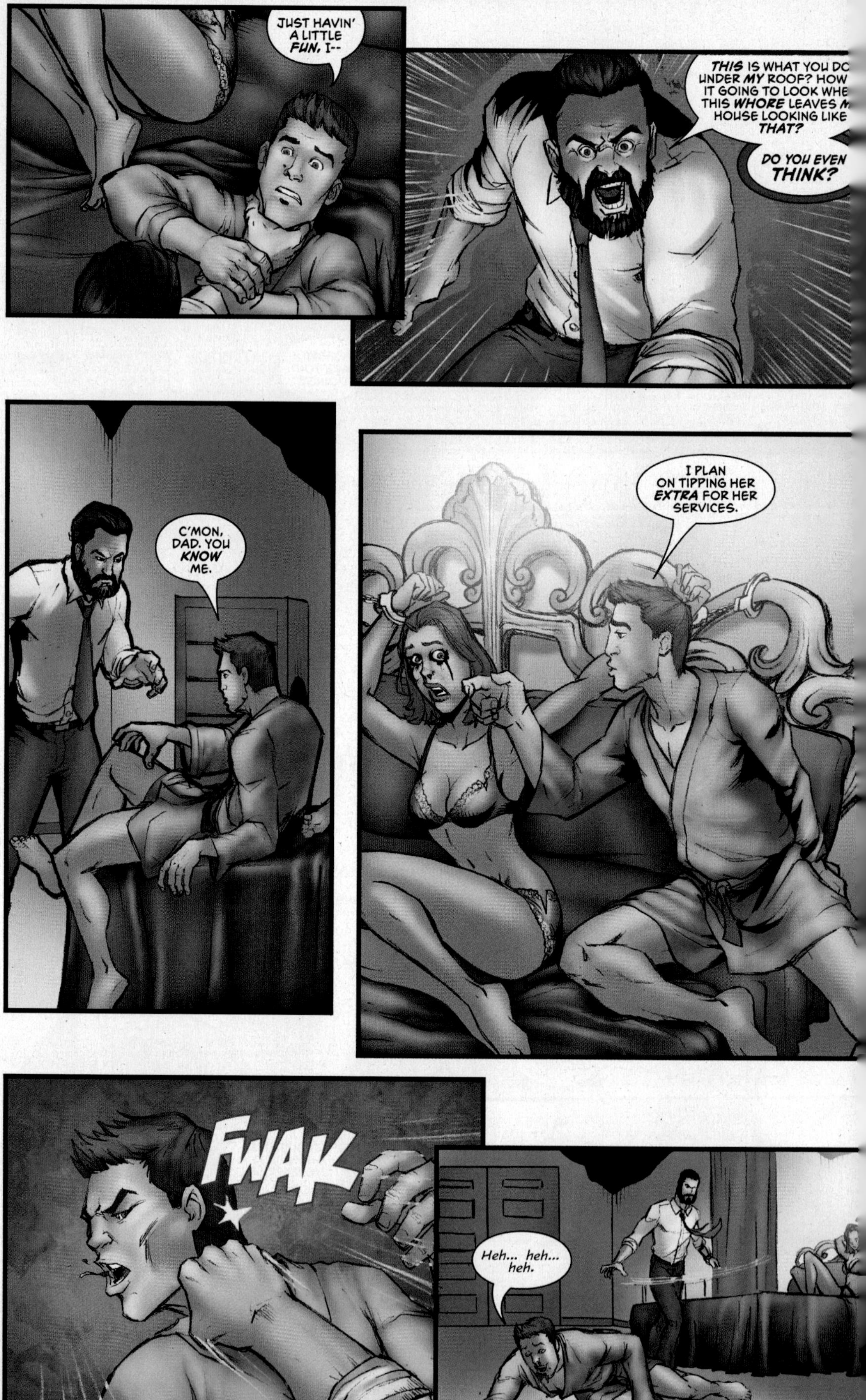

JUST HAVIN' A LITTLE FUN, I--
THIS IS WHAT YOU DO UNDER MY ROOF? HOW IT GOING TO LOOK WHE THIS WHORE LEAVES M HOUSE LOOKING LIKE THAT?
DO YOU EVEN THINK?
C'MON, DAD. YOU KNOW ME.
I PLAN ON TIPPING HER EXTRA FOR HER SERVICES.
FWAK
Heh... heh... heh.

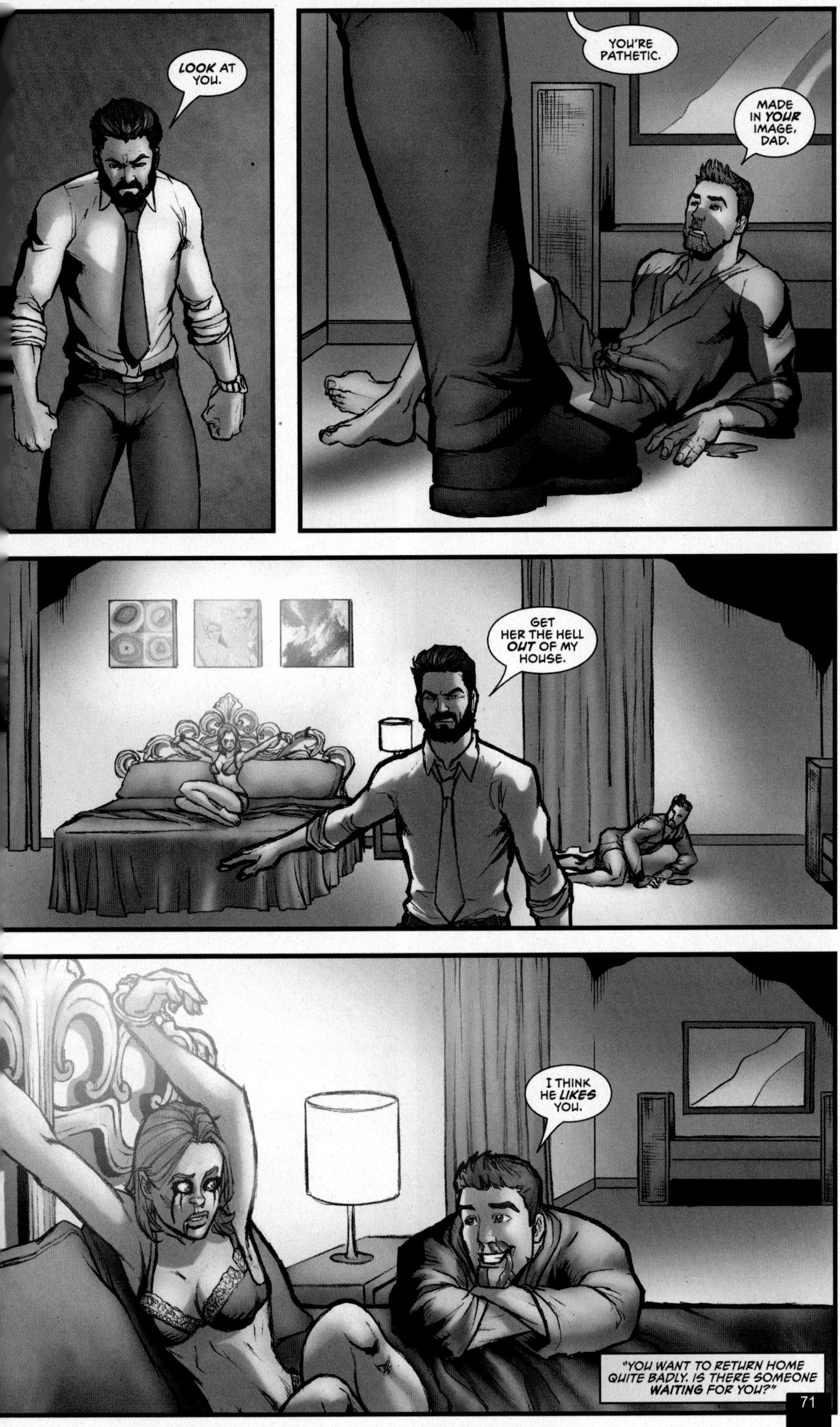
LOOK AT YOU.
YOU'RE PATHETIC.
MADE IN YOUR IMAGE, DAD.
GET HER THE HELL OUT OF MY HOUSE.
I THINK HE LIKES YOU.
"YOU WANT TO RETURN HOME QUITE BADLY. IS THERE SOMEONE WAITING FOR YOU?"

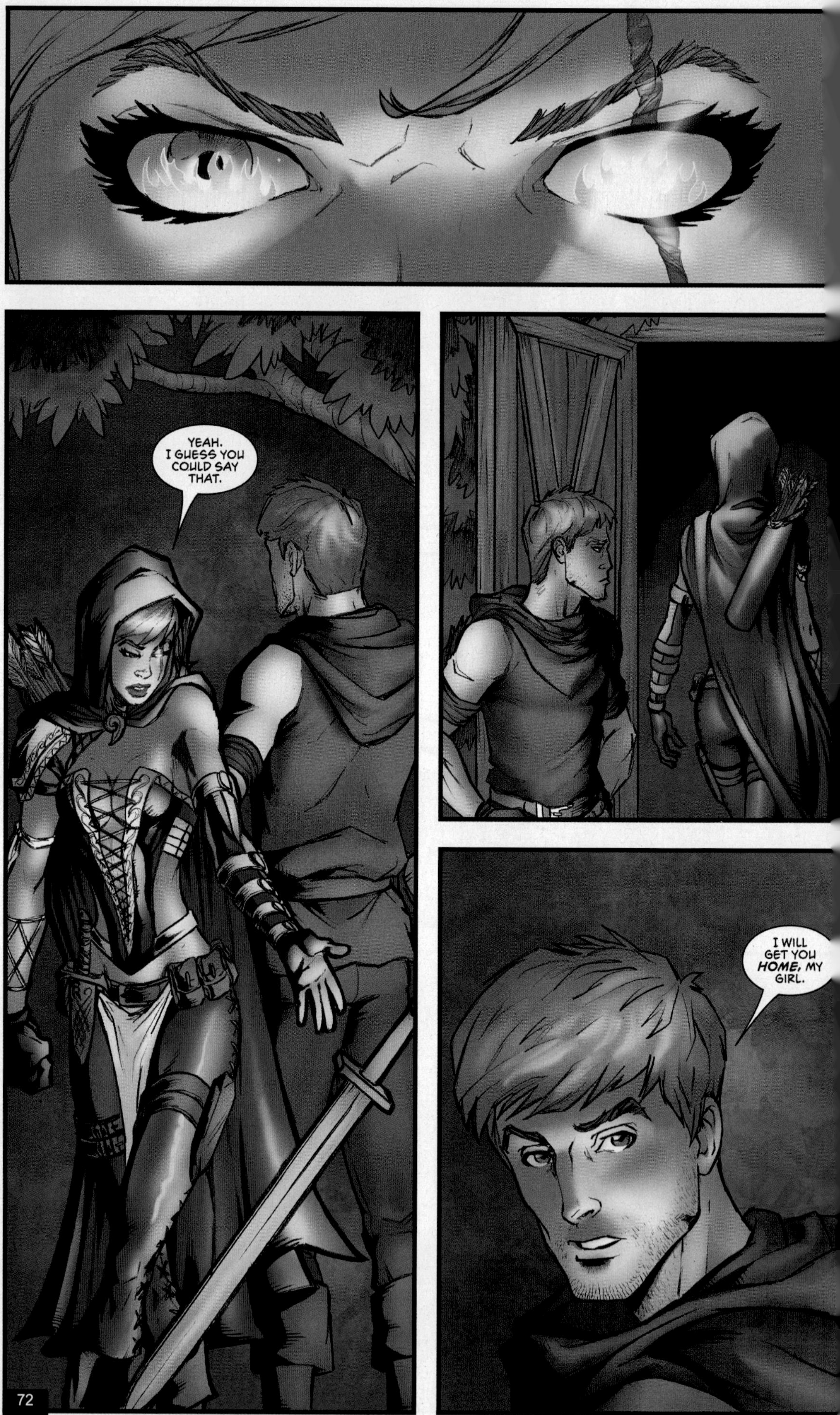
YEAH. I GUESS YOU COULD SAY THAT.
I WILL GET YOU *HOME*, MY GIRL.

THAT NIGHT, I DREAM OF KING JOHN STANDING OVER ME. HIS FACE DISTORTS, AND THEN HE BECOMES CAL. HOLDING ME DOWN. GRINNING.

AT FIRST, I'M HORRIFIED. I WAKE UP WITH A START AND BITE MY LIP TO KEEP FROM SCREAMING.

BUT I TAKE A MOMENT; I GO OUTSIDE.

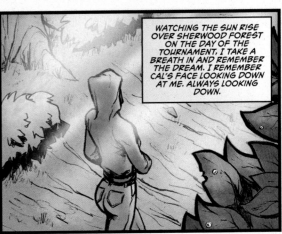

WATCHING THE SUN RISE OVER SHERWOOD FOREST ON THE DAY OF THE TOURNAMENT, I TAKE A BREATH IN AND REMEMBER THE DREAM. I REMEMBER CAL'S FACE LOOKING DOWN AT ME. ALWAYS LOOKING DOWN.

I'M GOING TO USE THAT.

HERE. WE SHALL ALL WEAR THESE. AND PULL YOUR HAIR BACK, OR THE KING WILL HAVE YOU SHOT ON SIGHT AND END OUR REVOLUTION.

YEAH, NOW I'LL BLEND IN.

JUST LONG ENOUGH TO MAKE A STAND. THEN, WE SHALL HANDLE IT.

"MAKE A STAND."

I'VE SPENT MY WHOLE LIFE DOING THINGS MY WAY. THE ONLY PERSON THAT EVER DEPENDED ON ME WAS MY MOTHER, AND SHE DIED.

73

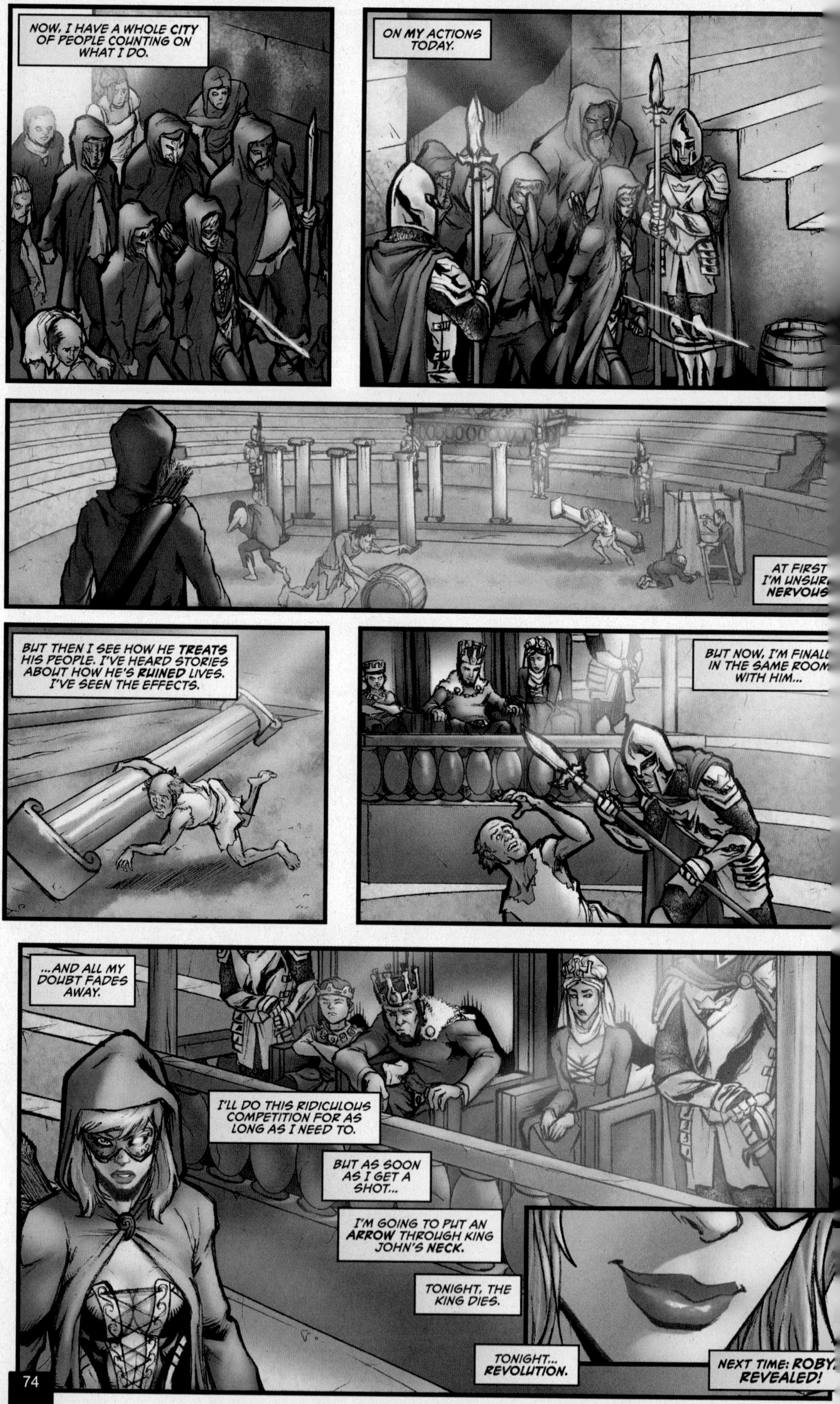
NOW, I HAVE A WHOLE CITY OF PEOPLE COUNTING ON WHAT I DO.
ON MY ACTIONS TODAY.
AT FIRST I'M UNSUR NERVOUS
BUT THEN I SEE HOW HE TREATS HIS PEOPLE. I'VE HEARD STORIES ABOUT HOW HE'S RUINED LIVES. I'VE SEEN THE EFFECTS.
BUT NOW, I'M FINALL IN THE SAME ROOM WITH HIM...
...AND ALL MY DOUBT FADES AWAY.
I'LL DO THIS RIDICULOUS COMPETITION FOR AS LONG AS I NEED TO.
BUT AS SOON AS I GET A SHOT...
I'M GOING TO PUT AN ARROW THROUGH KING JOHN'S NECK.
TONIGHT, THE KING DIES.
TONIGHT... REVOLUTION.
NEXT TIME: ROBY REVEALED!

# Grimm Fairy Tales
### presents:

# ROBYN HOOD
## ORIGIN

# CHAPTER FOUR

*Writer* Pat Shand
*Artwork* Larry Watts
*Colors* Adam Metcalfe
*Letters* Jim Campbell

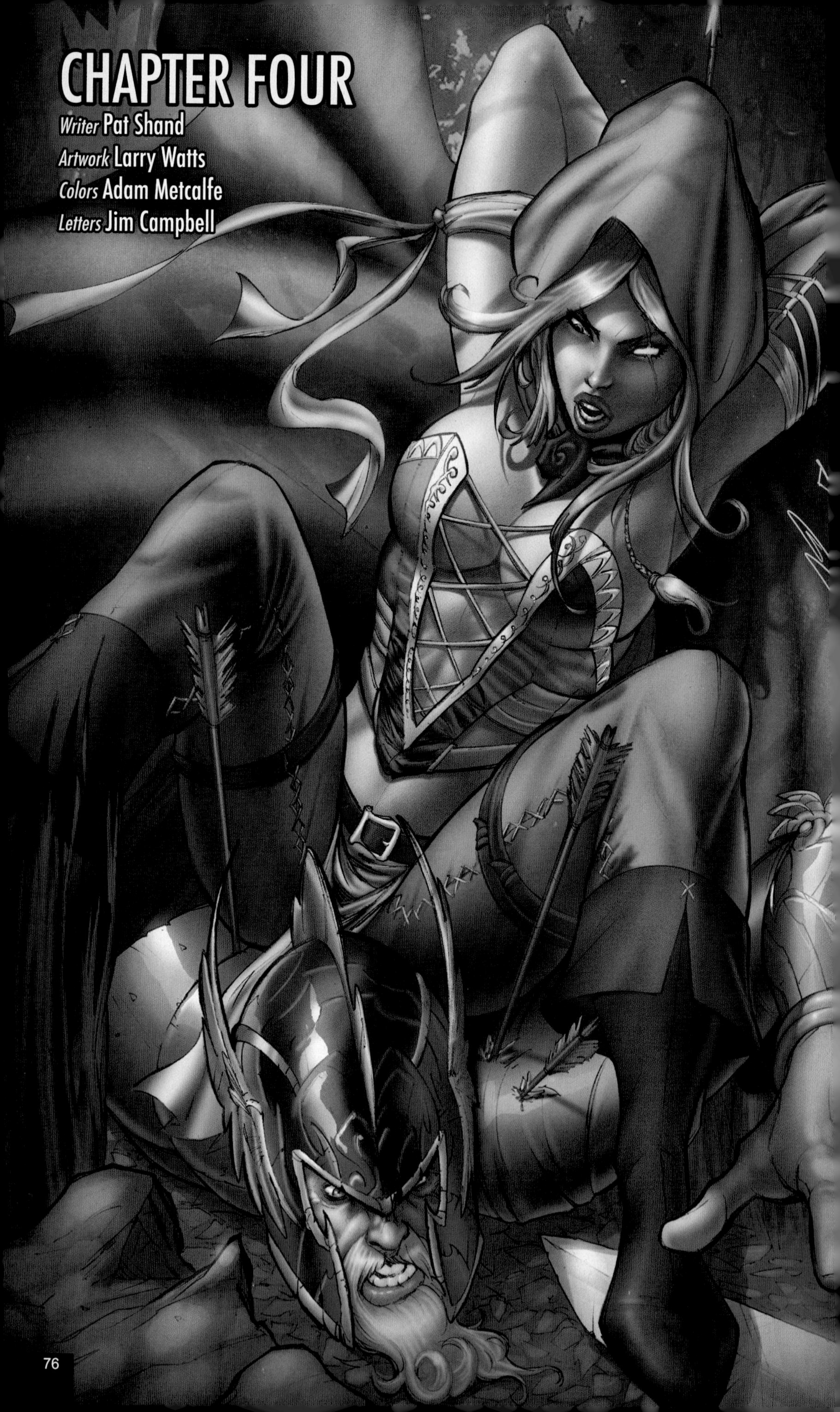

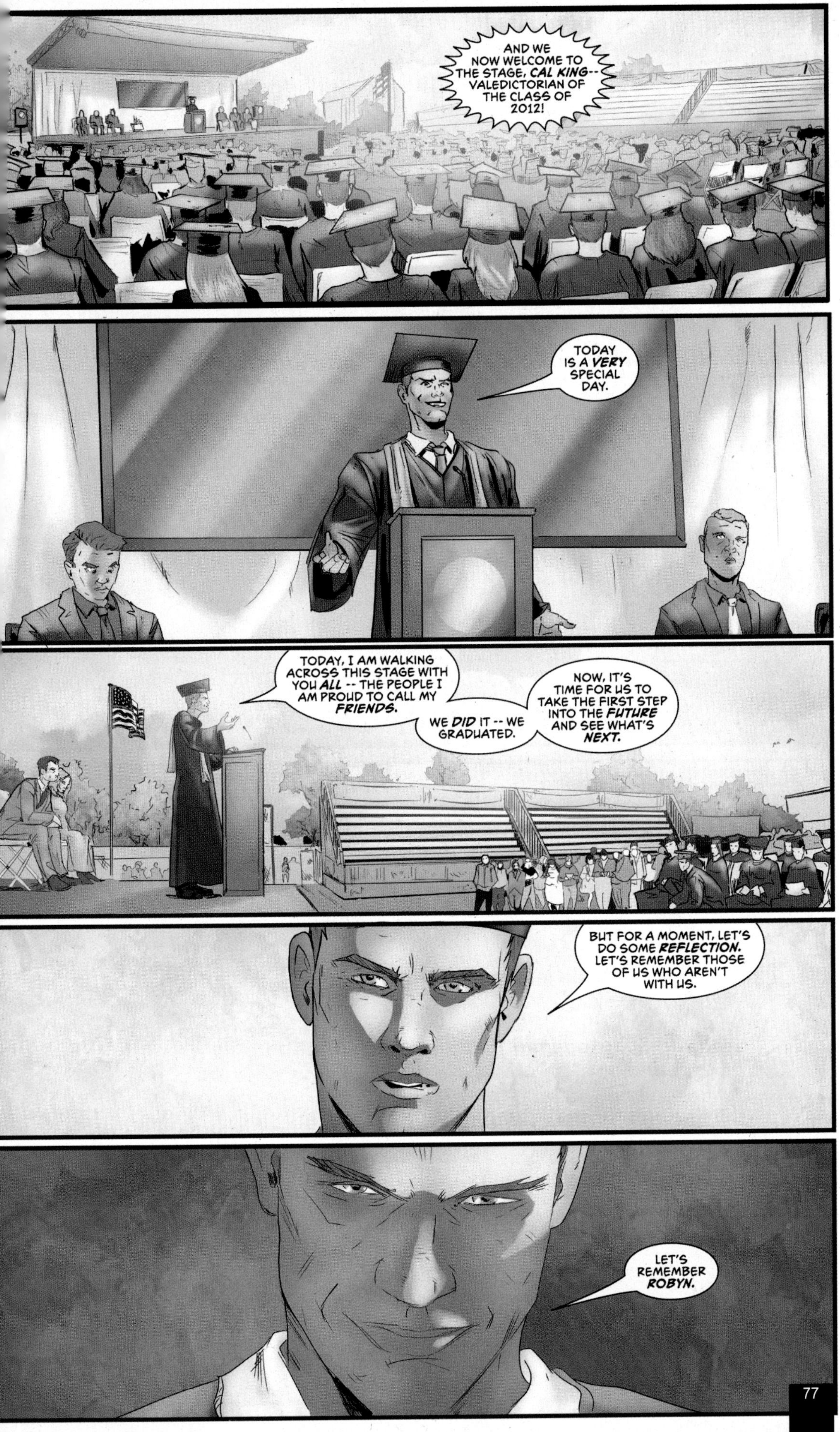
AND WE NOW WELCOME TO THE STAGE, CAL KING-- VALEDICTORIAN OF THE CLASS OF 2012!
TODAY IS A VERY SPECIAL DAY.
TODAY, I AM WALKING ACROSS THIS STAGE WITH YOU ALL -- THE PEOPLE I AM PROUD TO CALL MY FRIENDS.
WE DID IT -- WE GRADUATED.
NOW, IT'S TIME FOR US TO TAKE THE FIRST STEP INTO THE FUTURE AND SEE WHAT'S NEXT.
BUT FOR A MOMENT, LET'S DO SOME REFLECTION. LET'S REMEMBER THOSE OF US WHO AREN'T WITH US.
LET'S REMEMBER ROBYN.

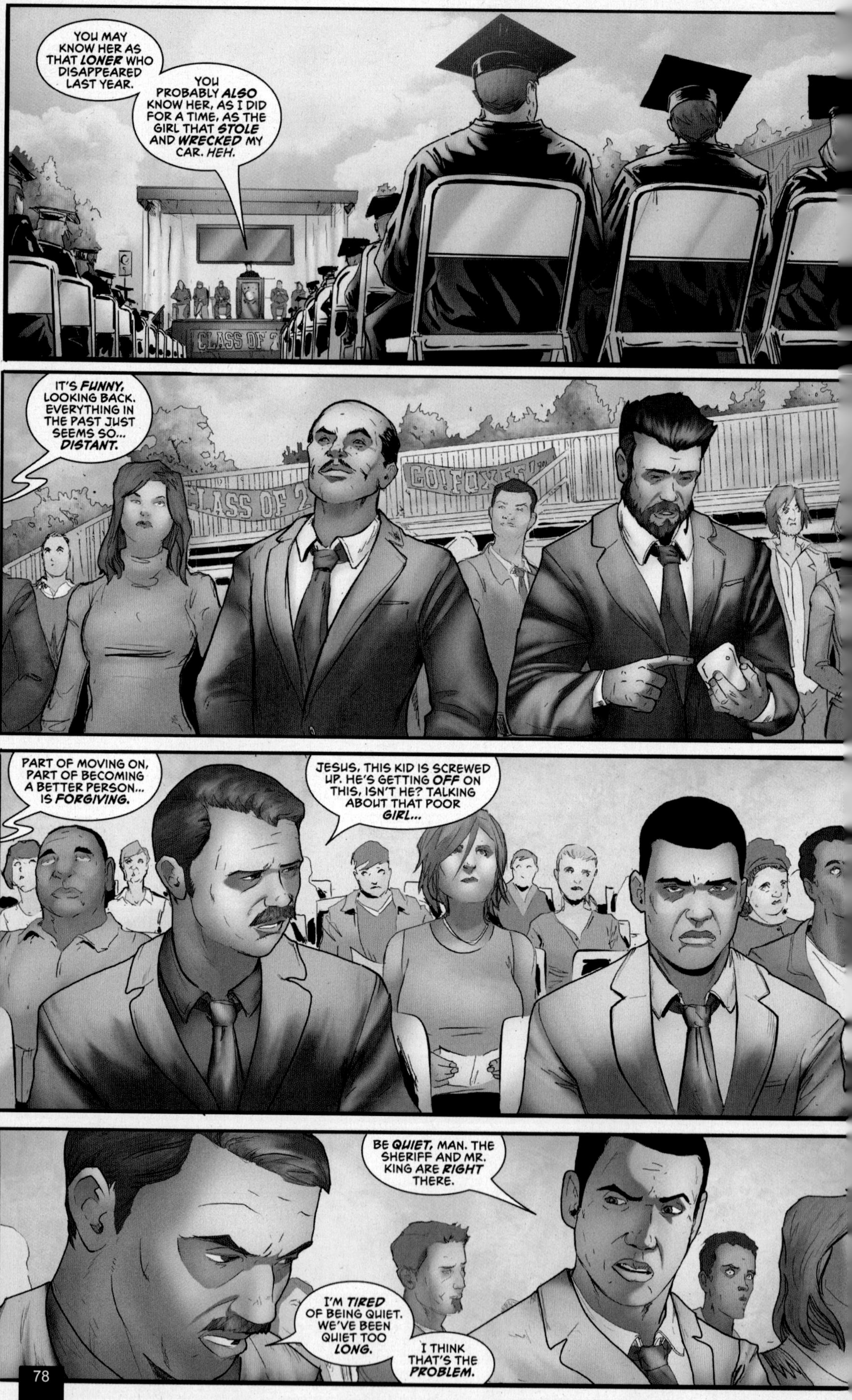
YOU MAY KNOW HER AS THAT LONER WHO DISAPPEARED LAST YEAR.
YOU PROBABLY ALSO KNOW HER, AS I DID FOR A TIME, AS THE GIRL THAT STOLE AND WRECKED MY CAR. HEH.
CLASS OF 2
IT'S FUNNY, LOOKING BACK. EVERYTHING IN THE PAST JUST SEEMS SO... DISTANT.
CLASS OF 2
GO! FOXES
PART OF MOVING ON, PART OF BECOMING A BETTER PERSON... IS FORGIVING.
JESUS, THIS KID IS SCREWED UP. HE'S GETTING OFF ON THIS, ISN'T HE? TALKING ABOUT THAT POOR GIRL...
BE QUIET, MAN. THE SHERIFF AND MR. KING ARE RIGHT THERE.
I'M TIRED OF BEING QUIET. WE'VE BEEN QUIET TOO LONG.
I THINK THAT'S THE PROBLEM.

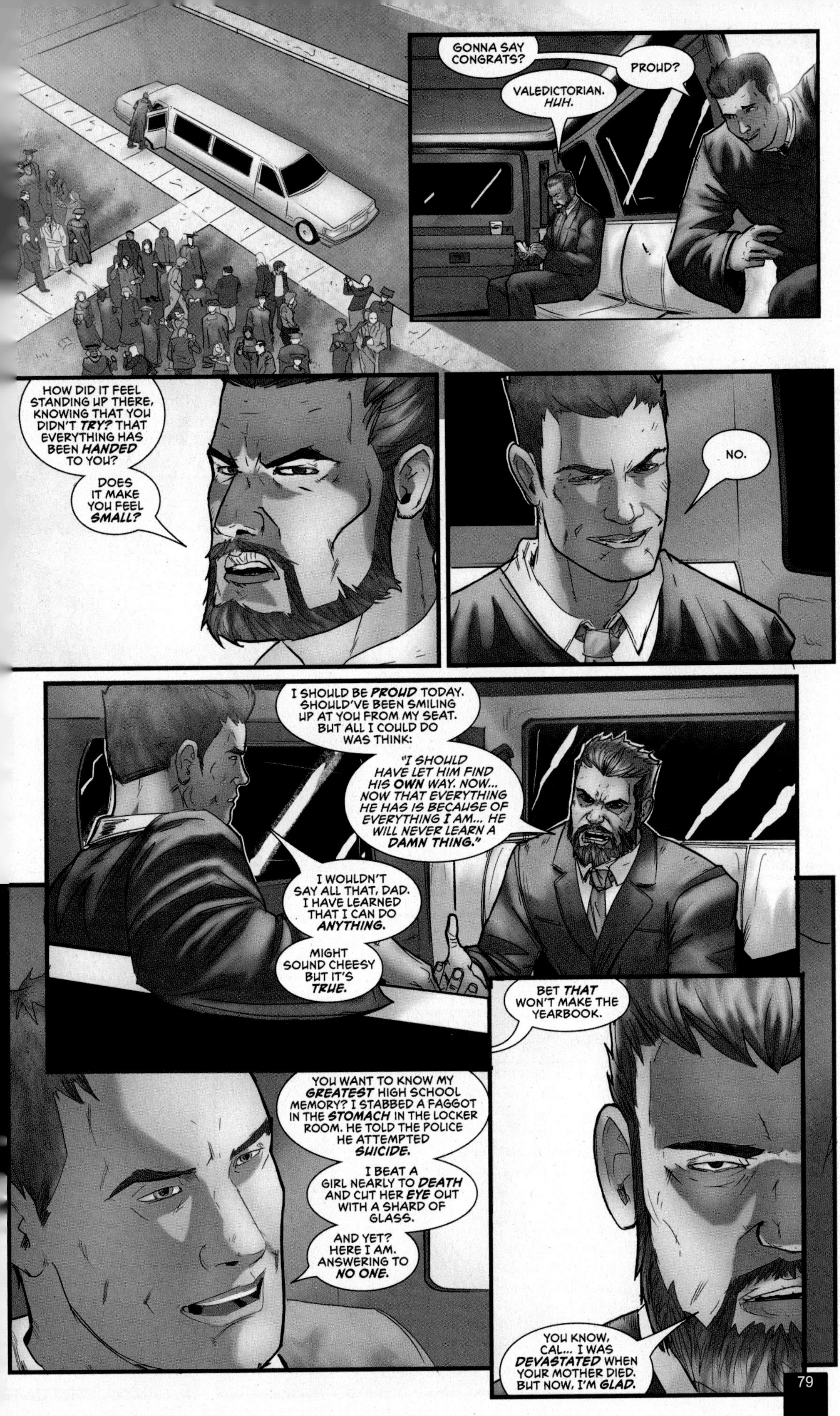
GONNA SAY CONGRATS?
PROUD?
VALEDICTORIAN. HUH.
HOW DID IT FEEL STANDING UP THERE, KNOWING THAT YOU DIDN'T TRY? THAT EVERYTHING HAS BEEN HANDED TO YOU?
DOES IT MAKE YOU FEEL SMALL?
NO.
I SHOULD BE PROUD TODAY. SHOULD'VE BEEN SMILING UP AT YOU FROM MY SEAT. BUT ALL I COULD DO WAS THINK:
"I SHOULD HAVE LET HIM FIND HIS OWN WAY. NOW... NOW THAT EVERYTHING HE HAS IS BECAUSE OF EVERYTHING I AM... HE WILL NEVER LEARN A DAMN THING."
I WOULDN'T SAY ALL THAT, DAD. I HAVE LEARNED THAT I CAN DO ANYTHING.
MIGHT SOUND CHEESY BUT IT'S TRUE.
BET THAT WON'T MAKE THE YEARBOOK.
YOU WANT TO KNOW MY GREATEST HIGH SCHOOL MEMORY? I STABBED A FAGGOT IN THE STOMACH IN THE LOCKER ROOM. HE TOLD THE POLICE HE ATTEMPTED SUICIDE.
I BEAT A GIRL NEARLY TO DEATH AND CUT HER EYE OUT WITH A SHARD OF GLASS.
AND YET? HERE I AM. ANSWERING TO NO ONE.
YOU KNOW, CAL... I WAS DEVASTATED WHEN YOUR MOTHER DIED. BUT NOW, I'M GLAD.

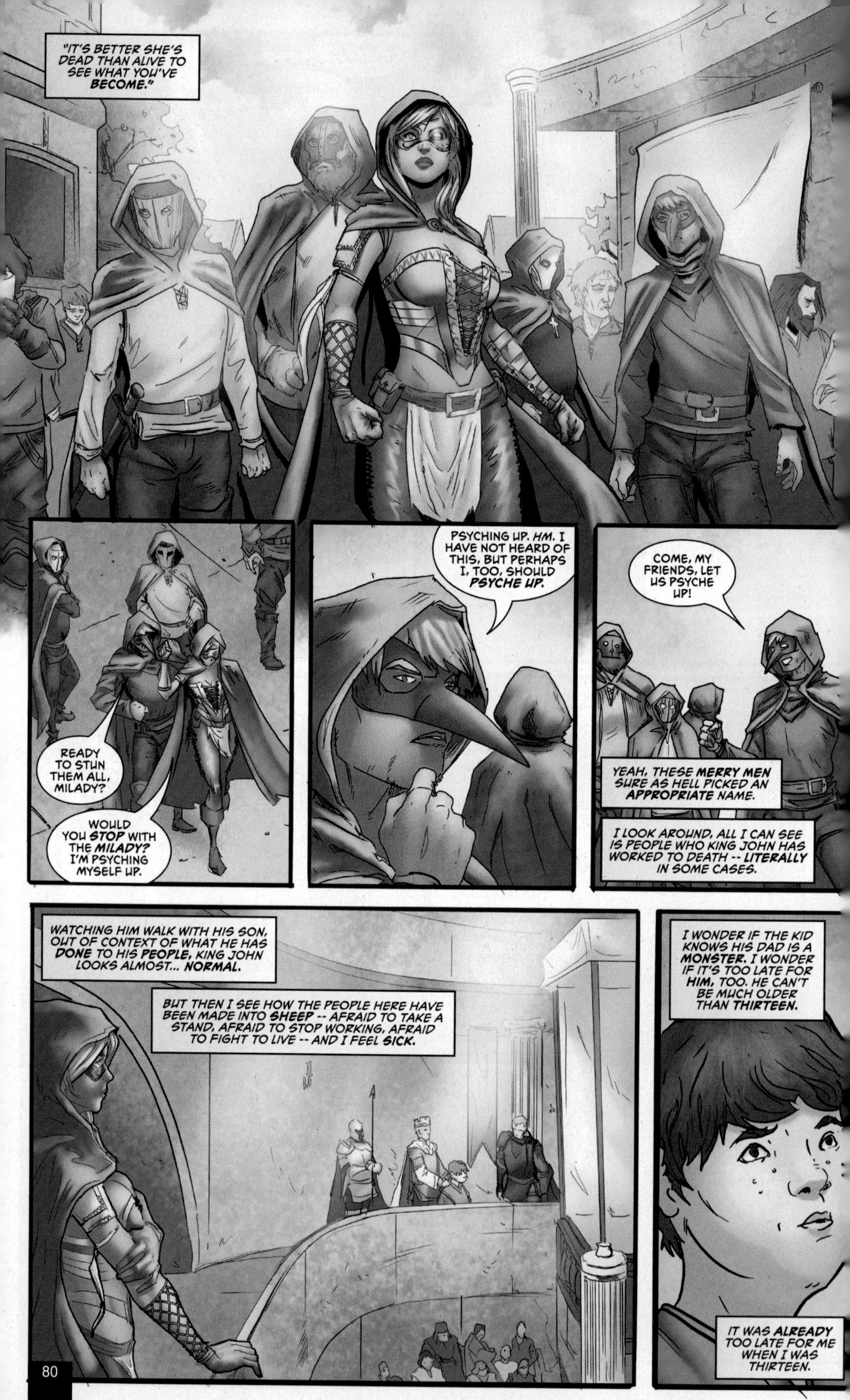

"IT'S BETTER SHE'S DEAD THAN ALIVE TO SEE WHAT YOU'VE BECOME."
READY TO STUN THEM ALL, MILADY?
WOULD YOU STOP WITH THE MILADY? I'M PSYCHING MYSELF UP.
PSYCHING UP. HM. I HAVE NOT HEARD OF THIS, BUT PERHAPS I, TOO, SHOULD PSYCHE UP.
COME, MY FRIENDS, LET US PSYCHE UP!
YEAH, THESE MERRY MEN SURE AS HELL PICKED AN APPROPRIATE NAME.
I LOOK AROUND, ALL I CAN SEE IS PEOPLE WHO KING JOHN HAS WORKED TO DEATH -- LITERALLY IN SOME CASES.
WATCHING HIM WALK WITH HIS SON, OUT OF CONTEXT OF WHAT HE HAS DONE TO HIS PEOPLE, KING JOHN LOOKS ALMOST... NORMAL.
BUT THEN I SEE HOW THE PEOPLE HERE HAVE BEEN MADE INTO SHEEP -- AFRAID TO TAKE A STAND, AFRAID TO STOP WORKING, AFRAID TO FIGHT TO LIVE -- AND I FEEL SICK.
I WONDER IF THE KID KNOWS HIS DAD IS A MONSTER. I WONDER IF IT'S TOO LATE FOR HIM, TOO. HE CAN'T BE MUCH OLDER THAN THIRTEEN.
IT WAS ALREADY TOO LATE FOR ME WHEN I WAS THIRTEEN.

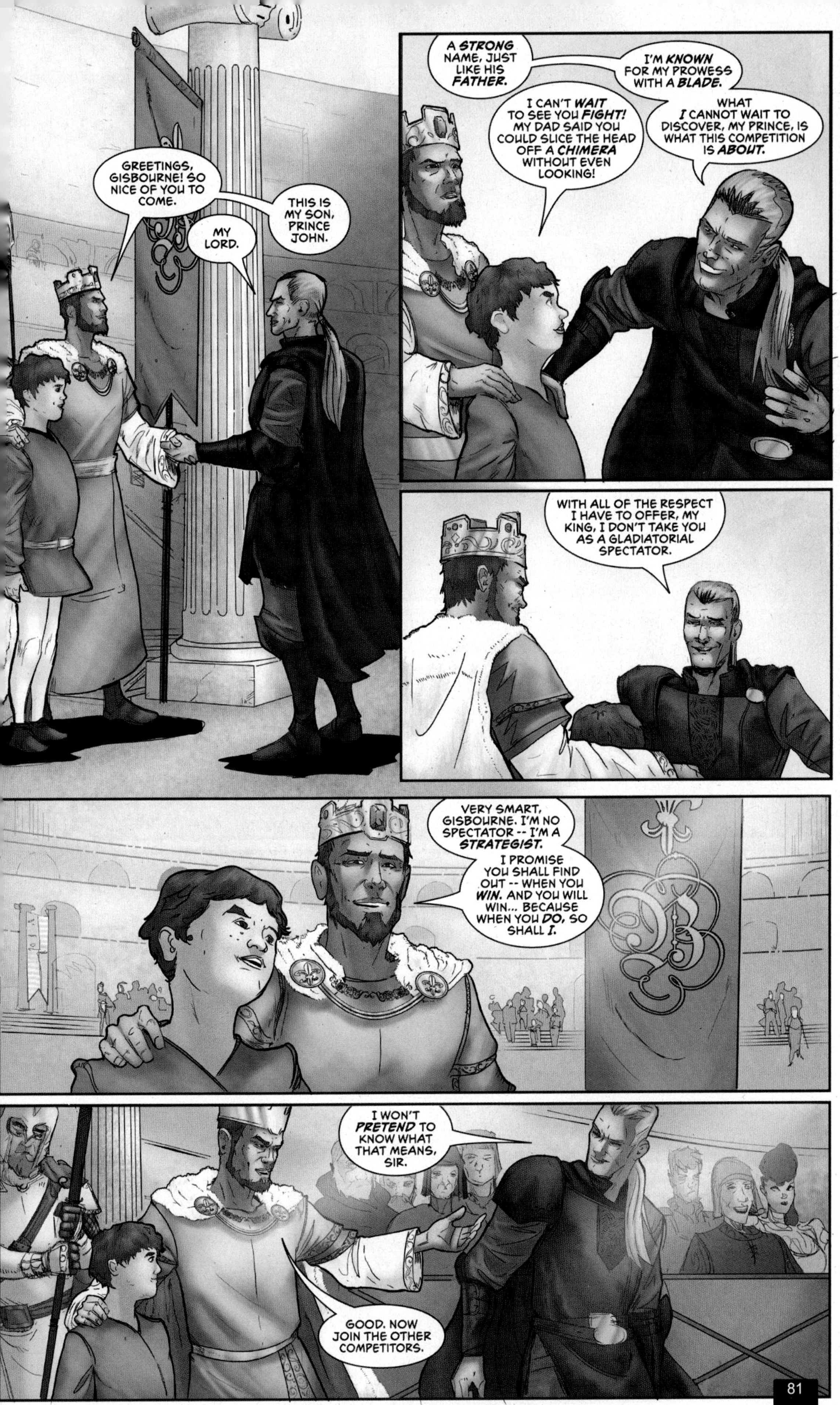
GREETINGS, GISBOURNE! SO NICE OF YOU TO COME.
MY LORD.
THIS IS MY SON, PRINCE JOHN.
A STRONG NAME, JUST LIKE HIS FATHER.
I'M KNOWN FOR MY PROWESS WITH A BLADE.
I CAN'T WAIT TO SEE YOU FIGHT! MY DAD SAID YOU COULD SLICE THE HEAD OFF A CHIMERA WITHOUT EVEN LOOKING!
WHAT I CANNOT WAIT TO DISCOVER, MY PRINCE, IS WHAT THIS COMPETITION IS ABOUT.
WITH ALL OF THE RESPECT I HAVE TO OFFER, MY KING, I DON'T TAKE YOU AS A GLADIATORIAL SPECTATOR.
VERY SMART, GISBOURNE. I'M NO SPECTATOR -- I'M A STRATEGIST.
I PROMISE YOU SHALL FIND OUT -- WHEN YOU WIN. AND YOU WILL WIN... BECAUSE WHEN YOU DO, SO SHALL I.
I WON'T PRETEND TO KNOW WHAT THAT MEANS, SIR.
GOOD. NOW JOIN THE OTHER COMPETITORS.

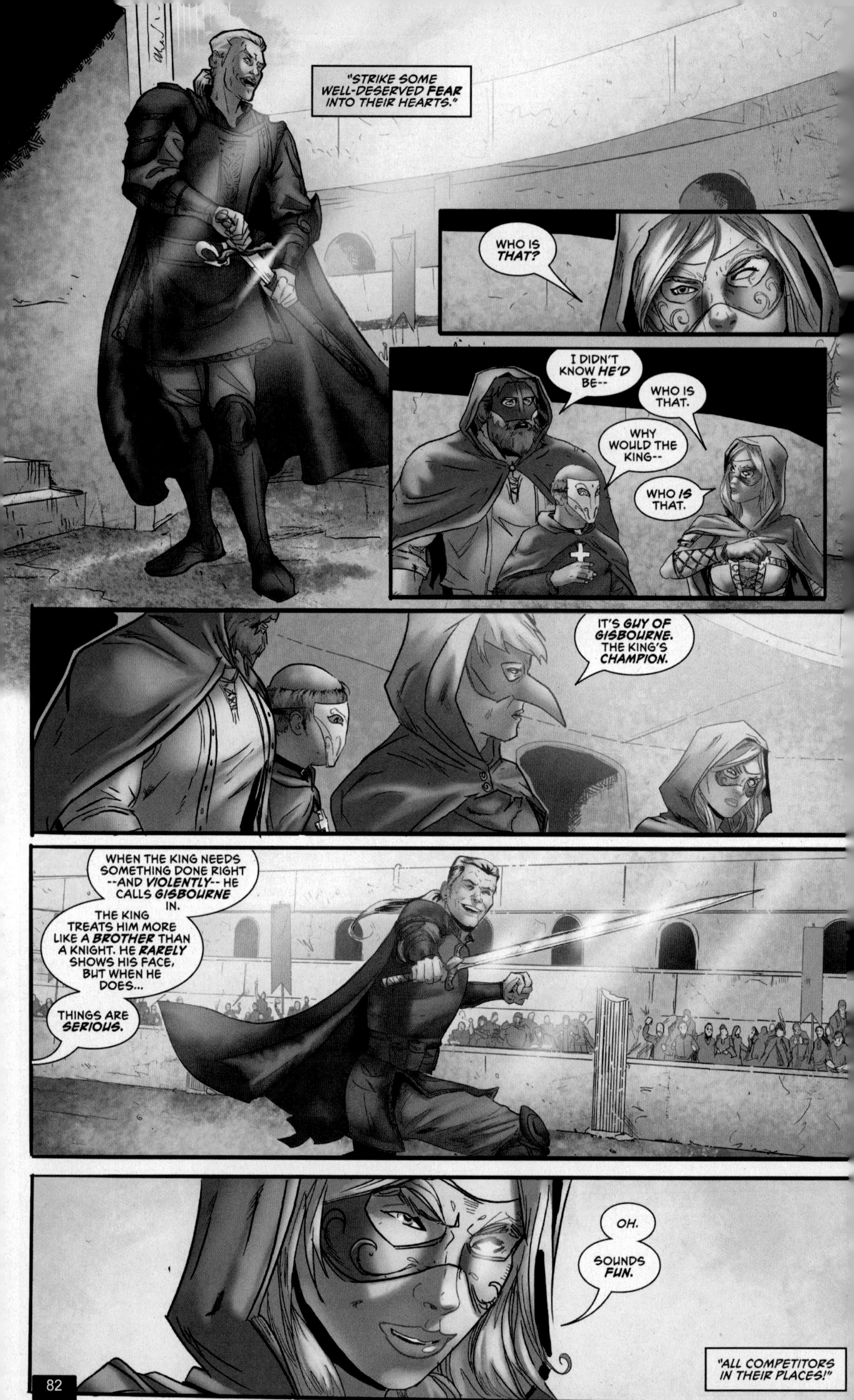
"STRIKE SOME WELL-DESERVED FEAR INTO THEIR HEARTS."
WHO IS THAT?
I DIDN'T KNOW HE'D BE--
WHO IS THAT.
WHY WOULD THE KING--
WHO IS THAT.
IT'S GUY OF GISBOURNE. THE KING'S CHAMPION.
WHEN THE KING NEEDS SOMETHING DONE RIGHT --AND VIOLENTLY-- HE CALLS GISBOURNE IN.
THE KING TREATS HIM MORE LIKE A BROTHER THAN A KNIGHT. HE RARELY SHOWS HIS FACE, BUT WHEN HE DOES...
THINGS ARE SERIOUS.
OH.
SOUNDS FUN.
"ALL COMPETITORS IN THEIR PLACES!"

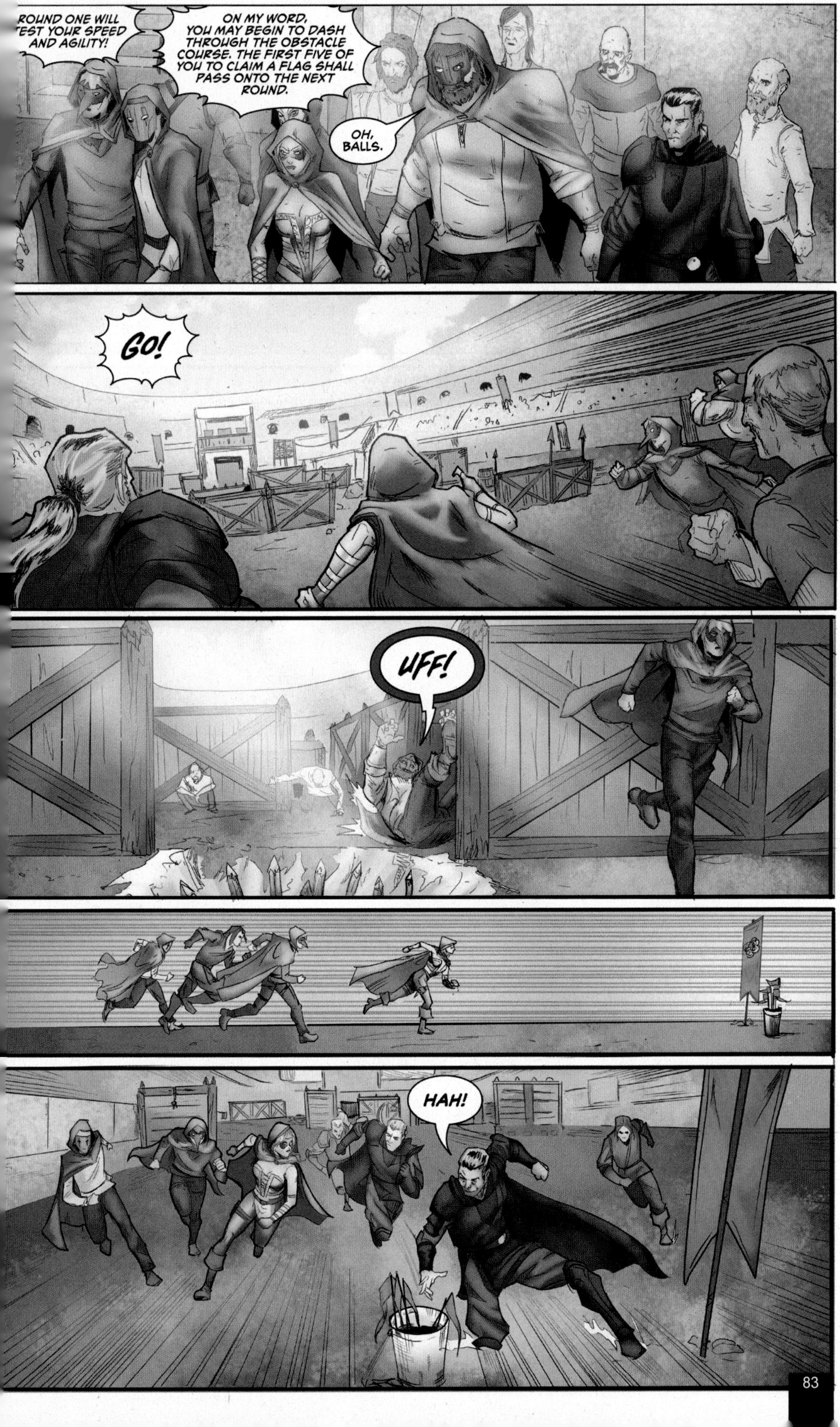
ROUND ONE WILL TEST YOUR SPEED AND AGILITY!
ON MY WORD, YOU MAY BEGIN TO DASH THROUGH THE OBSTACLE COURSE. THE FIRST FIVE OF YOU TO CLAIM A FLAG SHALL PASS ONTO THE NEXT ROUND.
OH, BALLS.
GO!
UFF!
HAH!

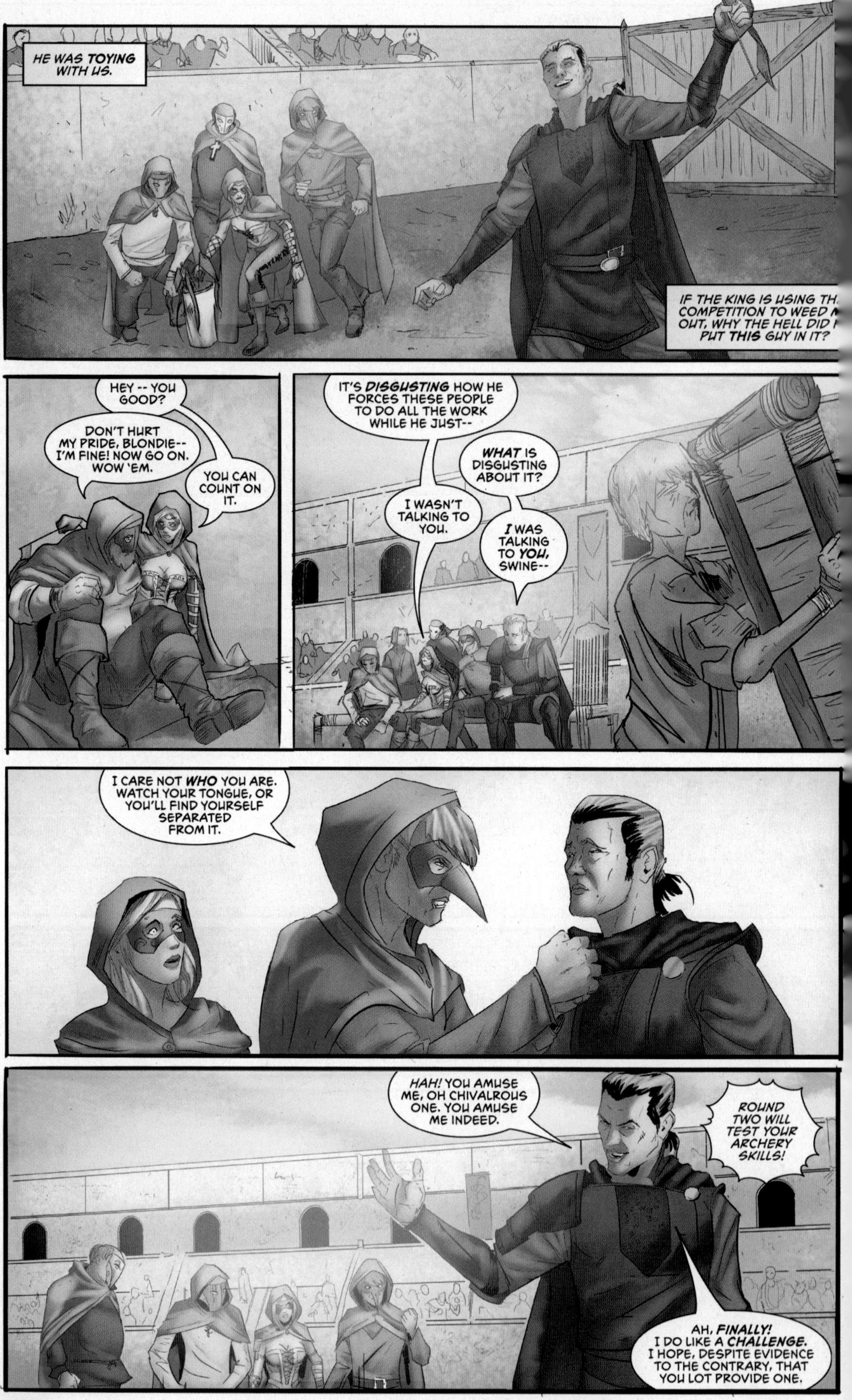
HE WAS TOYING WITH US.
IF THE KING IS USING TH COMPETITION TO WEED M OUT, WHY THE HELL DID PUT THIS GUY IN IT?
HEY -- YOU GOOD?
DON'T HURT MY PRIDE, BLONDIE-- I'M FINE! NOW GO ON. WOW 'EM.
YOU CAN COUNT ON IT.
IT'S DISGUSTING HOW HE FORCES THESE PEOPLE TO DO ALL THE WORK WHILE HE JUST--
WHAT IS DISGUSTING ABOUT IT?
I WASN'T TALKING TO YOU.
I WAS TALKING TO YOU, SWINE--
I CARE NOT WHO YOU ARE. WATCH YOUR TONGUE, OR YOU'LL FIND YOURSELF SEPARATED FROM IT.
HAH! YOU AMUSE ME, OH CHIVALROUS ONE. YOU AMUSE ME INDEED.
ROUND TWO WILL TEST YOUR ARCHERY SKILLS!
AH, FINALLY! I DO LIKE A CHALLENGE. I HOPE, DESPITE EVIDENCE TO THE CONTRARY, THAT YOU LOT PROVIDE ONE.

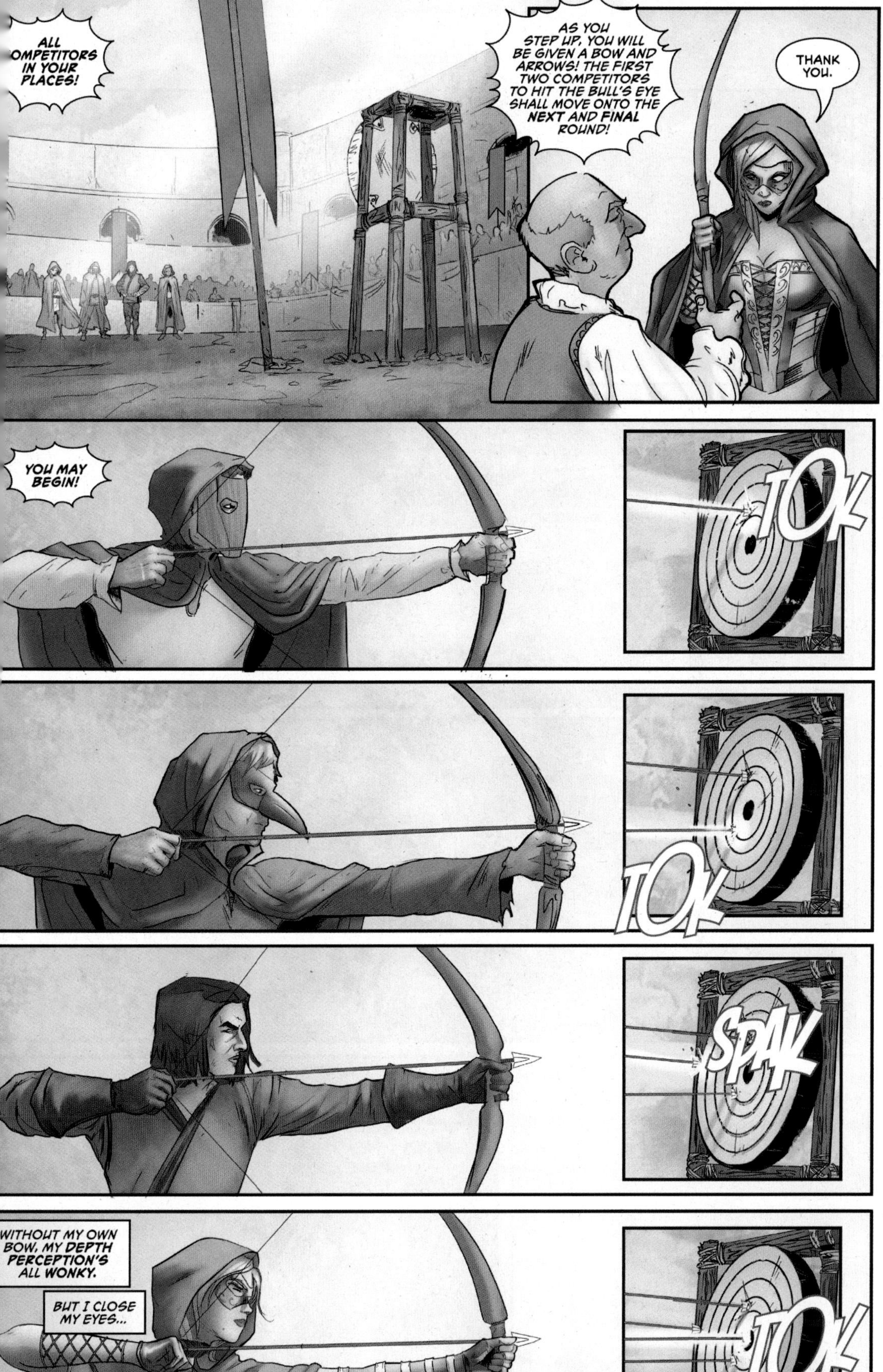
ALL COMPETITORS IN YOUR PLACES!
AS YOU STEP UP, YOU WILL BE GIVEN A BOW AND ARROWS! THE FIRST TWO COMPETITORS TO HIT THE BULL'S EYE SHALL MOVE ONTO THE NEXT AND FINAL ROUND!
THANK YOU.
YOU MAY BEGIN!
TOK
TOK
SPAK
WITHOUT MY OWN BOW, MY DEPTH PERCEPTION'S ALL WONKY.
BUT I CLOSE MY EYES...
...AND IT COMES TO ME AS NATURAL AS BREATHING.
TOK

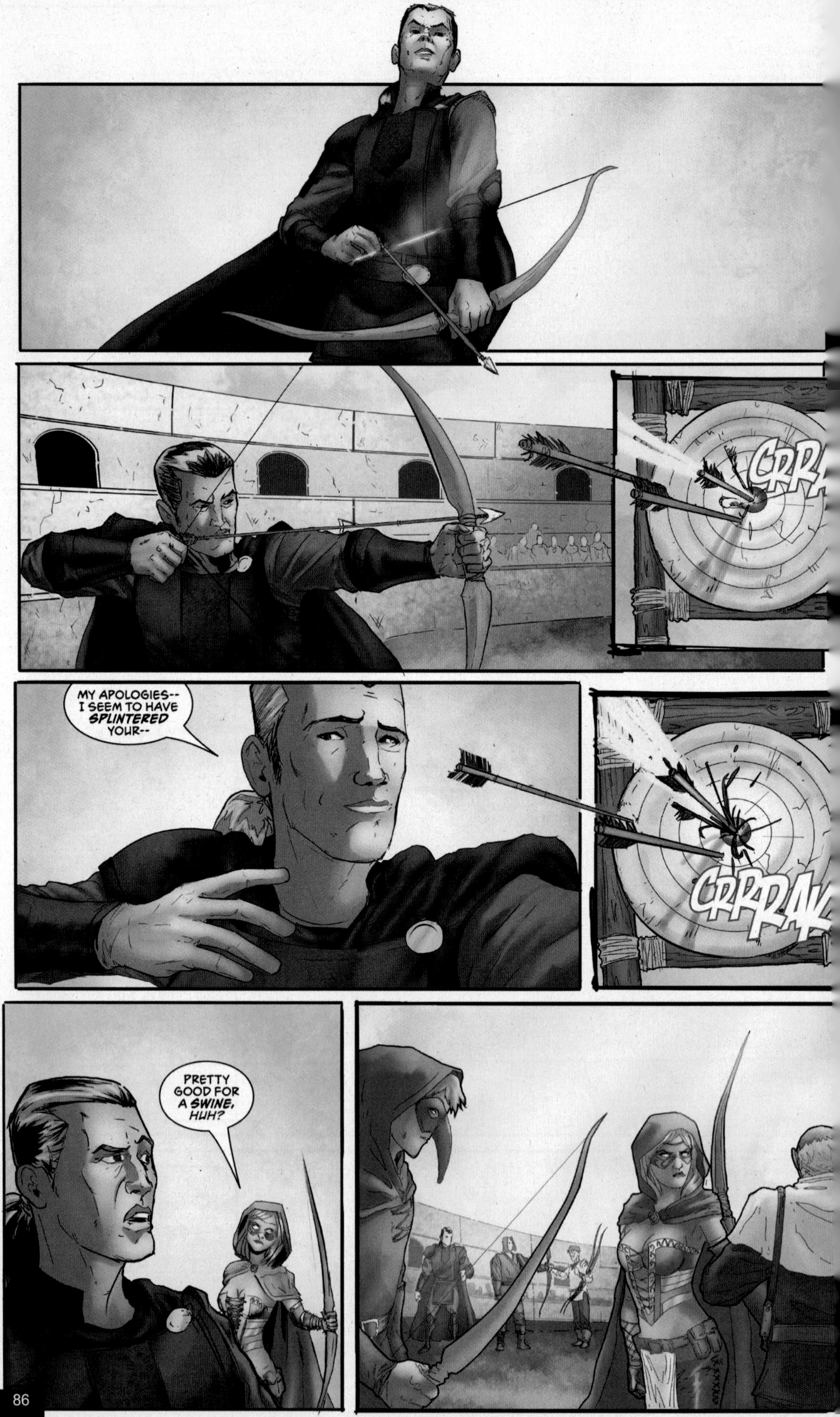
CRR
MY APOLOGIES-- I SEEM TO HAVE SPLINTERED YOUR--
CRRRAK
PRETTY GOOD FOR A SWINE, HUH?

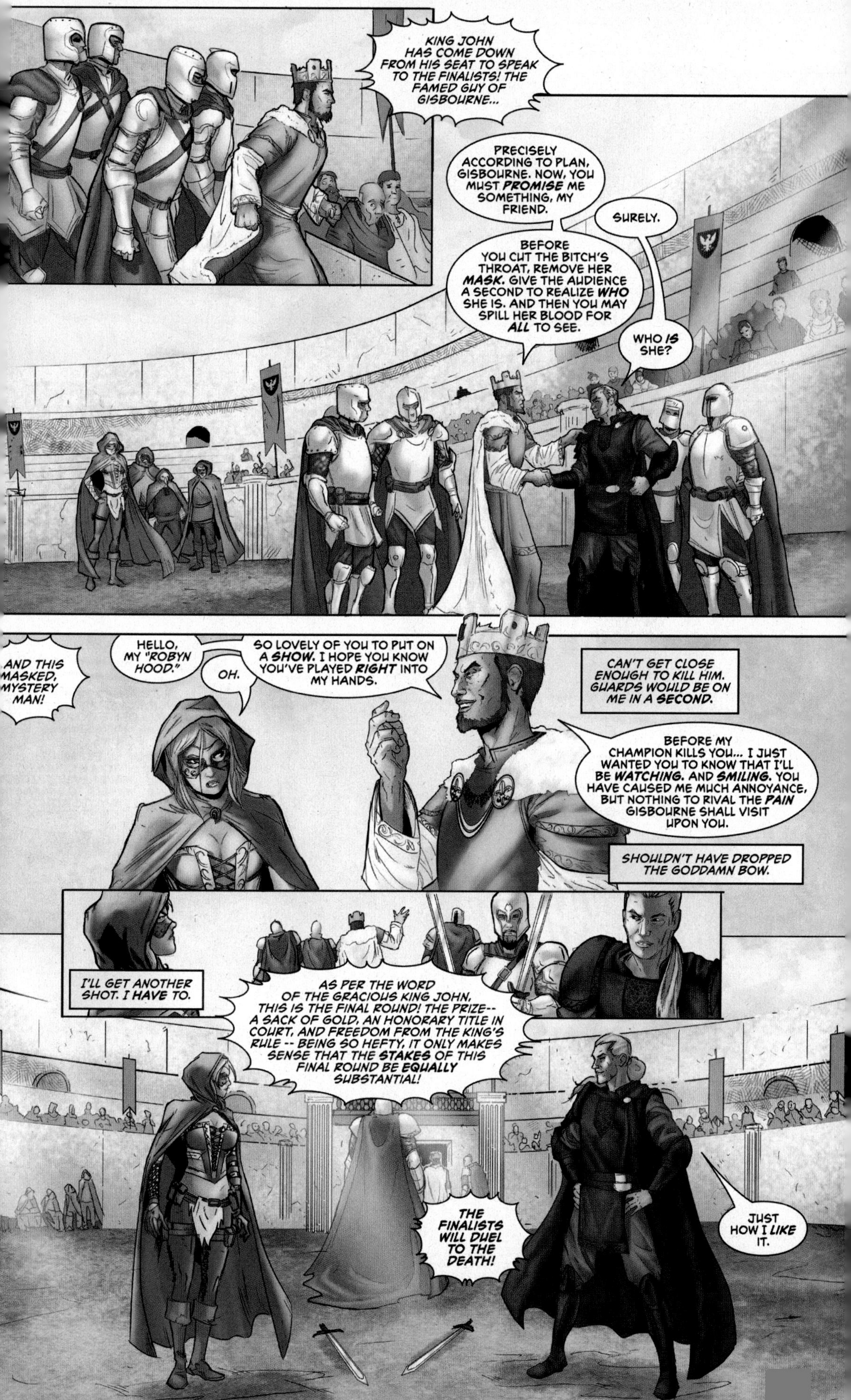
KING JOHN HAS COME DOWN FROM HIS SEAT TO SPEAK TO THE FINALISTS! THE FAMED GUY OF GISBOURNE...
PRECISELY ACCORDING TO PLAN, GISBOURNE. NOW, YOU MUST PROMISE ME SOMETHING, MY FRIEND.
SURELY.
BEFORE YOU CUT THE BITCH'S THROAT, REMOVE HER MASK. GIVE THE AUDIENCE A SECOND TO REALIZE WHO SHE IS. AND THEN YOU MAY SPILL HER BLOOD FOR ALL TO SEE.
WHO IS SHE?
AND THIS MASKED, MYSTERY MAN!
HELLO, MY "ROBYN HOOD."
OH.
SO LOVELY OF YOU TO PUT ON A SHOW. I HOPE YOU KNOW YOU'VE PLAYED RIGHT INTO MY HANDS.
CAN'T GET CLOSE ENOUGH TO KILL HIM. GUARDS WOULD BE ON ME IN A SECOND.
BEFORE MY CHAMPION KILLS YOU... I JUST WANTED YOU TO KNOW THAT I'LL BE WATCHING. AND SMILING. YOU HAVE CAUSED ME MUCH ANNOYANCE, BUT NOTHING TO RIVAL THE PAIN GISBOURNE SHALL VISIT UPON YOU.
SHOULDN'T HAVE DROPPED THE GODDAMN BOW.
I'LL GET ANOTHER SHOT. I HAVE TO.
AS PER THE WORD OF THE GRACIOUS KING JOHN, THIS IS THE FINAL ROUND! THE PRIZE-- A SACK OF GOLD, AN HONORARY TITLE IN COURT, AND FREEDOM FROM THE KING'S RULE -- BEING SO HEFTY, IT ONLY MAKES SENSE THAT THE STAKES OF THIS FINAL ROUND BE EQUALLY SUBSTANTIAL!
THE FINALISTS WILL DUEL TO THE DEATH!
JUST HOW I LIKE IT.

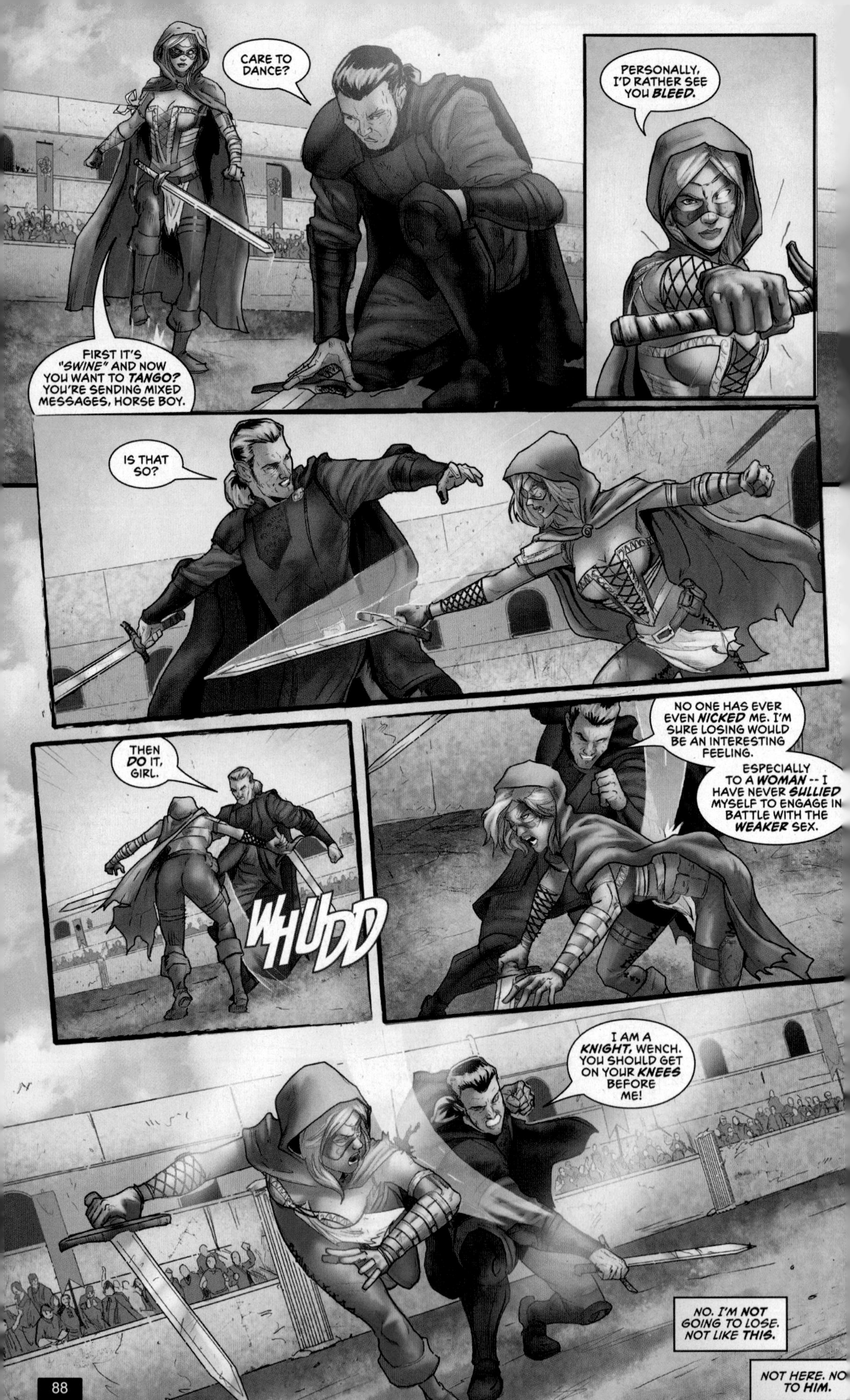
CARE TO DANCE?
FIRST IT'S "SWINE" AND NOW YOU WANT TO TANGO? YOU'RE SENDING MIXED MESSAGES, HORSE BOY.
PERSONALLY, I'D RATHER SEE YOU BLEED.
IS THAT SO?
THEN DO IT, GIRL.
WHUDD
NO ONE HAS EVER EVEN NICKED ME. I'M SURE LOSING WOULD BE AN INTERESTING FEELING.
ESPECIALLY TO A WOMAN -- I HAVE NEVER SULLIED MYSELF TO ENGAGE IN BATTLE WITH THE WEAKER SEX.
I AM A KNIGHT, WENCH. YOU SHOULD GET ON YOUR KNEES BEFORE ME!
NO. I'M NOT GOING TO LOSE. NOT LIKE THIS.
NOT HERE. NO TO HIM.

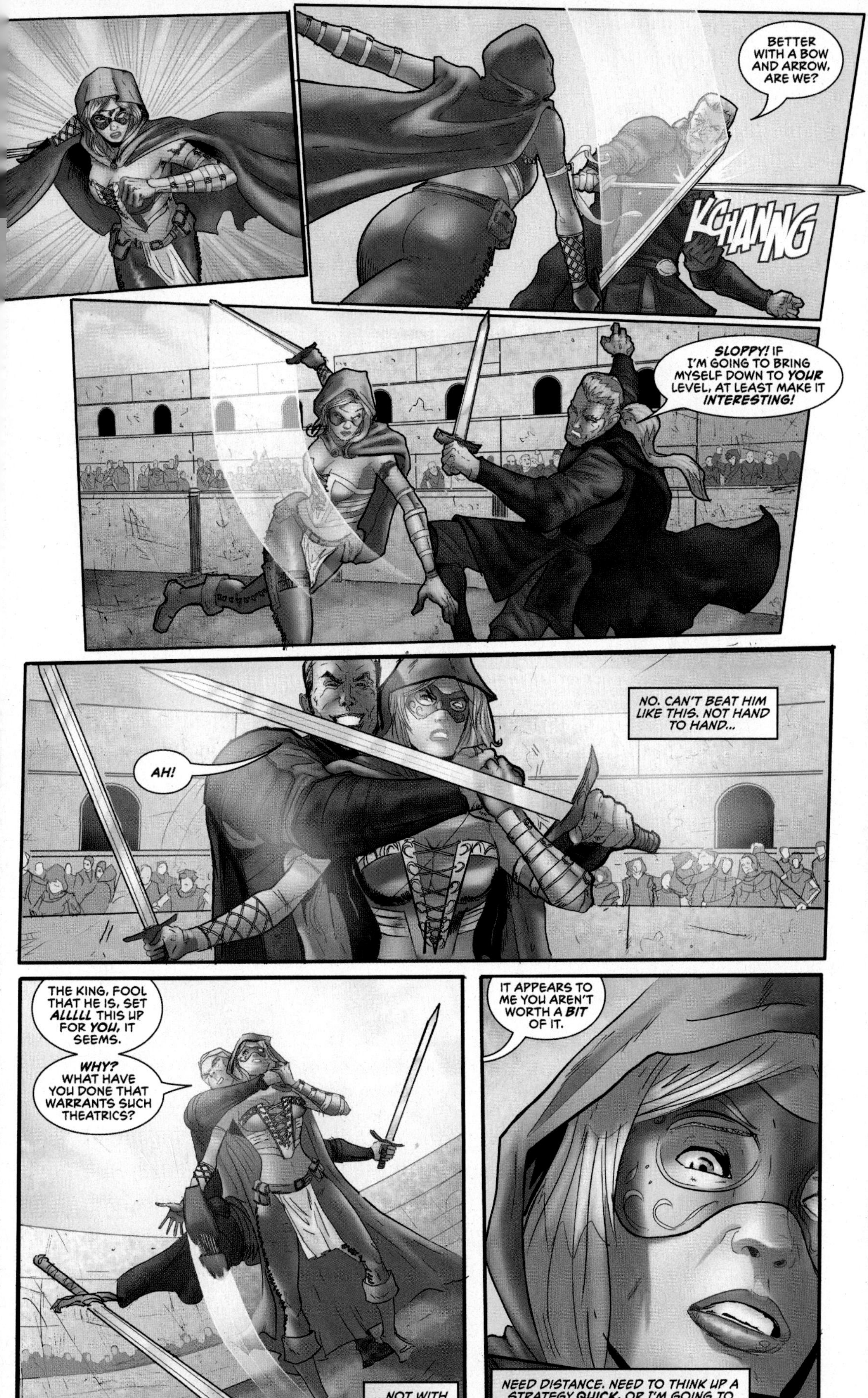
BETTER WITH A BOW AND ARROW, ARE WE?
K'CHANNG
SLOPPY! IF I'M GOING TO BRING MYSELF DOWN TO YOUR LEVEL, AT LEAST MAKE IT INTERESTING!
NO. CAN'T BEAT HIM LIKE THIS. NOT HAND TO HAND...
AH!
THE KING, FOOL THAT HE IS, SET ALLLLL THIS UP FOR YOU, IT SEEMS.
WHY? WHAT HAVE YOU DONE THAT WARRANTS SUCH THEATRICS?
...NOT WITH SWORDS.
IT APPEARS TO ME YOU AREN'T WORTH A BIT OF IT.
NEED DISTANCE. NEED TO THINK UP A STRATEGY QUICK, OR I'M GOING TO DIE IN FREAKIN' FAIRY TALE LAND.

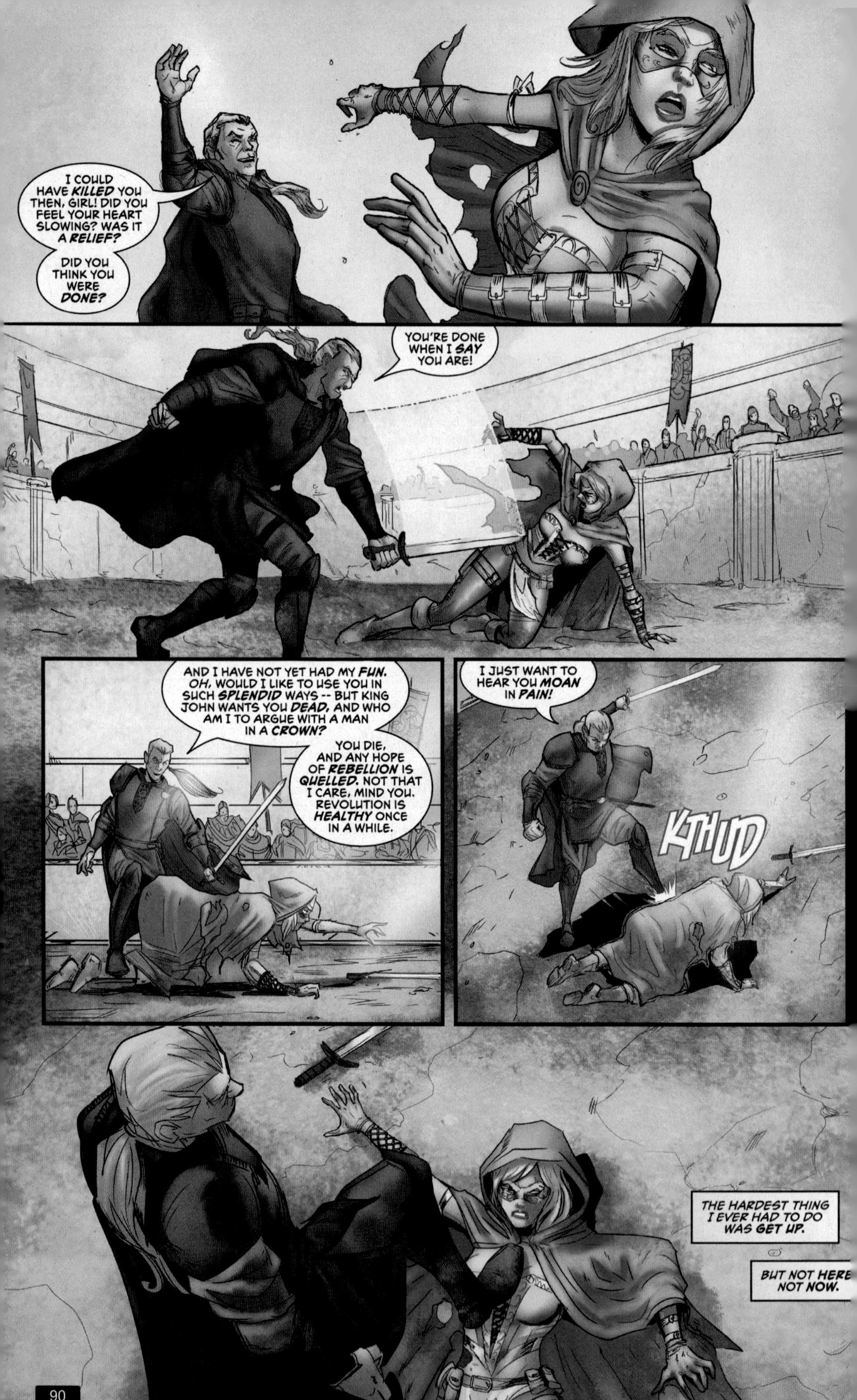
I COULD HAVE *KILLED* YOU THEN, GIRL! DID YOU FEEL YOUR HEART SLOWING? WAS IT A *RELIEF?*
DID YOU THINK YOU WERE *DONE?*
YOU'RE DONE WHEN I *SAY* YOU ARE!
AND I HAVE NOT YET HAD MY *FUN. OH,* WOULD I LIKE TO USE YOU IN SUCH *SPLENDID* WAYS -- BUT KING JOHN WANTS YOU *DEAD,* AND WHO AM I TO ARGUE WITH A MAN IN A *CROWN?*
YOU DIE, AND ANY HOPE OF *REBELLION* IS *QUELLED.* NOT THAT I CARE, MIND YOU. REVOLUTION IS *HEALTHY* ONCE IN A WHILE.
I JUST WANT TO HEAR YOU *MOAN* IN *PAIN!*
KTHUD
THE HARDEST THING I EVER HAD TO DO WAS *GET UP.*
BUT NOT HERE NOT NOW.

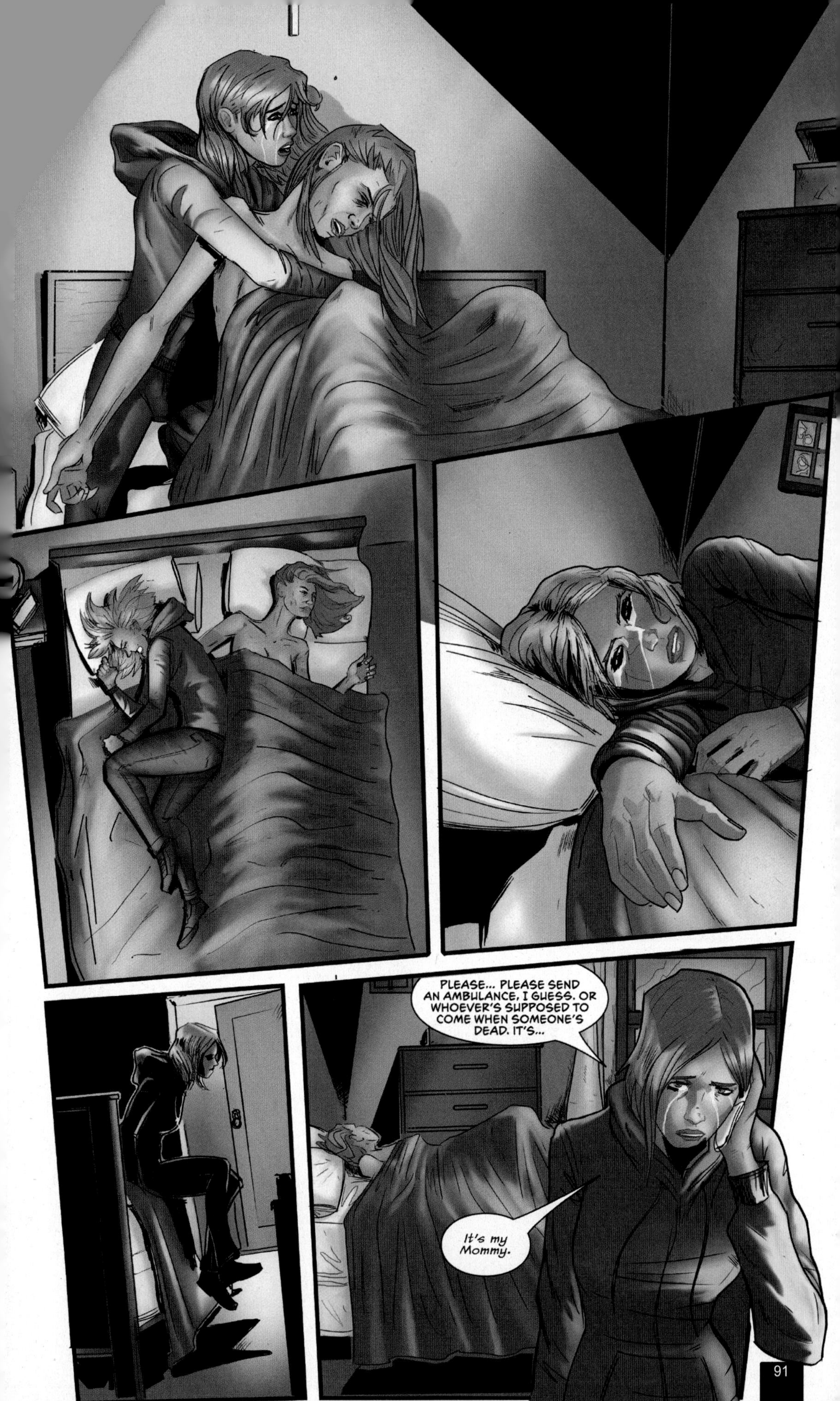
PLEASE... PLEASE SEND AN AMBULANCE, I GUESS. OR WHOEVER'S SUPPOSED TO COME WHEN SOMEONE'S DEAD. IT'S...
It's my Mommy.

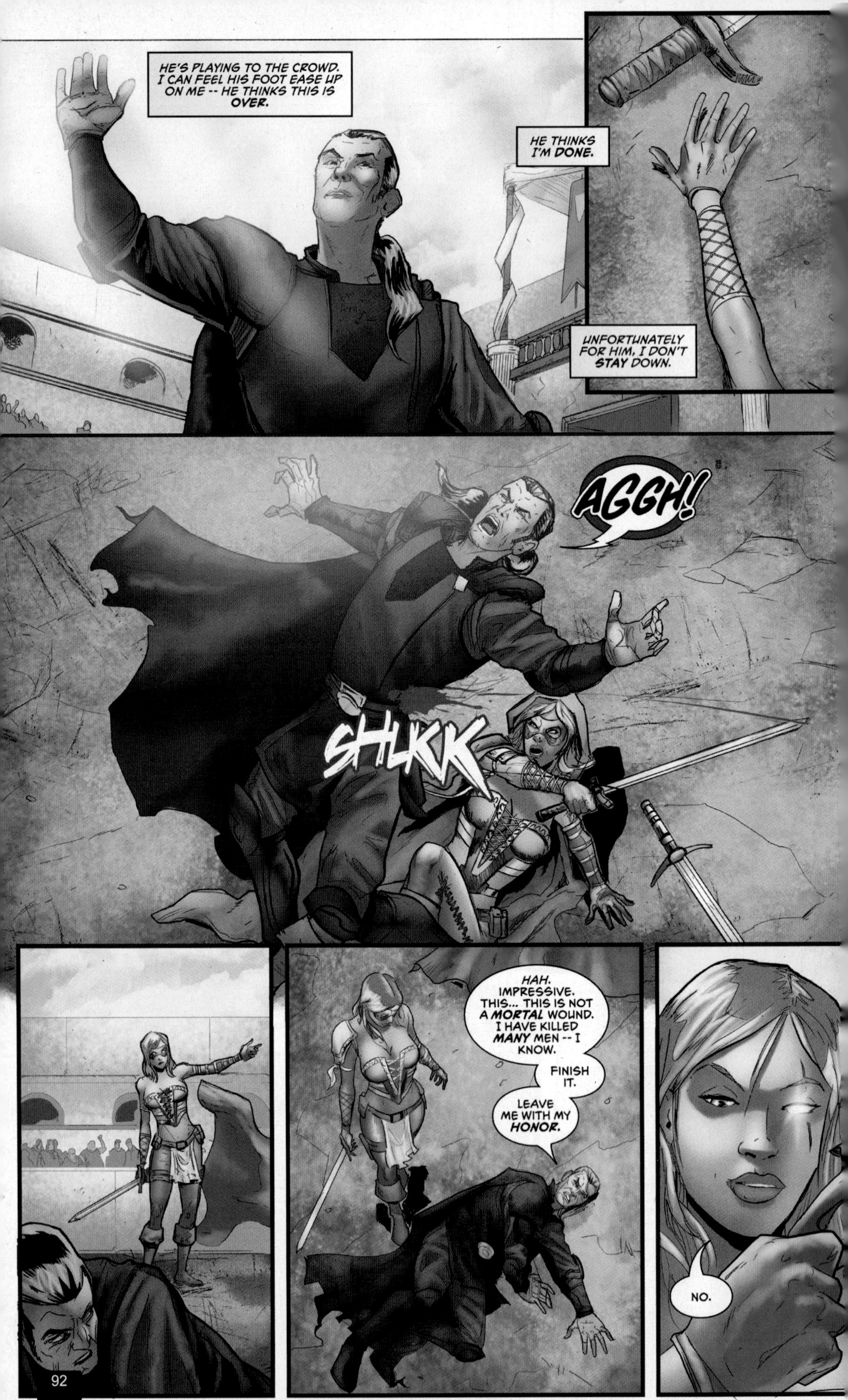
HE'S PLAYING TO THE CROWD. I CAN FEEL HIS FOOT EASE UP ON ME -- HE THINKS THIS IS OVER.
HE THINKS I'M DONE.
UNFORTUNATELY FOR HIM, I DON'T STAY DOWN.
AGGH!
SHLKK
HAH. IMPRESSIVE. THIS... THIS IS NOT A MORTAL WOUND. I HAVE KILLED MANY MEN -- I KNOW.
FINISH IT.
LEAVE ME WITH MY HONOR.
NO.

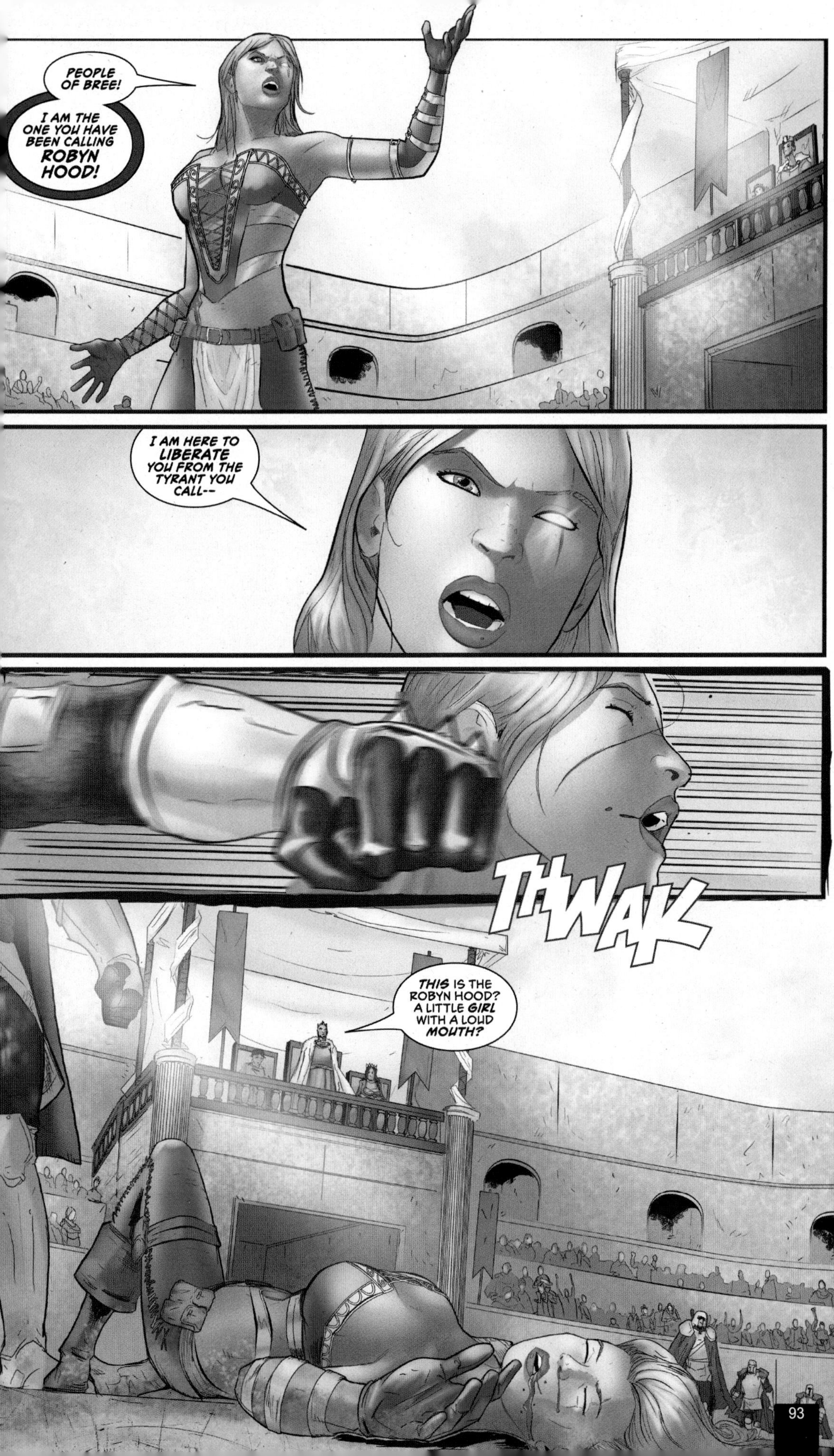
PEOPLE OF BREE!
I AM THE ONE YOU HAVE BEEN CALLING ROBYN HOOD!
I AM HERE TO LIBERATE YOU FROM THE TYRANT YOU CALL--
THWAK
THIS IS THE ROBYN HOOD? A LITTLE GIRL WITH A LOUD MOUTH?

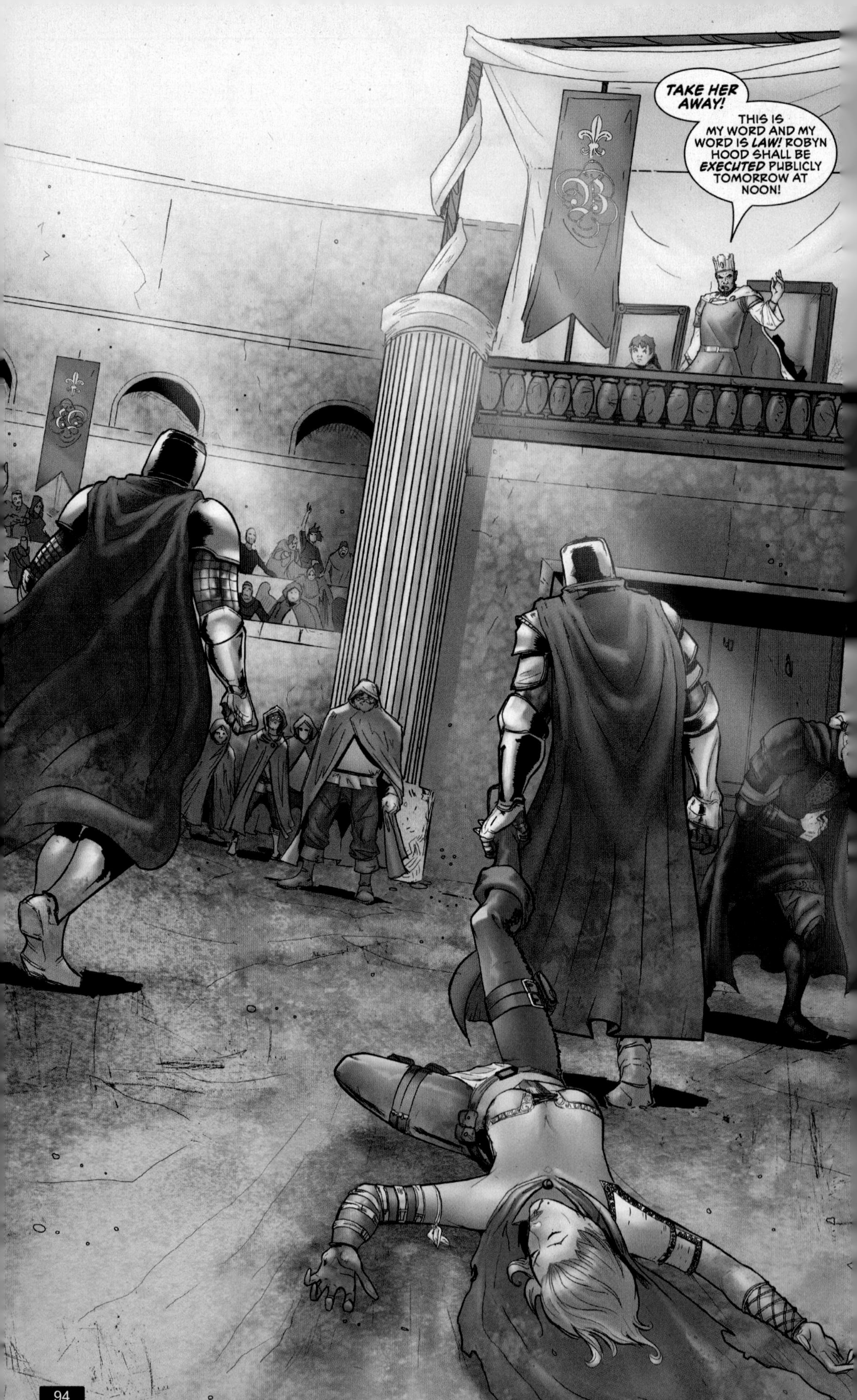
TAKE HER AWAY!
THIS IS MY WORD AND MY WORD IS LAW! ROBYN HOOD SHALL BE EXECUTED PUBLICLY TOMORROW AT NOON!

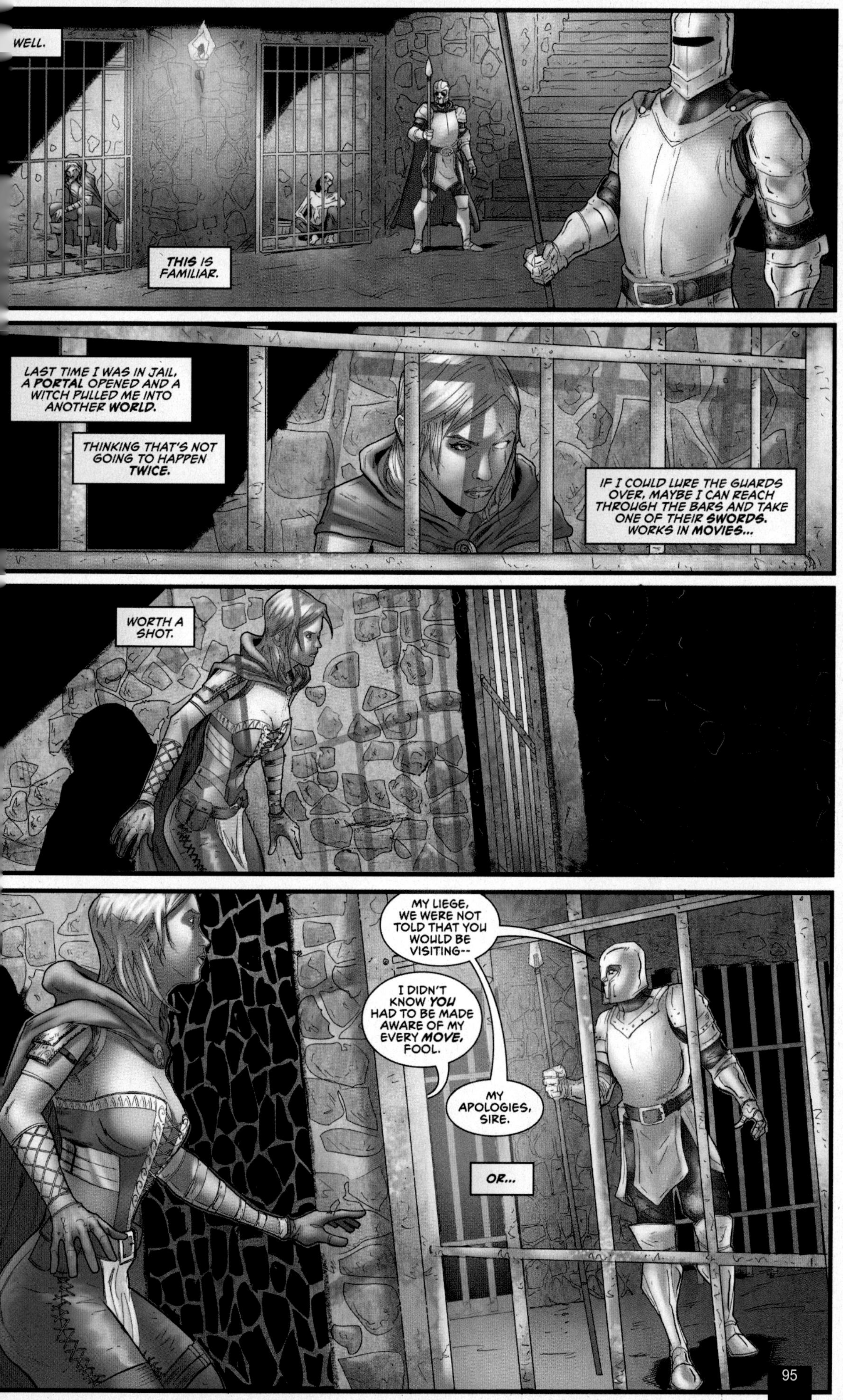
WELL.
THIS IS FAMILIAR.
LAST TIME I WAS IN JAIL, A PORTAL OPENED AND A WITCH PULLED ME INTO ANOTHER WORLD.
THINKING THAT'S NOT GOING TO HAPPEN TWICE.
IF I COULD LURE THE GUARDS OVER, MAYBE I CAN REACH THROUGH THE BARS AND TAKE ONE OF THEIR SWORDS. WORKS IN MOVIES...
WORTH A SHOT.
MY LIEGE, WE WERE NOT TOLD THAT YOU WOULD BE VISITING--
I DIDN'T KNOW YOU HAD TO BE MADE AWARE OF MY EVERY MOVE, FOOL.
MY APOLOGIES, SIRE.
OR...

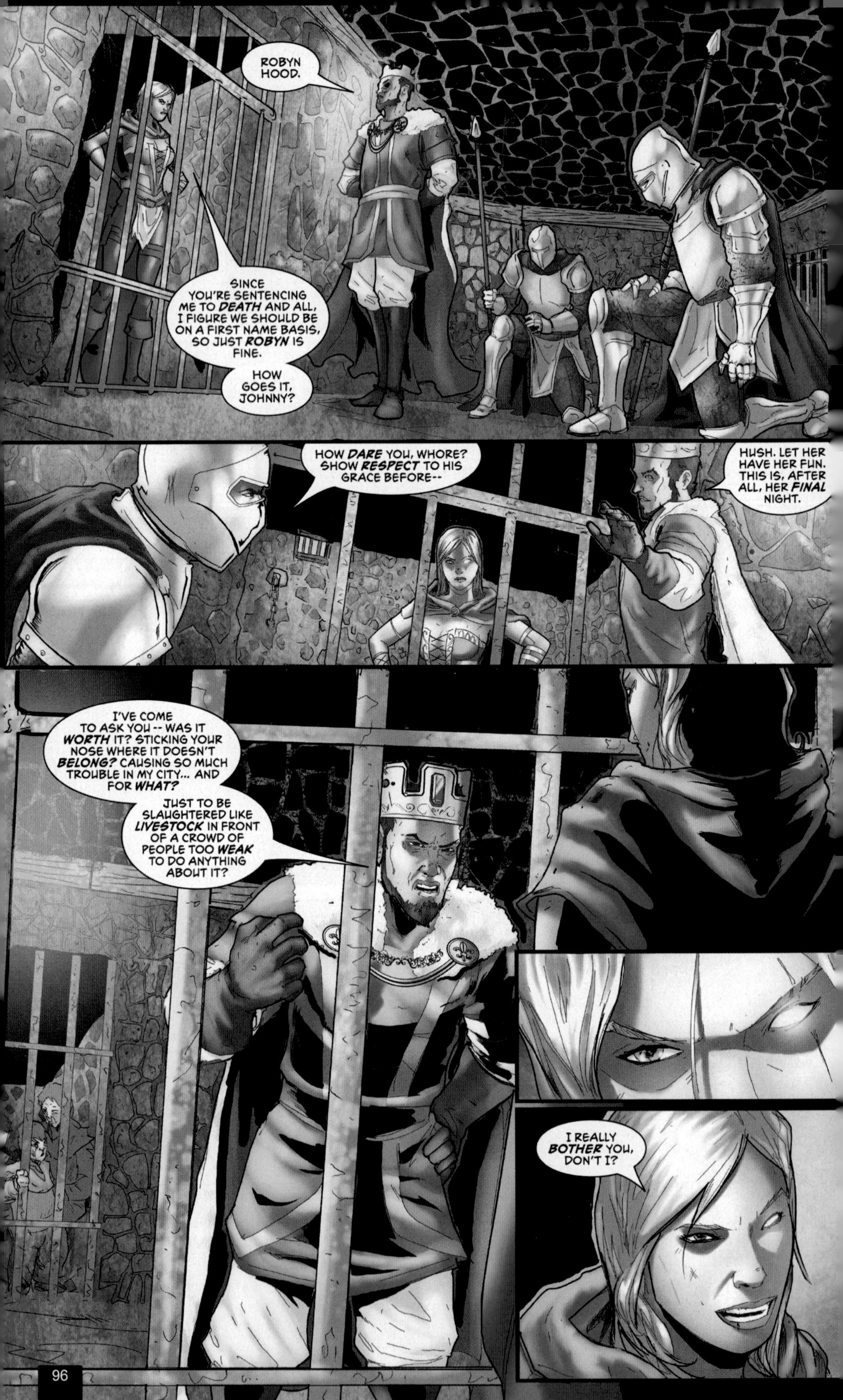
ROBYN HOOD.
SINCE YOU'RE SENTENCING ME TO DEATH AND ALL, I FIGURE WE SHOULD BE ON A FIRST NAME BASIS, SO JUST ROBYN IS FINE.
HOW GOES IT, JOHNNY?
HOW DARE YOU, WHORE? SHOW RESPECT TO HIS GRACE BEFORE--
HUSH. LET HER HAVE HER FUN. THIS IS, AFTER ALL, HER FINAL NIGHT.
I'VE COME TO ASK YOU -- WAS IT WORTH IT? STICKING YOUR NOSE WHERE IT DOESN'T BELONG? CAUSING SO MUCH TROUBLE IN MY CITY... AND FOR WHAT?
JUST TO BE SLAUGHTERED LIKE LIVESTOCK IN FRONT OF A CROWD OF PEOPLE TOO WEAK TO DO ANYTHING ABOUT IT?
I REALLY BOTHER YOU, DON'T I?

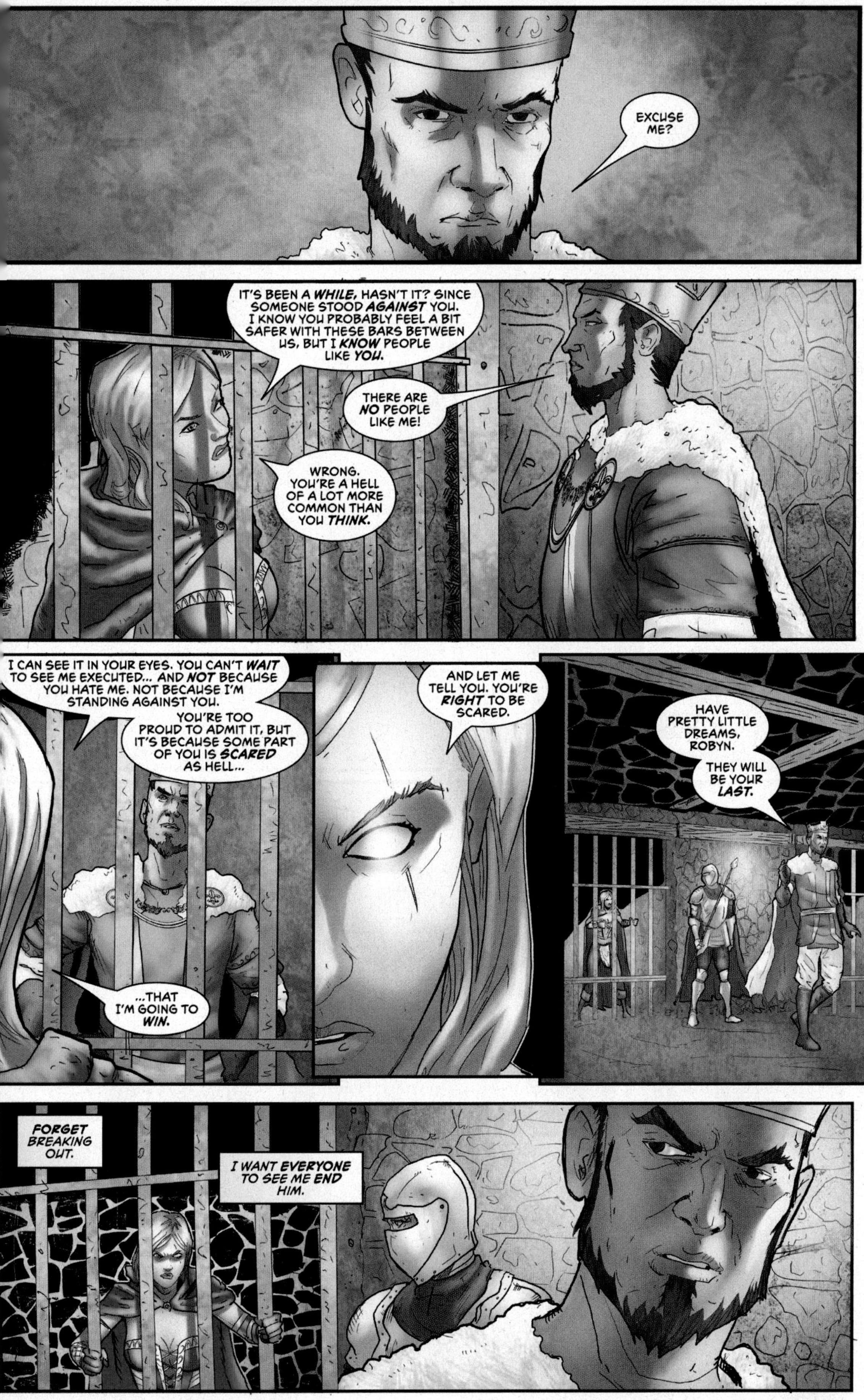
EXCUSE ME?
IT'S BEEN A WHILE, HASN'T IT? SINCE SOMEONE STOOD AGAINST YOU. I KNOW YOU PROBABLY FEEL A BIT SAFER WITH THESE BARS BETWEEN US, BUT I KNOW PEOPLE LIKE YOU.
THERE ARE NO PEOPLE LIKE ME!
WRONG. YOU'RE A HELL OF A LOT MORE COMMON THAN YOU THINK.
I CAN SEE IT IN YOUR EYES. YOU CAN'T WAIT TO SEE ME EXECUTED... AND NOT BECAUSE YOU HATE ME. NOT BECAUSE I'M STANDING AGAINST YOU.
YOU'RE TOO PROUD TO ADMIT IT, BUT IT'S BECAUSE SOME PART OF YOU IS SCARED AS HELL...
...THAT I'M GOING TO WIN.
AND LET ME TELL YOU. YOU'RE RIGHT TO BE SCARED.
HAVE PRETTY LITTLE DREAMS, ROBYN.
THEY WILL BE YOUR LAST.
FORGET BREAKING OUT.
I WANT EVERYONE TO SEE ME END HIM.

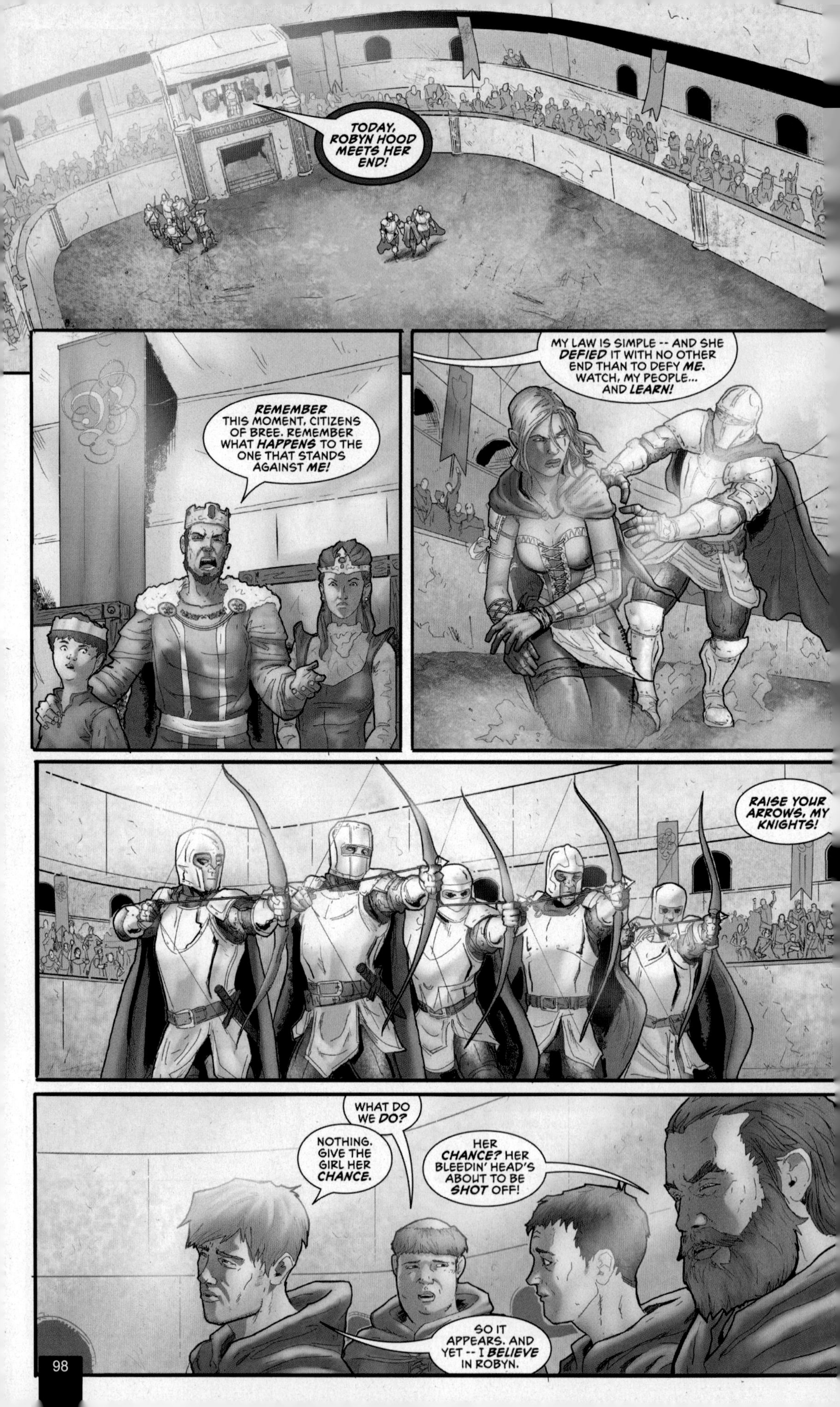
TODAY, ROBYN HOOD MEETS HER END!
REMEMBER THIS MOMENT, CITIZENS OF BREE. REMEMBER WHAT HAPPENS TO THE ONE THAT STANDS AGAINST ME!
MY LAW IS SIMPLE -- AND SHE DEFIED IT WITH NO OTHER END THAN TO DEFY ME. WATCH, MY PEOPLE... AND LEARN!
RAISE YOUR ARROWS, MY KNIGHTS!
WHAT DO WE DO?
NOTHING. GIVE THE GIRL HER CHANCE.
HER CHANCE? HER BLEEDIN' HEAD'S ABOUT TO BE SHOT OFF!
SO IT APPEARS. AND YET -- I BELIEVE IN ROBYN.

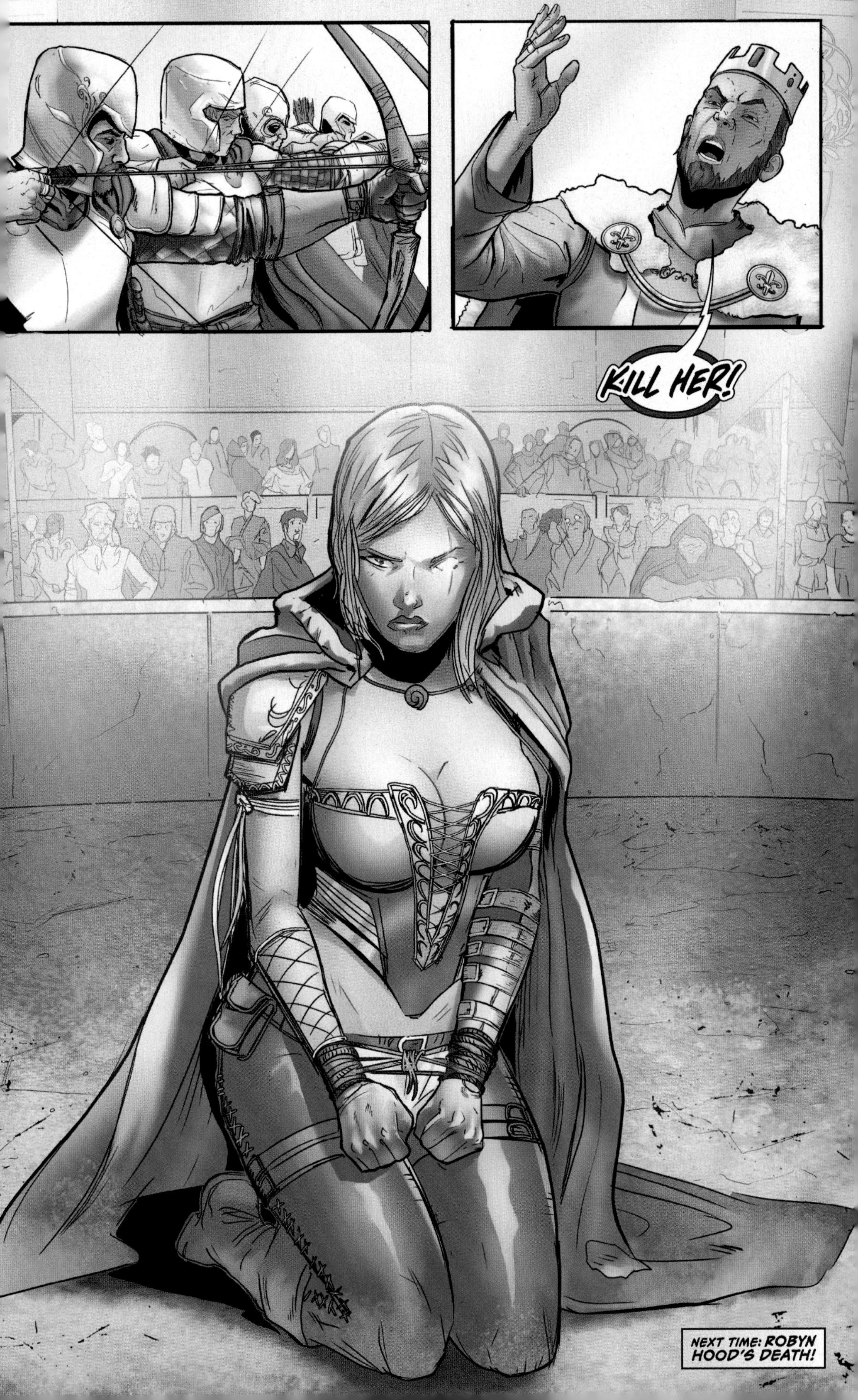
KILL HER!
NEXT TIME: ROBYN HOOD'S DEATH!

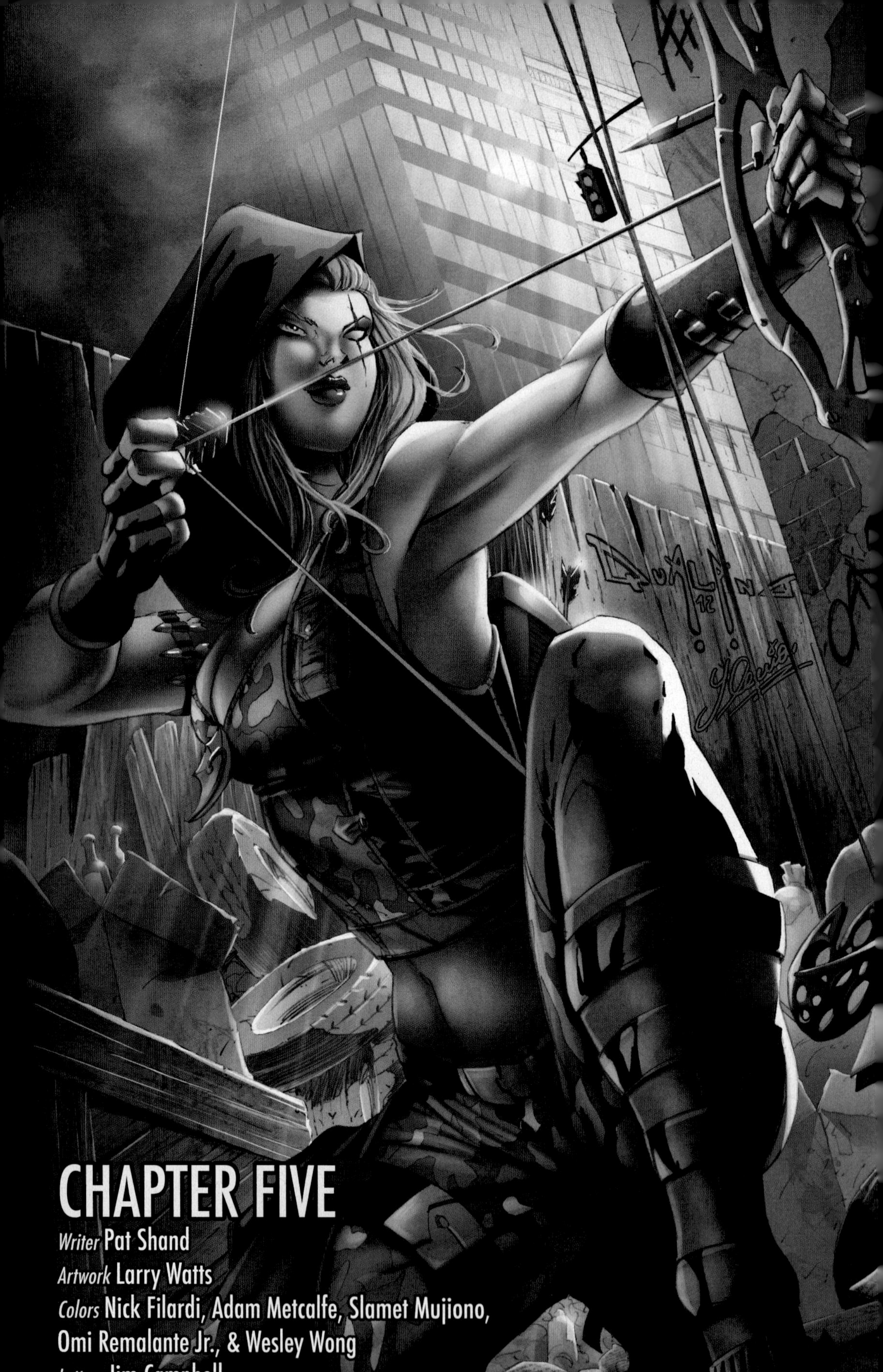

# CHAPTER FIVE

*Writer* Pat Shand
*Artwork* Larry Watts
*Colors* Nick Filardi, Adam Metcalfe, Slamet Mujiono, Omi Remalante Jr., & Wesley Wong
*Letters* Jim Campbell

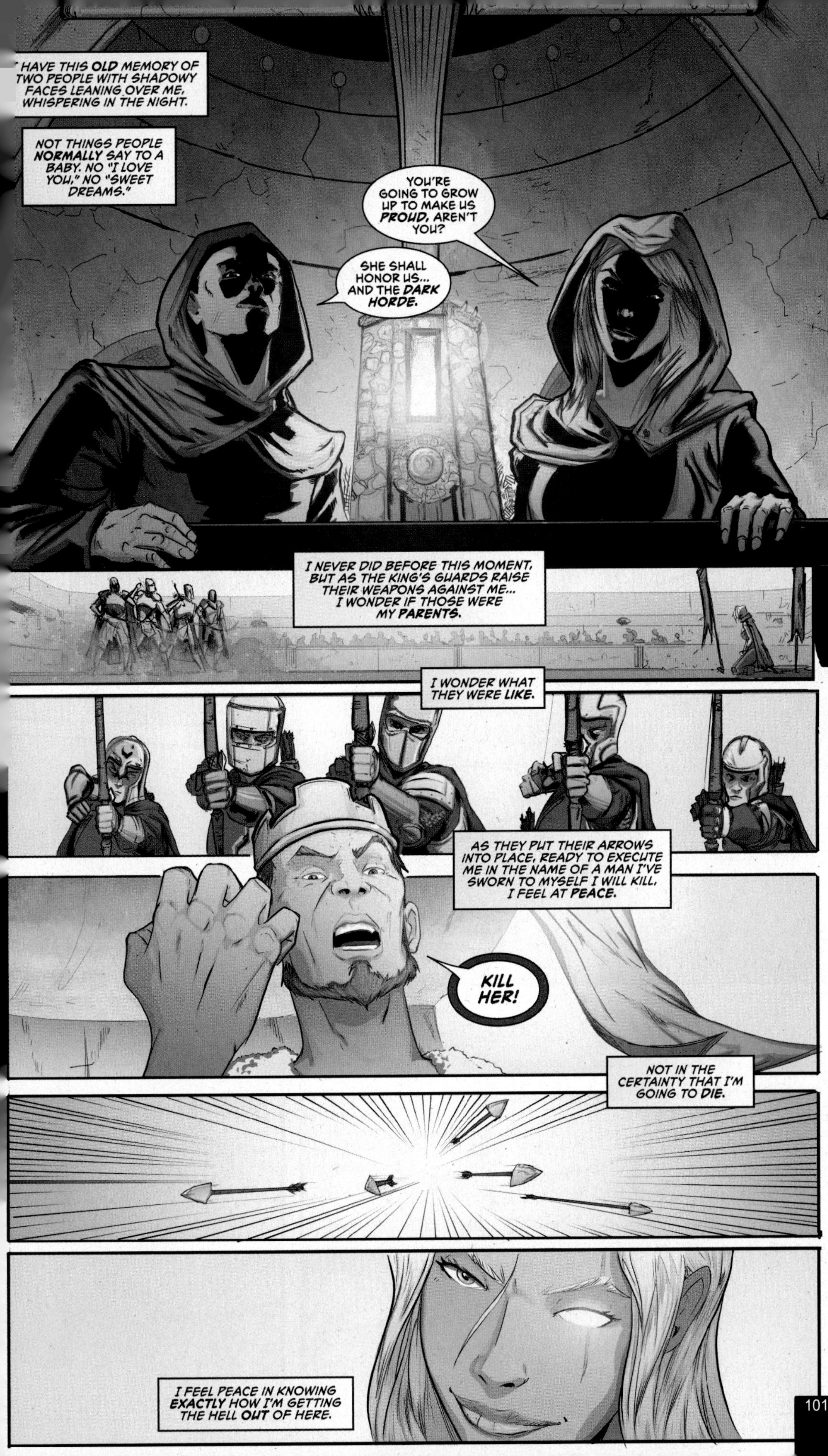
I HAVE THIS OLD MEMORY OF TWO PEOPLE WITH SHADOWY FACES LEANING OVER ME, WHISPERING IN THE NIGHT.
NOT THINGS PEOPLE NORMALLY SAY TO A BABY. NO "I LOVE YOU," NO "SWEET DREAMS."
YOU'RE GOING TO GROW UP TO MAKE US PROUD, AREN'T YOU?
SHE SHALL HONOR US... AND THE DARK HORDE.
I NEVER DID BEFORE THIS MOMENT, BUT AS THE KING'S GUARDS RAISE THEIR WEAPONS AGAINST ME... I WONDER IF THOSE WERE MY PARENTS.
I WONDER WHAT THEY WERE LIKE.
AS THEY PUT THEIR ARROWS INTO PLACE, READY TO EXECUTE ME IN THE NAME OF A MAN I'VE SWORN TO MYSELF I WILL KILL, I FEEL AT PEACE.
KILL HER!
NOT IN THE CERTAINTY THAT I'M GOING TO DIE.
I FEEL PEACE IN KNOWING EXACTLY HOW I'M GETTING THE HELL OUT OF HERE.

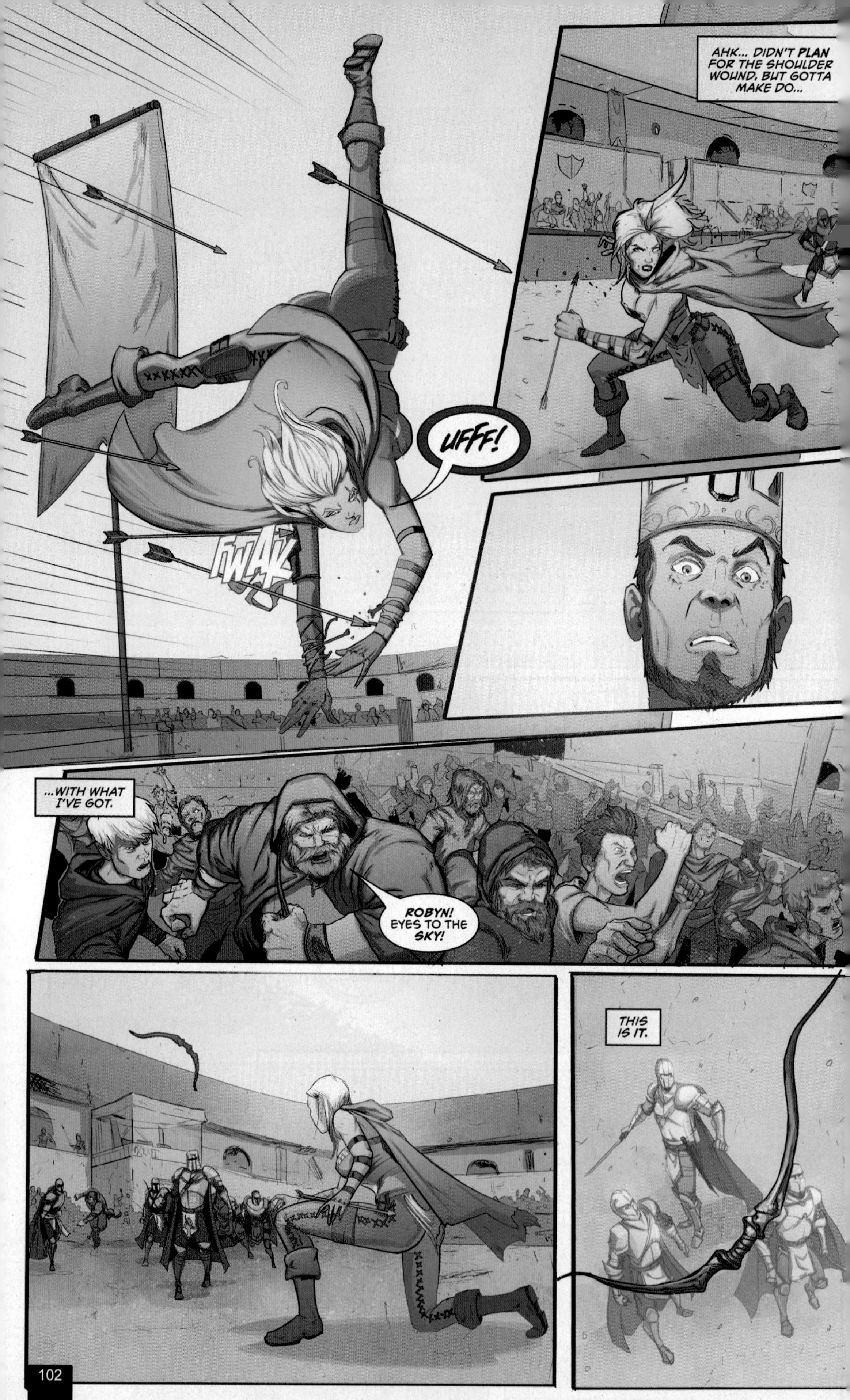
UFFF!
FWAK
AHK... DIDN'T PLAN FOR THE SHOULDER WOUND, BUT GOTTA MAKE DO...
...WITH WHAT I'VE GOT.
ROBYN! EYES TO THE SKY!
THIS IS IT.

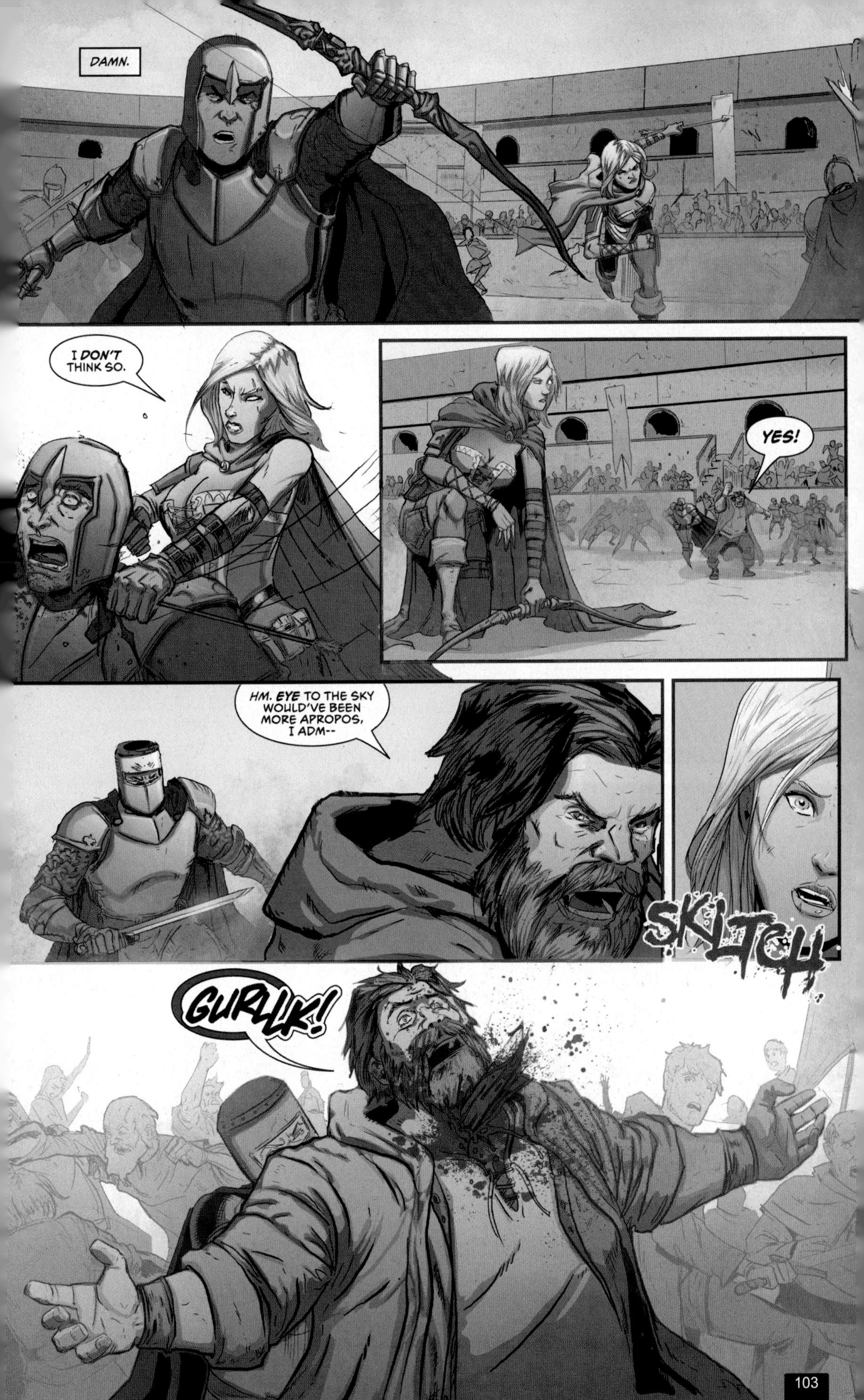
DAMN.
I DON'T THINK SO.
YES!
HM. EYE TO THE SKY WOULD'VE BEEN MORE APROPOS, I ADM--
SKLTCH
GURLLK!

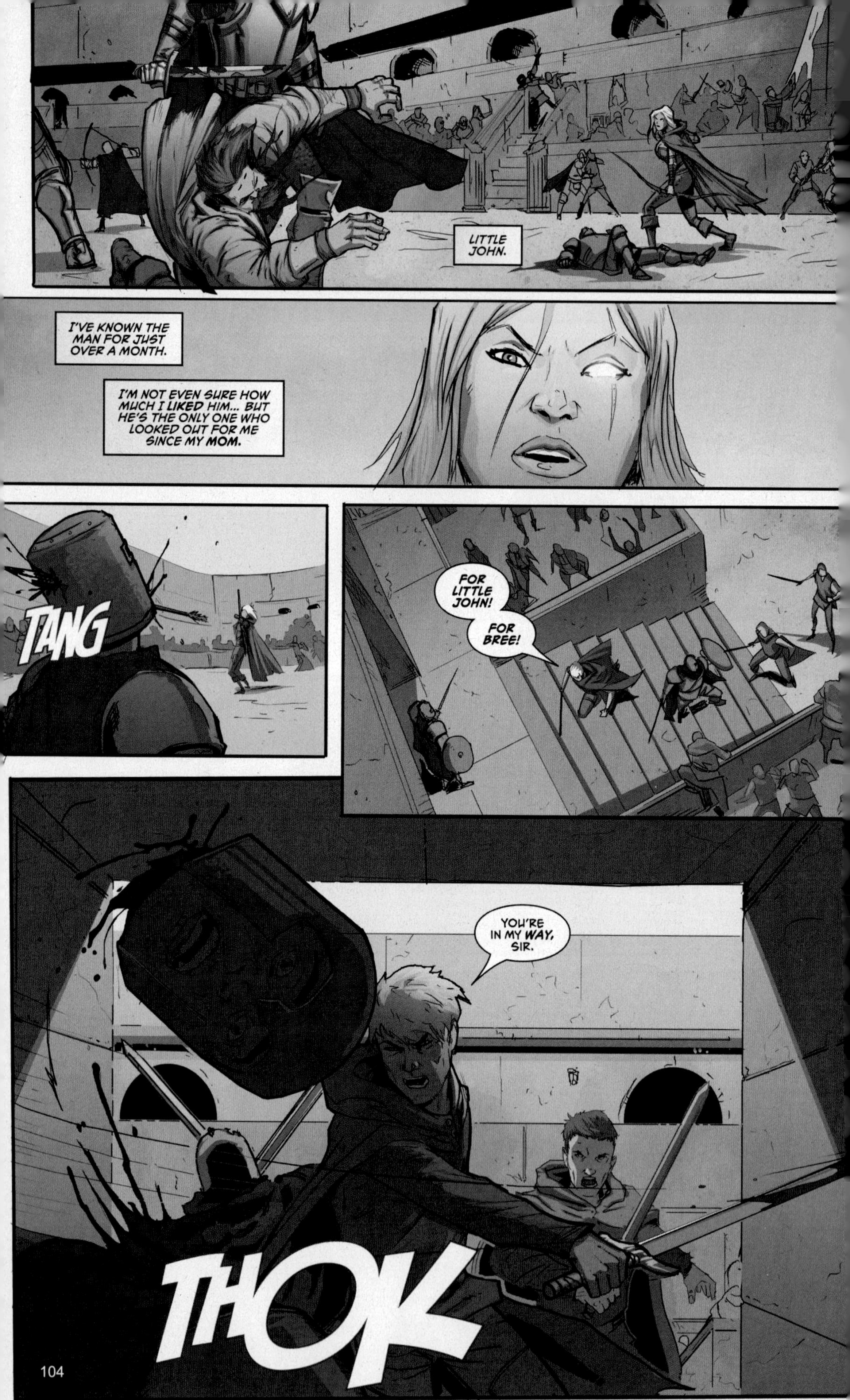
LITTLE JOHN.
I'VE KNOWN THE MAN FOR JUST OVER A MONTH.
I'M NOT EVEN SURE HOW MUCH I LIKED HIM... BUT HE'S THE ONLY ONE WHO LOOKED OUT FOR ME SINCE MY MOM.
TANG
FOR LITTLE JOHN!
FOR BREE!
YOU'RE IN MY WAY, SIR.
THOK

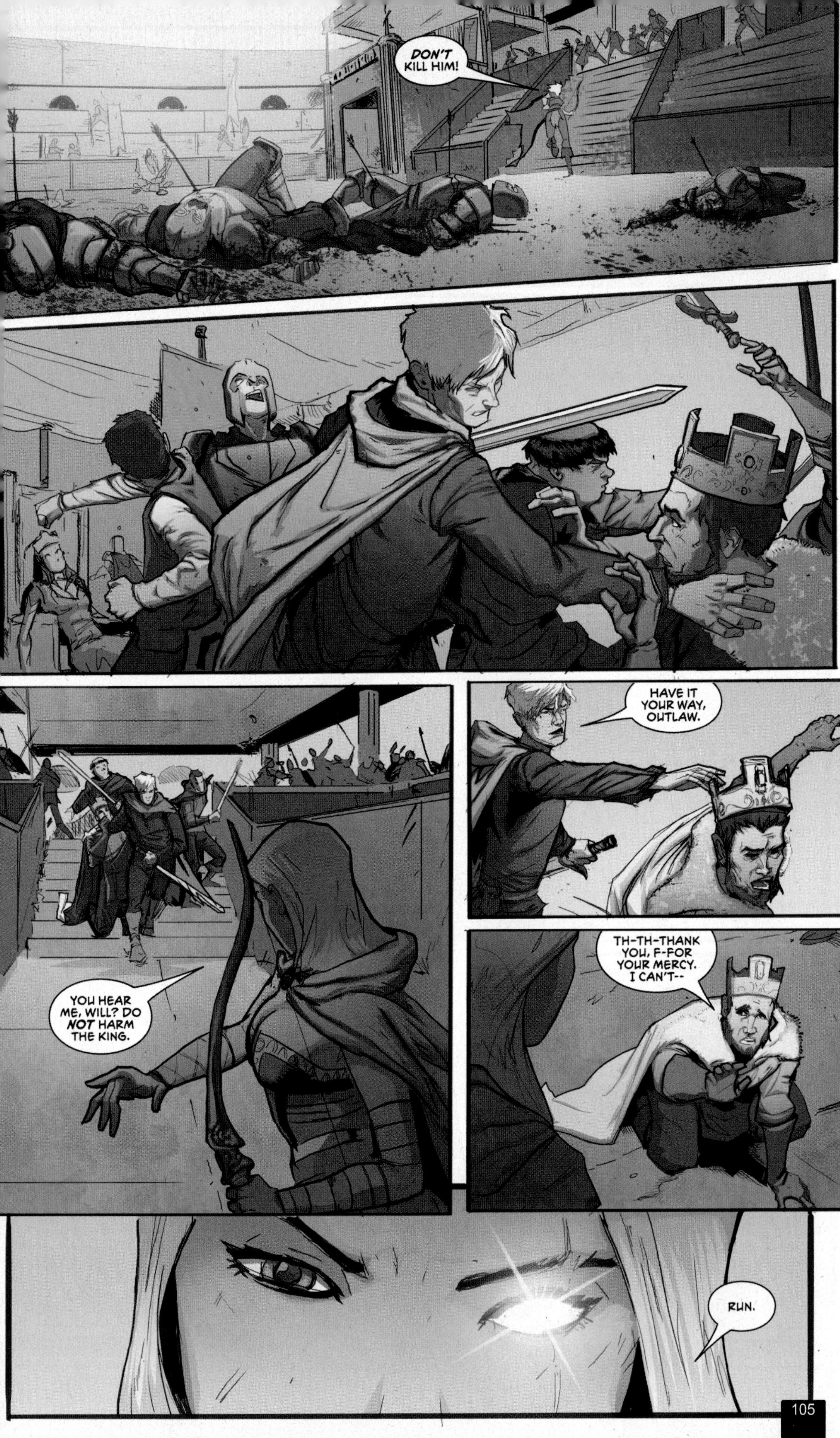

DON'T KILL HIM!
YOU HEAR ME, WILL? DO NOT HARM THE KING.
HAVE IT YOUR WAY, OUTLAW.
TH-TH-THANK YOU, F-FOR YOUR MERCY. I CAN'T--
RUN.

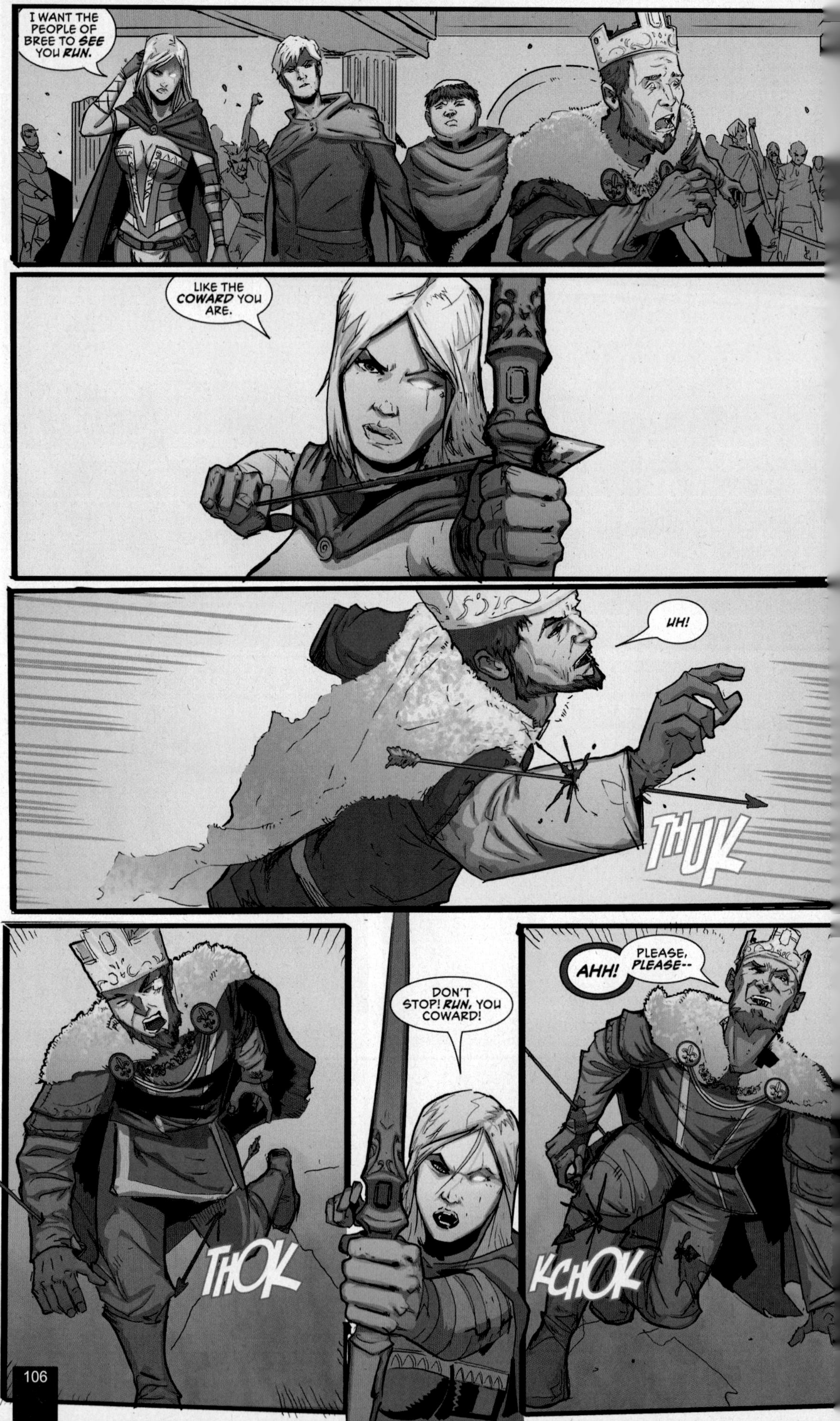
I WANT THE PEOPLE OF BREE TO SEE YOU RUN.
LIKE THE COWARD YOU ARE.
UH!
THUK
DON'T STOP! RUN, YOU COWARD!
THOK
AHH!
PLEASE, PLEASE--
KCHOK

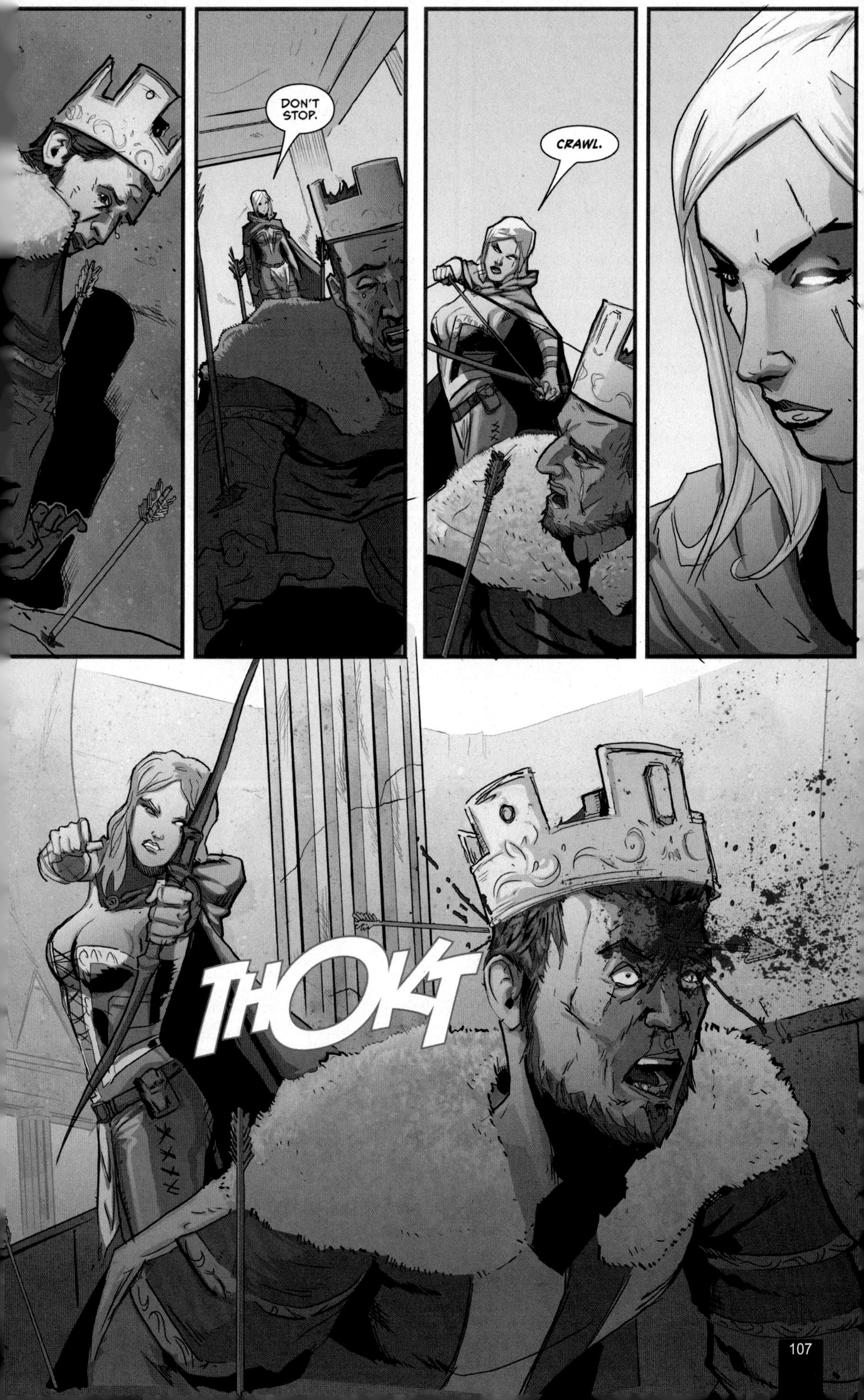
DON'T STOP.
CRAWL.
THOKT

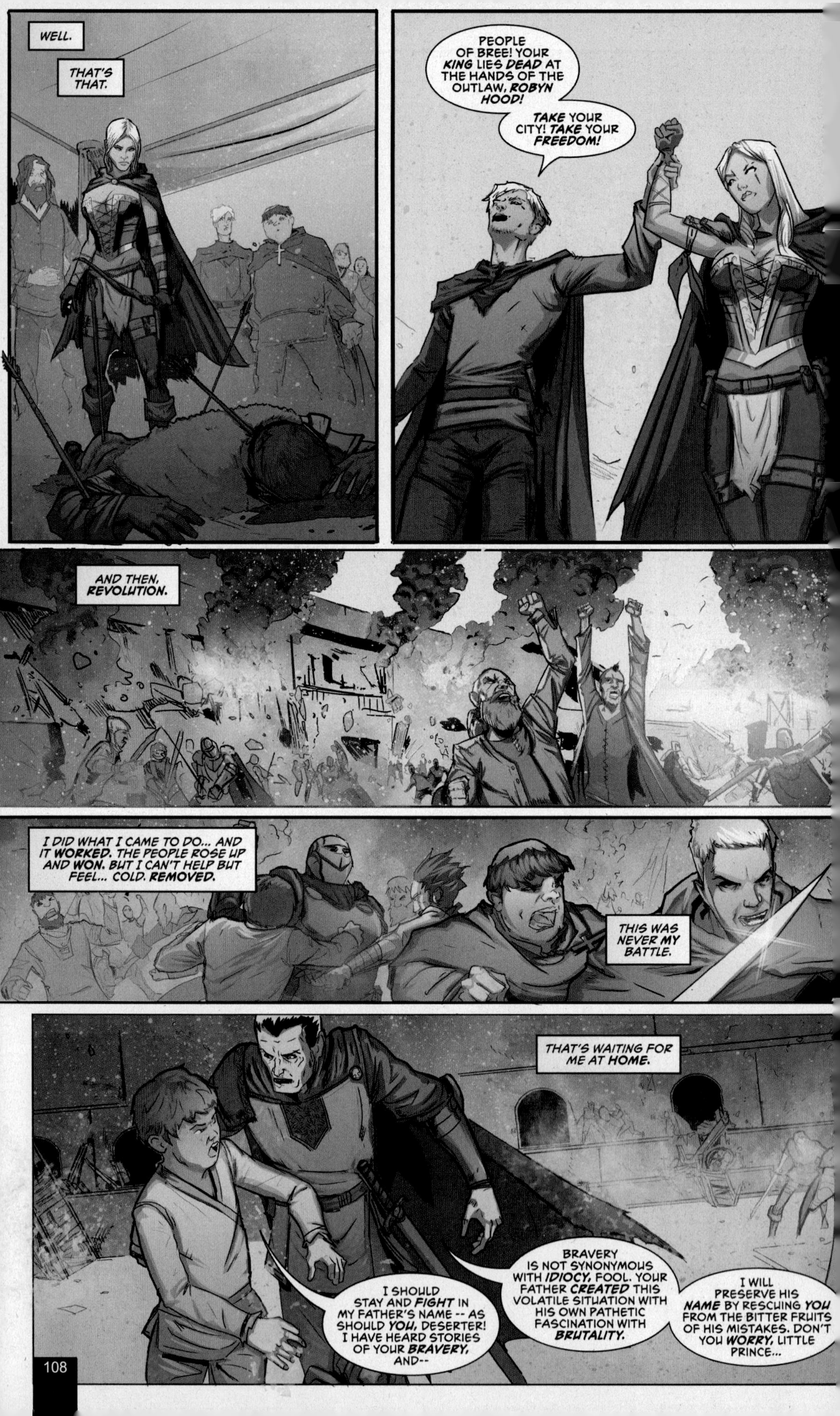
WELL.
THAT'S THAT.
PEOPLE OF BREE! YOUR KING LIES DEAD AT THE HANDS OF THE OUTLAW, ROBYN HOOD!
TAKE YOUR CITY! TAKE YOUR FREEDOM!
AND THEN, REVOLUTION.
I DID WHAT I CAME TO DO... AND IT WORKED. THE PEOPLE ROSE UP AND WON. BUT I CAN'T HELP BUT FEEL... COLD. REMOVED.
THIS WAS NEVER MY BATTLE.
THAT'S WAITING FOR ME AT HOME.
I SHOULD STAY AND FIGHT IN MY FATHER'S NAME -- AS SHOULD YOU, DESERTER! I HAVE HEARD STORIES OF YOUR BRAVERY, AND--
BRAVERY IS NOT SYNONYMOUS WITH IDIOCY, FOOL. YOUR FATHER CREATED THIS VOLATILE SITUATION WITH HIS OWN PATHETIC FASCINATION WITH BRUTALITY.
I WILL PRESERVE HIS NAME BY RESCUING YOU FROM THE BITTER FRUITS OF HIS MISTAKES. DON'T YOU WORRY, LITTLE PRINCE...

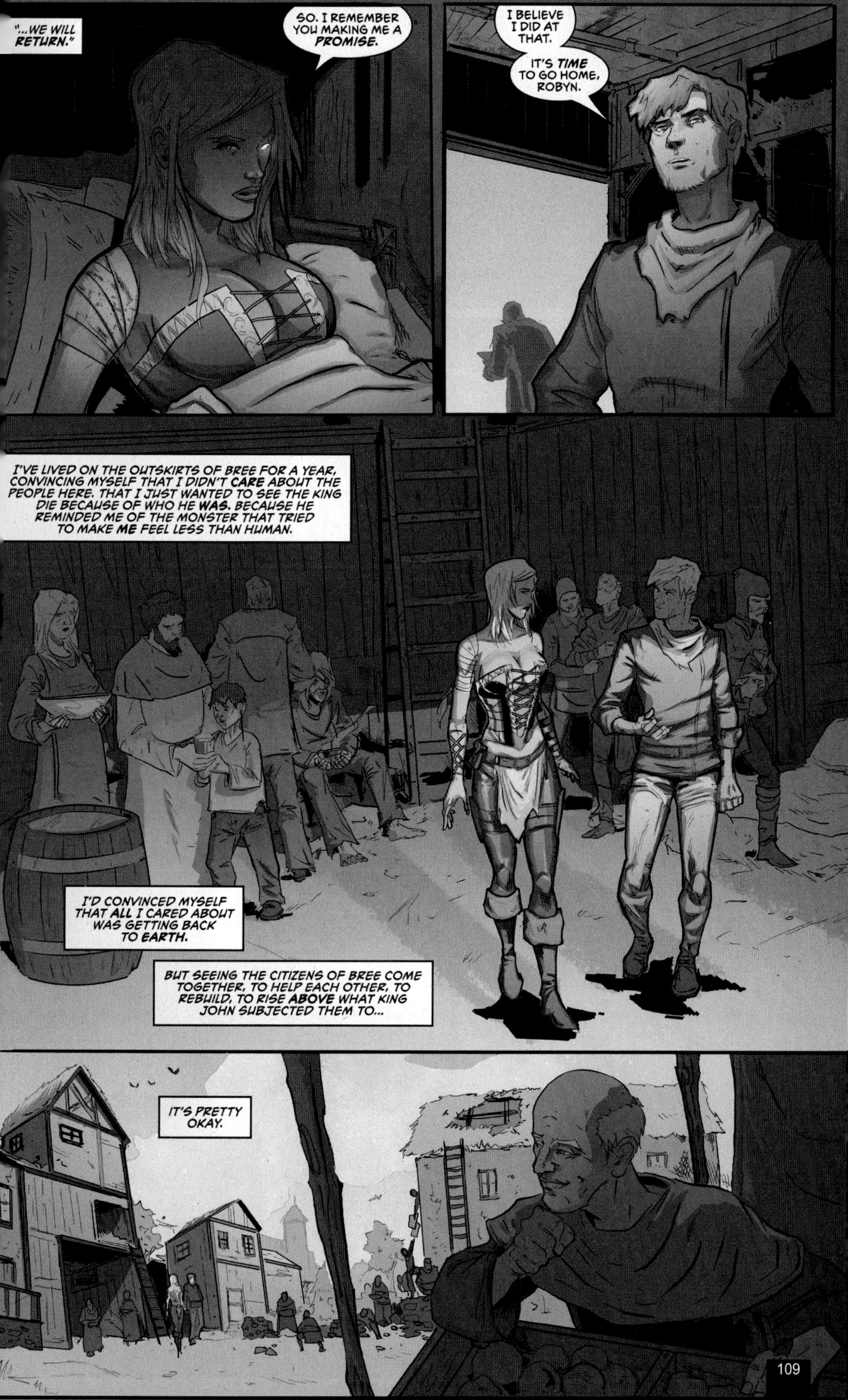
"...WE WILL RETURN."
SO. I REMEMBER YOU MAKING ME A PROMISE.
I BELIEVE I DID AT THAT.
IT'S TIME TO GO HOME, ROBYN.
I'VE LIVED ON THE OUTSKIRTS OF BREE FOR A YEAR, CONVINCING MYSELF THAT I DIDN'T CARE ABOUT THE PEOPLE HERE. THAT I JUST WANTED TO SEE THE KING DIE BECAUSE OF WHO HE WAS. BECAUSE HE REMINDED ME OF THE MONSTER THAT TRIED TO MAKE ME FEEL LESS THAN HUMAN.
I'D CONVINCED MYSELF THAT ALL I CARED ABOUT WAS GETTING BACK TO EARTH.
BUT SEEING THE CITIZENS OF BREE COME TOGETHER, TO HELP EACH OTHER, TO REBUILD, TO RISE ABOVE WHAT KING JOHN SUBJECTED THEM TO...
IT'S PRETTY OKAY.

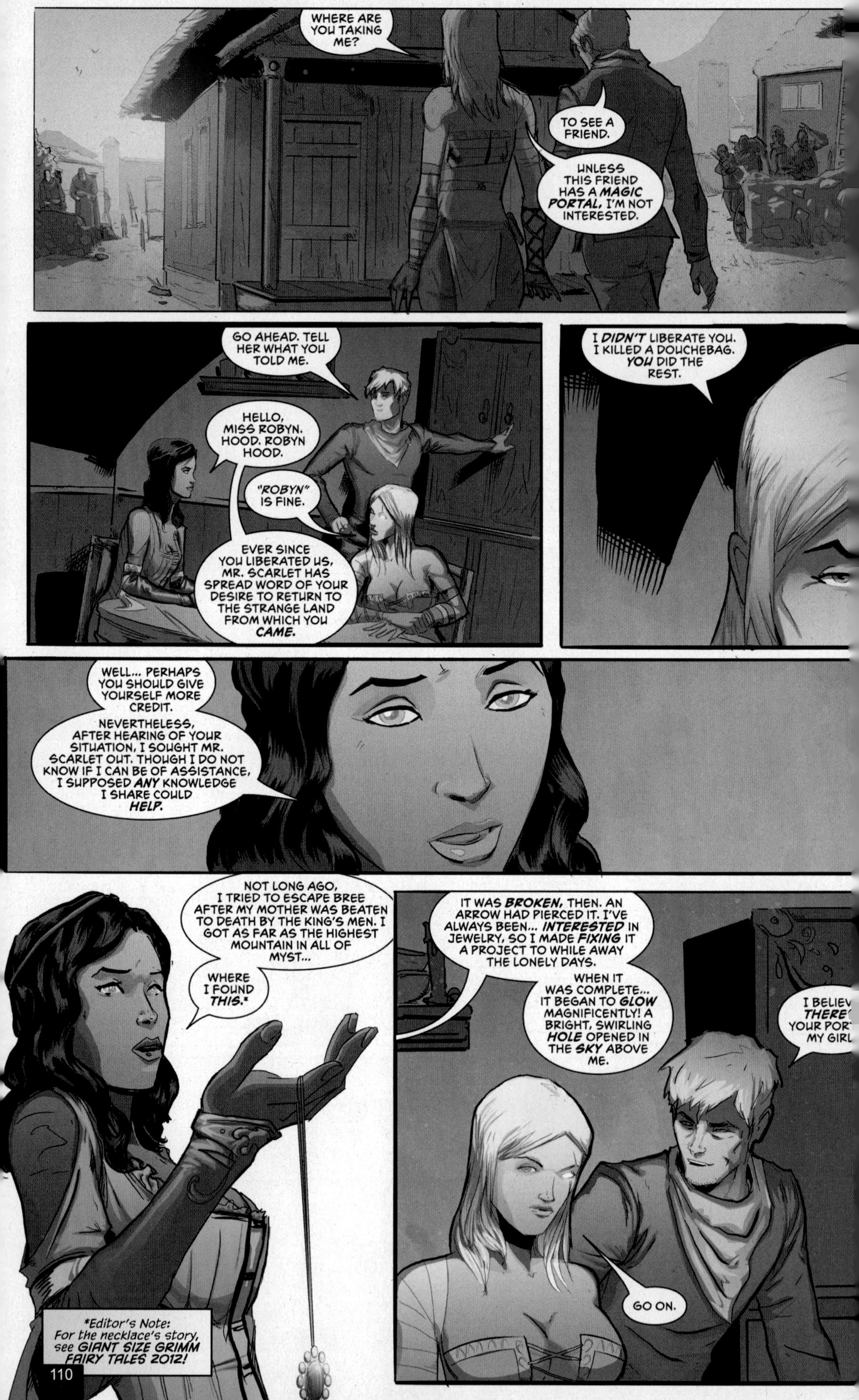
WHERE ARE YOU TAKING ME?
TO SEE A FRIEND.
UNLESS THIS FRIEND HAS A MAGIC PORTAL, I'M NOT INTERESTED.
GO AHEAD. TELL HER WHAT YOU TOLD ME.
HELLO, MISS ROBYN. HOOD. ROBYN HOOD.
"ROBYN" IS FINE.
EVER SINCE YOU LIBERATED US, MR. SCARLET HAS SPREAD WORD OF YOUR DESIRE TO RETURN TO THE STRANGE LAND FROM WHICH YOU CAME.
I DIDN'T LIBERATE YOU. I KILLED A DOUCHEBAG. YOU DID THE REST.
WELL... PERHAPS YOU SHOULD GIVE YOURSELF MORE CREDIT.
NEVERTHELESS, AFTER HEARING OF YOUR SITUATION, I SOUGHT MR. SCARLET OUT. THOUGH I DO NOT KNOW IF I CAN BE OF ASSISTANCE, I SUPPOSED ANY KNOWLEDGE I SHARE COULD HELP.
NOT LONG AGO, I TRIED TO ESCAPE BREE AFTER MY MOTHER WAS BEATEN TO DEATH BY THE KING'S MEN. I GOT AS FAR AS THE HIGHEST MOUNTAIN IN ALL OF MYST...
WHERE I FOUND THIS.*
*Editor's Note: For the necklace's story, see GIANT SIZE GRIMM FAIRY TALES 2012!
IT WAS BROKEN, THEN. AN ARROW HAD PIERCED IT. I'VE ALWAYS BEEN... INTERESTED IN JEWELRY, SO I MADE FIXING IT A PROJECT TO WHILE AWAY THE LONELY DAYS.
WHEN IT WAS COMPLETE... IT BEGAN TO GLOW MAGNIFICENTLY! A BRIGHT, SWIRLING HOLE OPENED IN THE SKY ABOVE ME.
I BELIEV THERE YOUR PORT MY GIRL
GO ON.

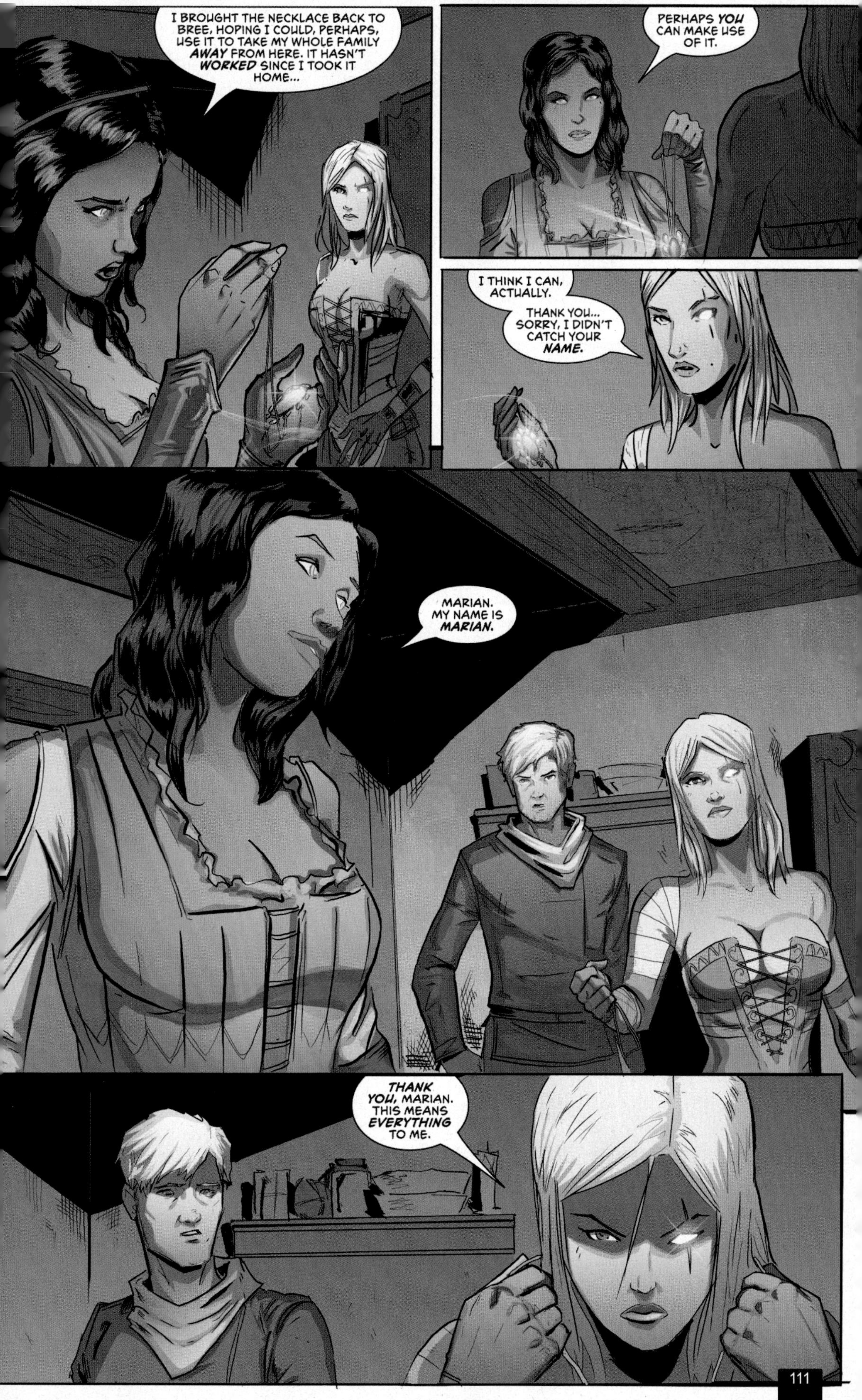
I BROUGHT THE NECKLACE BACK TO BREE, HOPING I COULD, PERHAPS, USE IT TO TAKE MY WHOLE FAMILY AWAY FROM HERE. IT HASN'T WORKED SINCE I TOOK IT HOME...
PERHAPS YOU CAN MAKE USE OF IT.
I THINK I CAN, ACTUALLY.
THANK YOU... SORRY, I DIDN'T CATCH YOUR NAME.
MARIAN. MY NAME IS MARIAN.
THANK YOU, MARIAN. THIS MEANS EVERYTHING TO ME.

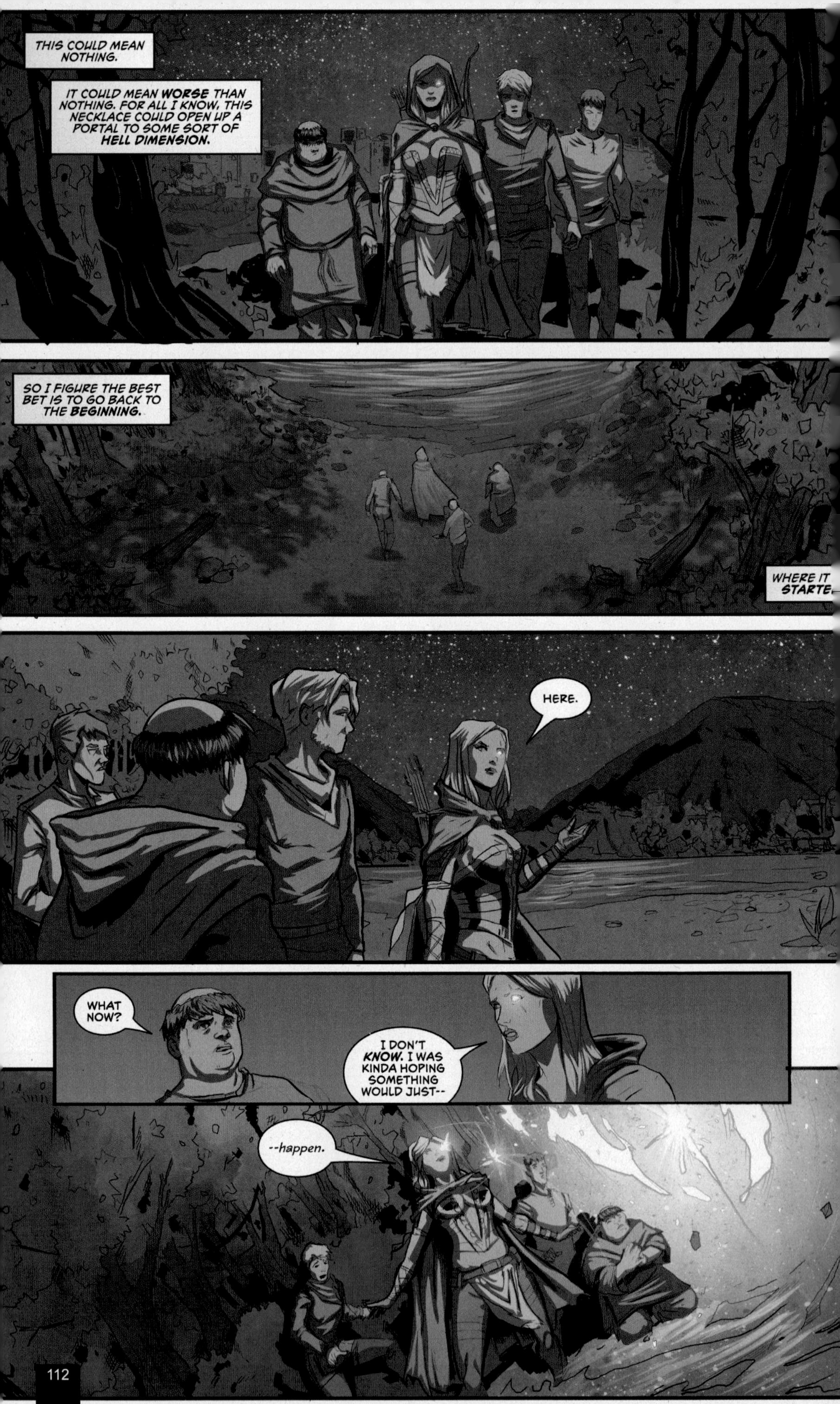

THIS COULD MEAN NOTHING.
IT COULD MEAN WORSE THAN NOTHING. FOR ALL I KNOW, THIS NECKLACE COULD OPEN UP A PORTAL TO SOME SORT OF HELL DIMENSION.
SO I FIGURE THE BEST BET IS TO GO BACK TO THE BEGINNING.
WHERE IT STARTE
HERE.
WHAT NOW?
I DON'T KNOW. I WAS KINDA HOPING SOMETHING WOULD JUST--
--happen.

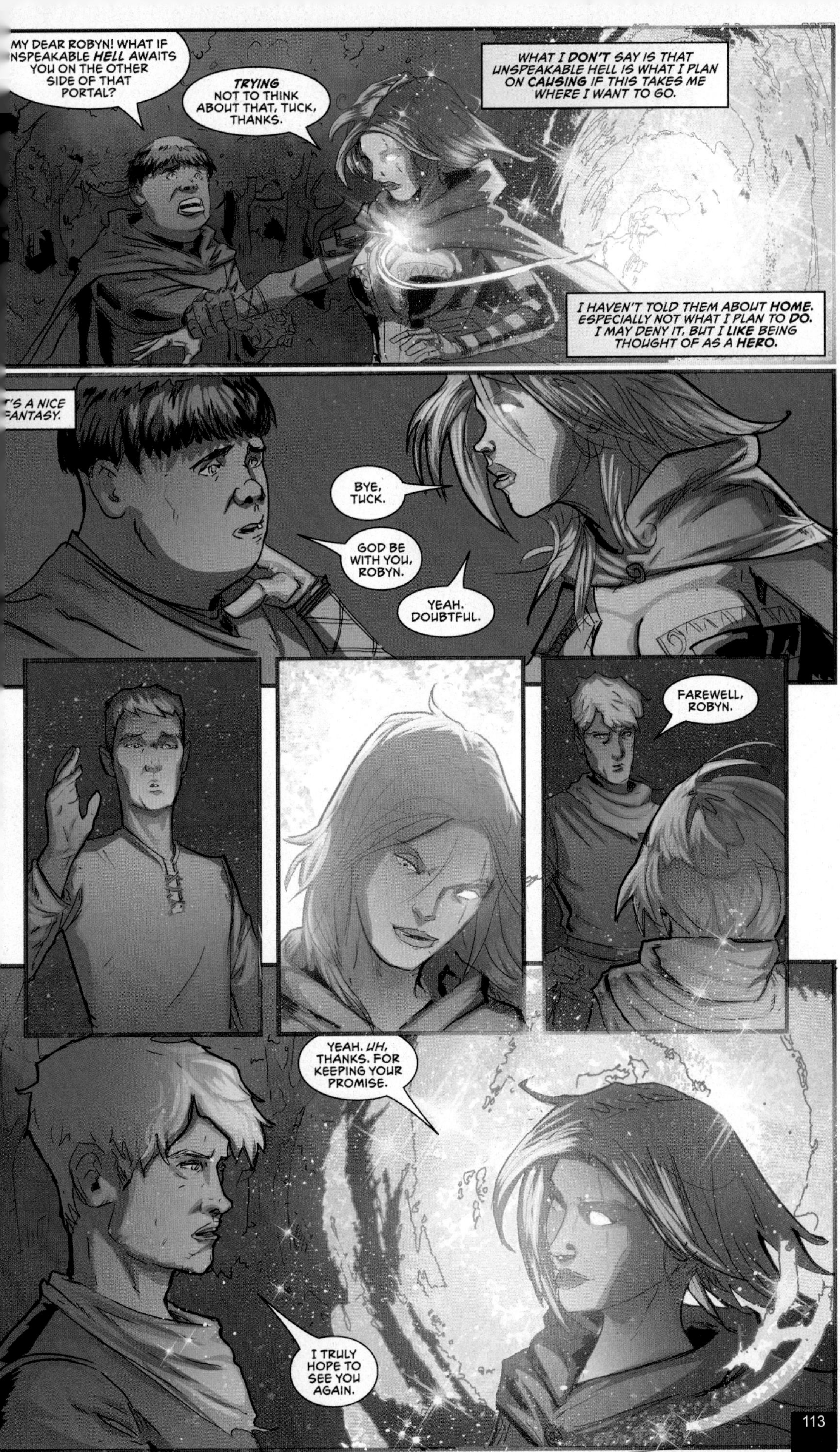
MY DEAR ROBYN! WHAT IF UNSPEAKABLE HELL AWAITS YOU ON THE OTHER SIDE OF THAT PORTAL?
TRYING NOT TO THINK ABOUT THAT, TUCK, THANKS.
WHAT I DON'T SAY IS THAT UNSPEAKABLE HELL IS WHAT I PLAN ON CAUSING IF THIS TAKES ME WHERE I WANT TO GO.
I HAVEN'T TOLD THEM ABOUT HOME. ESPECIALLY NOT WHAT I PLAN TO DO. I MAY DENY IT, BUT I LIKE BEING THOUGHT OF AS A HERO.
'S A NICE FANTASY.
BYE, TUCK.
GOD BE WITH YOU, ROBYN.
YEAH. DOUBTFUL.
FAREWELL, ROBYN.
YEAH. UH, THANKS. FOR KEEPING YOUR PROMISE.
I TRULY HOPE TO SEE YOU AGAIN.

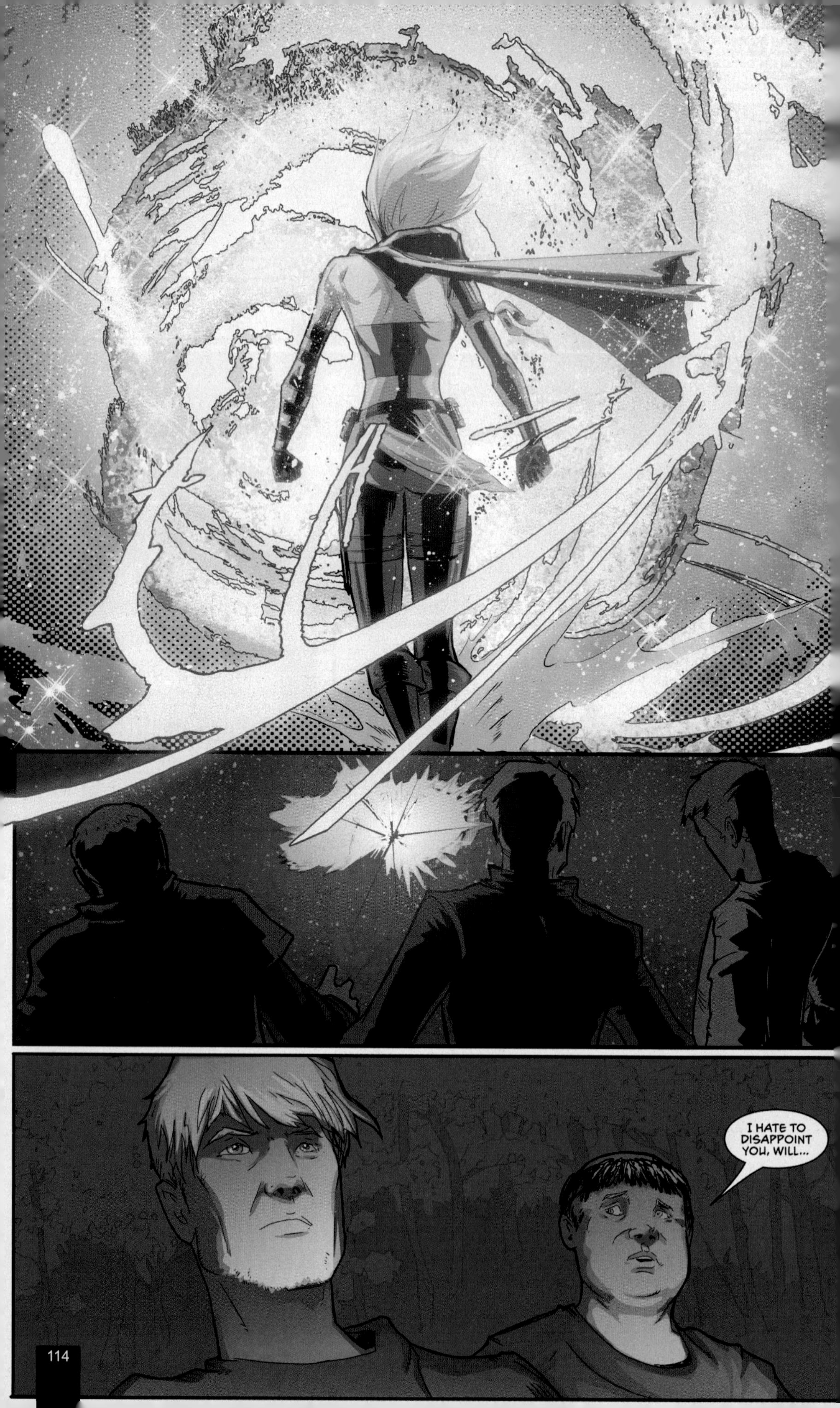
I HATE TO DISAPPOINT YOU, WILL...

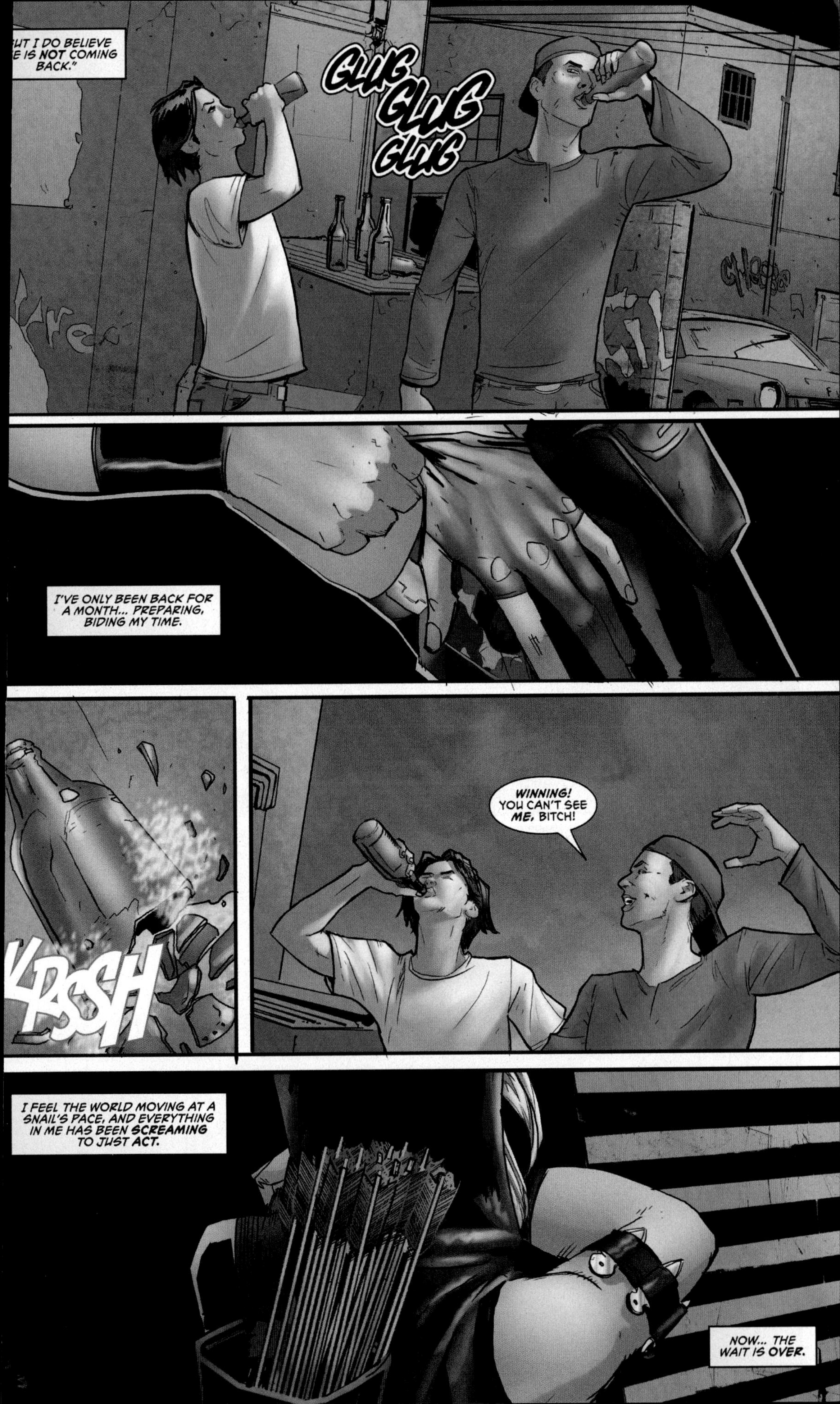

...UT I DO BELIEVE ...E IS NOT COMING BACK."
GLUG GLUG GLUG
I'VE ONLY BEEN BACK FOR A MONTH... PREPARING, BIDING MY TIME.
KRSSH
WINNING! YOU CAN'T SEE ME, BITCH!
I FEEL THE WORLD MOVING AT A SNAIL'S PACE, AND EVERYTHING IN ME HAS BEEN SCREAMING TO JUST ACT.
NOW... THE WAIT IS OVER.

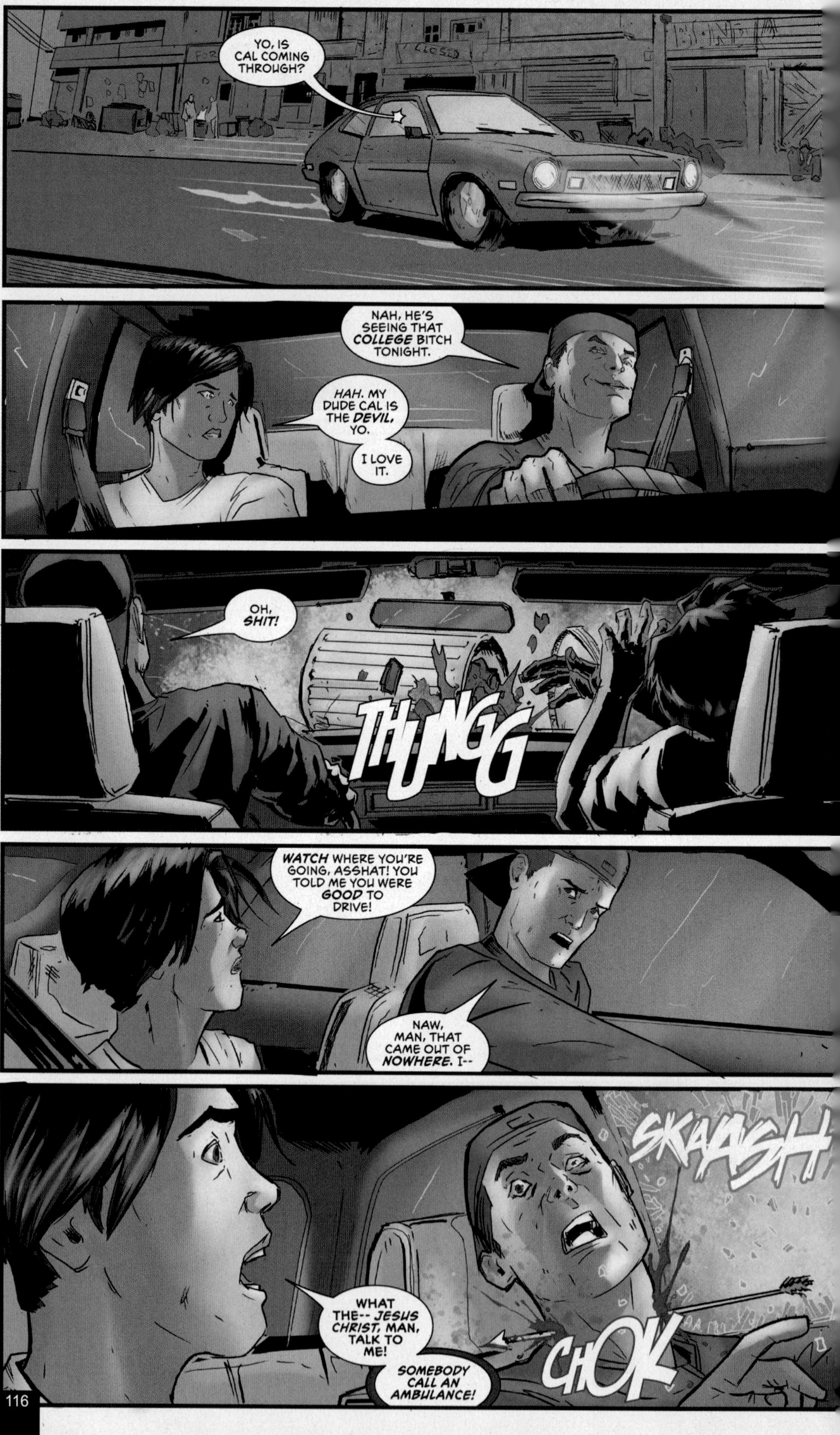
YO, IS CAL COMING THROUGH?
NAH, HE'S SEEING THAT COLLEGE BITCH TONIGHT.
HAH. MY DUDE CAL IS THE DEVIL, YO.
I LOVE IT.
OH, SHIT!
THUNGG
WATCH WHERE YOU'RE GOING, ASSHAT! YOU TOLD ME YOU WERE GOOD TO DRIVE!
NAW, MAN, THAT CAME OUT OF NOWHERE. I--
SKAASH
WHAT THE-- JESUS CHRIST, MAN, TALK TO ME!
SOMEBODY CALL AN AMBULANCE!
CHOK

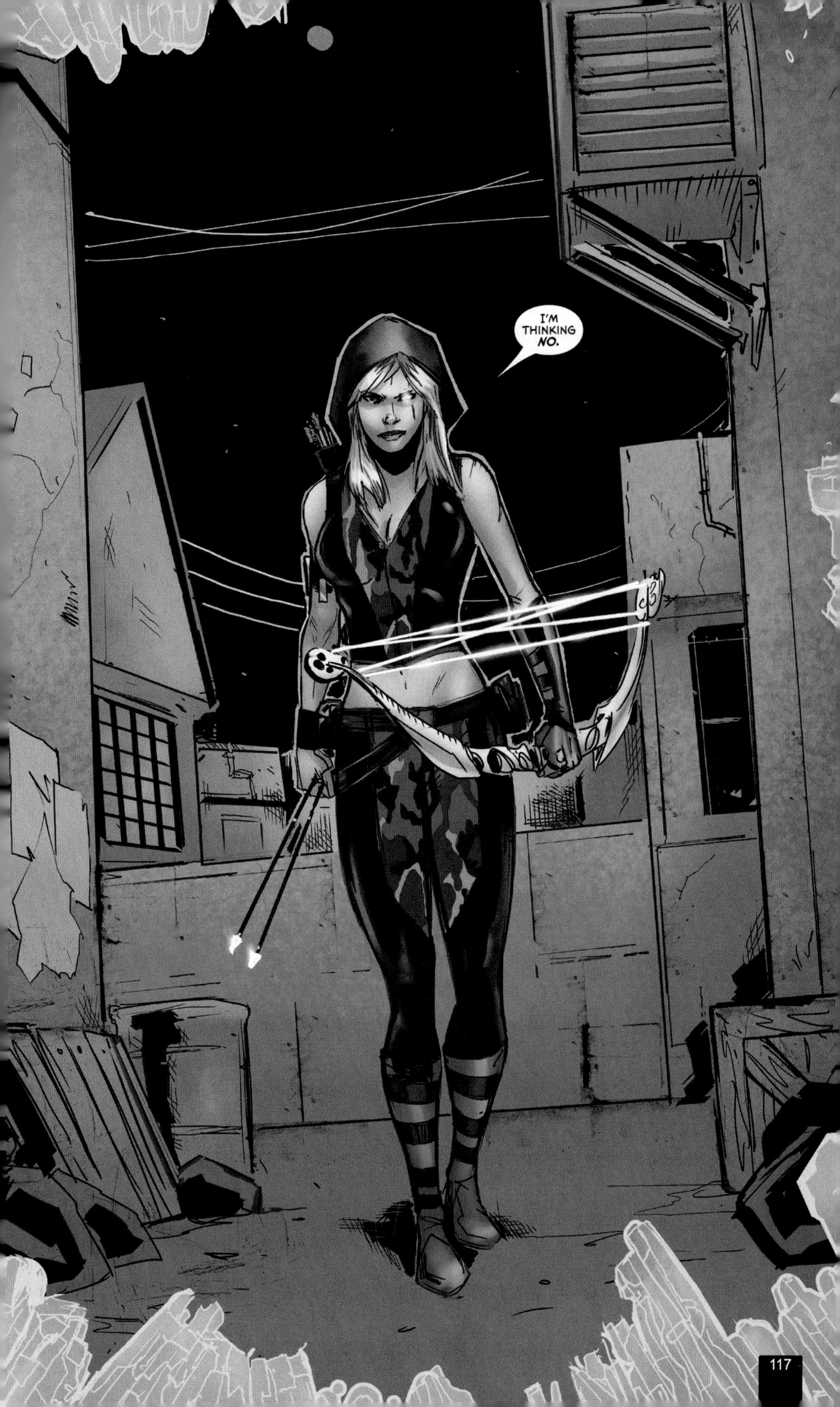
I'M THINKING *NO.*

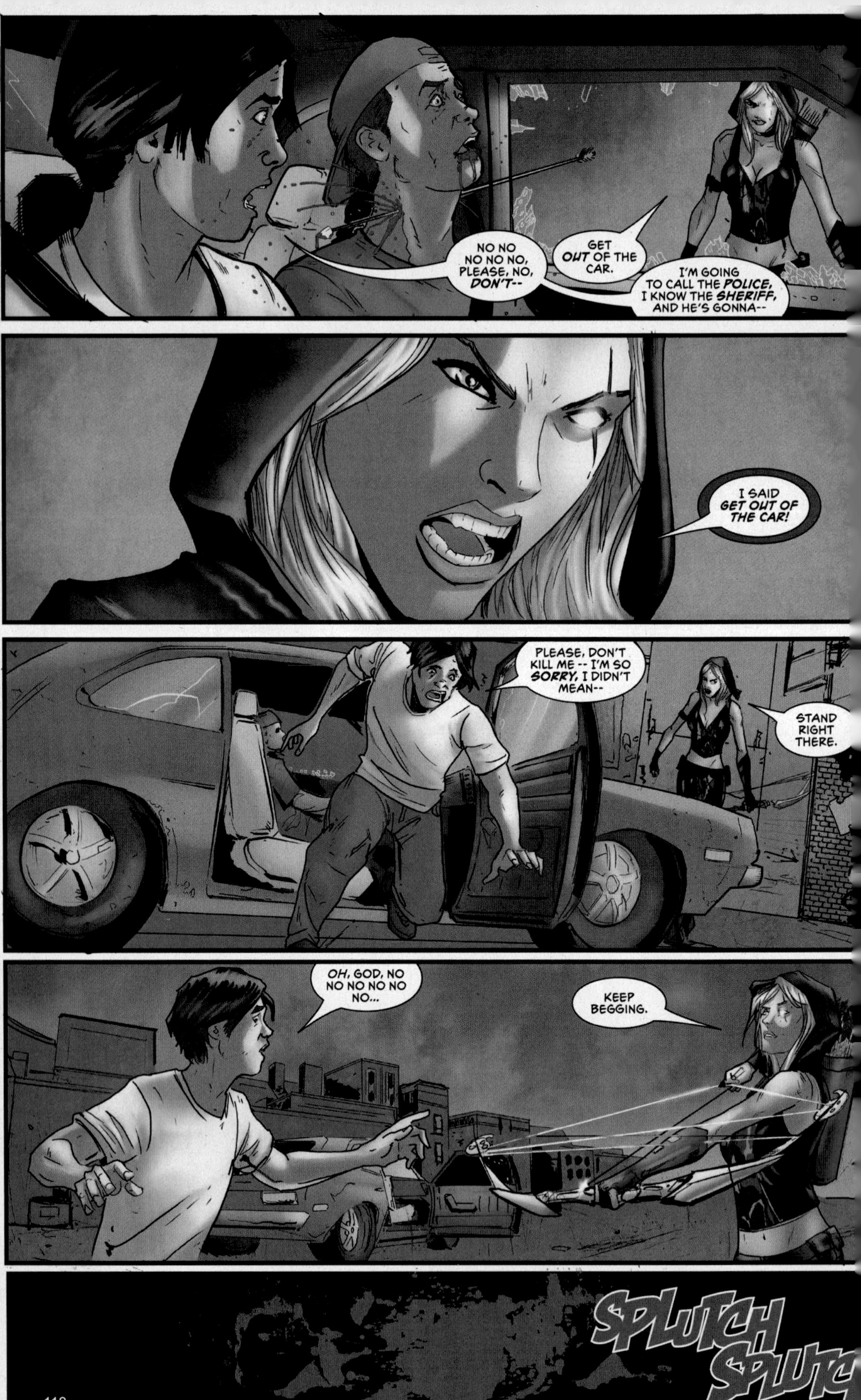
NO NO NO NO NO, PLEASE, NO, DON'T--
GET OUT OF THE CAR.
I'M GOING TO CALL THE POLICE, I KNOW THE SHERIFF, AND HE'S GONNA--
I SAID GET OUT OF THE CAR!
PLEASE, DON'T KILL ME -- I'M SO SORRY, I DIDN'T MEAN--
STAND RIGHT THERE.
OH, GOD, NO NO NO NO NO NO...
KEEP BEGGING.
SPLUTCH

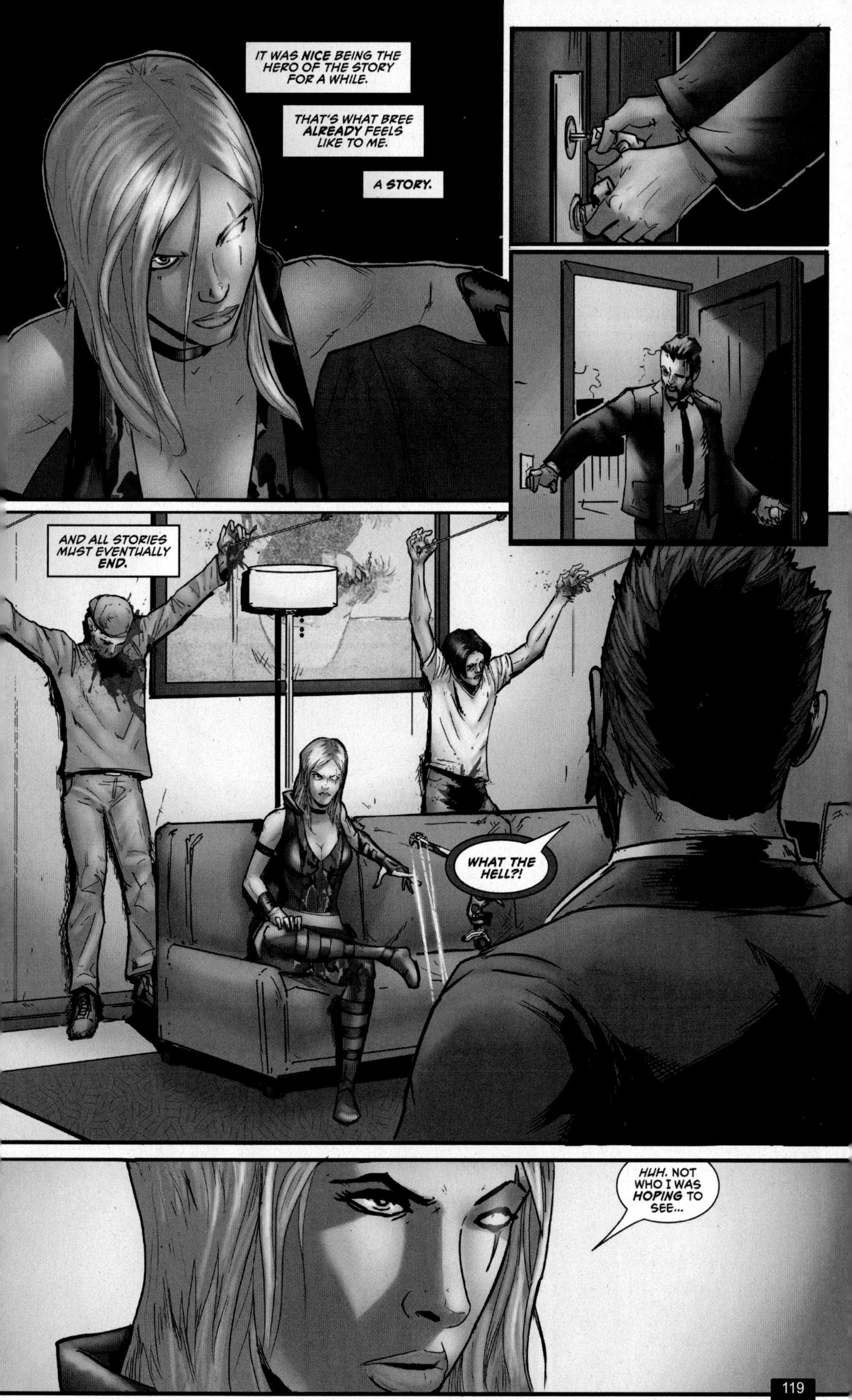
IT WAS NICE BEING THE HERO OF THE STORY FOR A WHILE.
THAT'S WHAT BREE ALREADY FEELS LIKE TO ME.
A STORY.
AND ALL STORIES MUST EVENTUALLY END.
WHAT THE HELL?!
HUH. NOT WHO I WAS HOPING TO SEE...

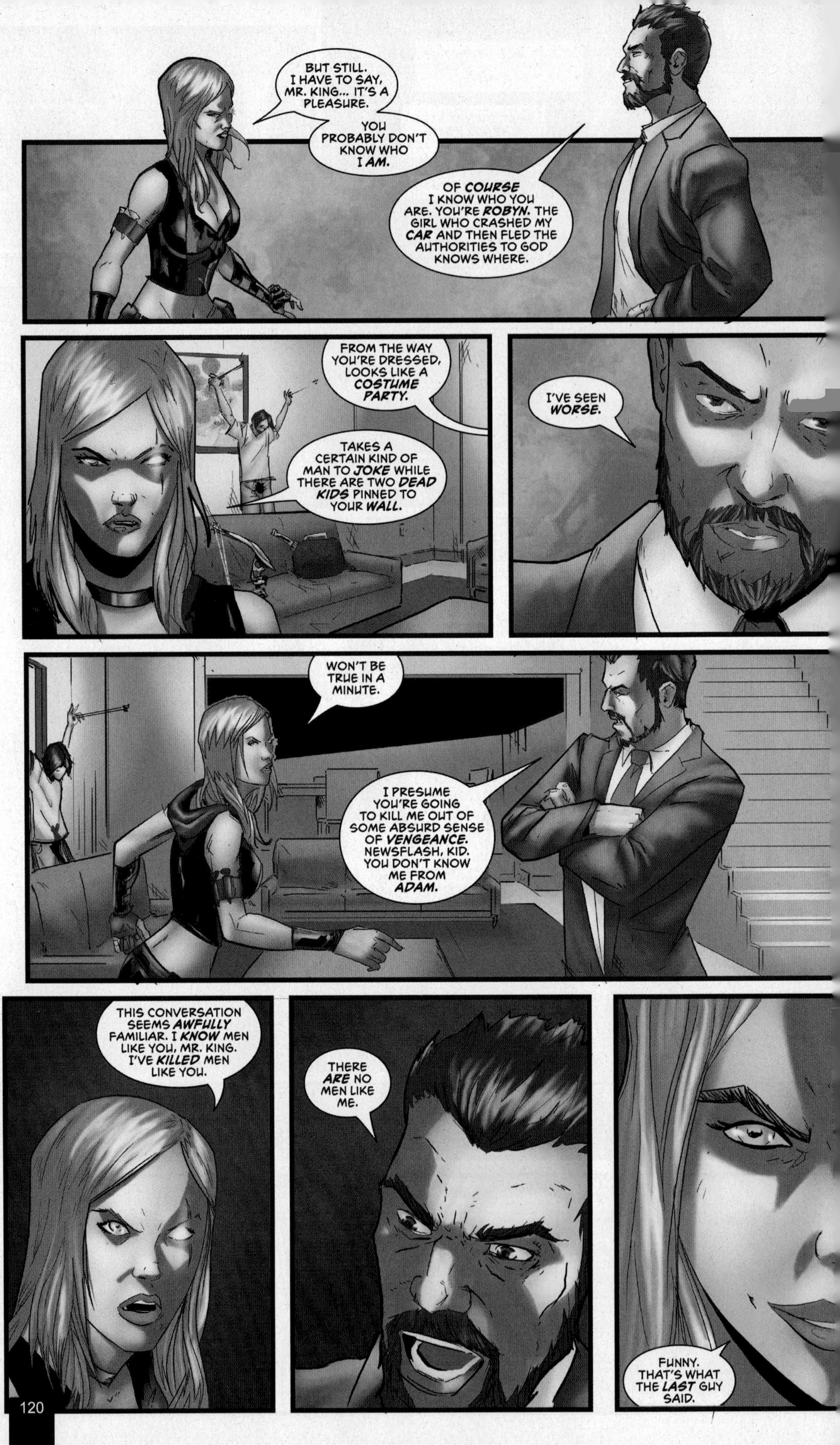
BUT STILL. I HAVE TO SAY, MR. KING... IT'S A PLEASURE.
YOU PROBABLY DON'T KNOW WHO I AM.
OF COURSE I KNOW WHO YOU ARE. YOU'RE ROBYN. THE GIRL WHO CRASHED MY CAR AND THEN FLED THE AUTHORITIES TO GOD KNOWS WHERE.
FROM THE WAY YOU'RE DRESSED, LOOKS LIKE A COSTUME PARTY.
TAKES A CERTAIN KIND OF MAN TO JOKE WHILE THERE ARE TWO DEAD KIDS PINNED TO YOUR WALL.
I'VE SEEN WORSE.
WON'T BE TRUE IN A MINUTE.
I PRESUME YOU'RE GOING TO KILL ME OUT OF SOME ABSURD SENSE OF VENGEANCE. NEWSFLASH, KID. YOU DON'T KNOW ME FROM ADAM.
THIS CONVERSATION SEEMS AWFULLY FAMILIAR. I KNOW MEN LIKE YOU, MR. KING. I'VE KILLED MEN LIKE YOU.
THERE ARE NO MEN LIKE ME.
FUNNY. THAT'S WHAT THE LAST GUY SAID.

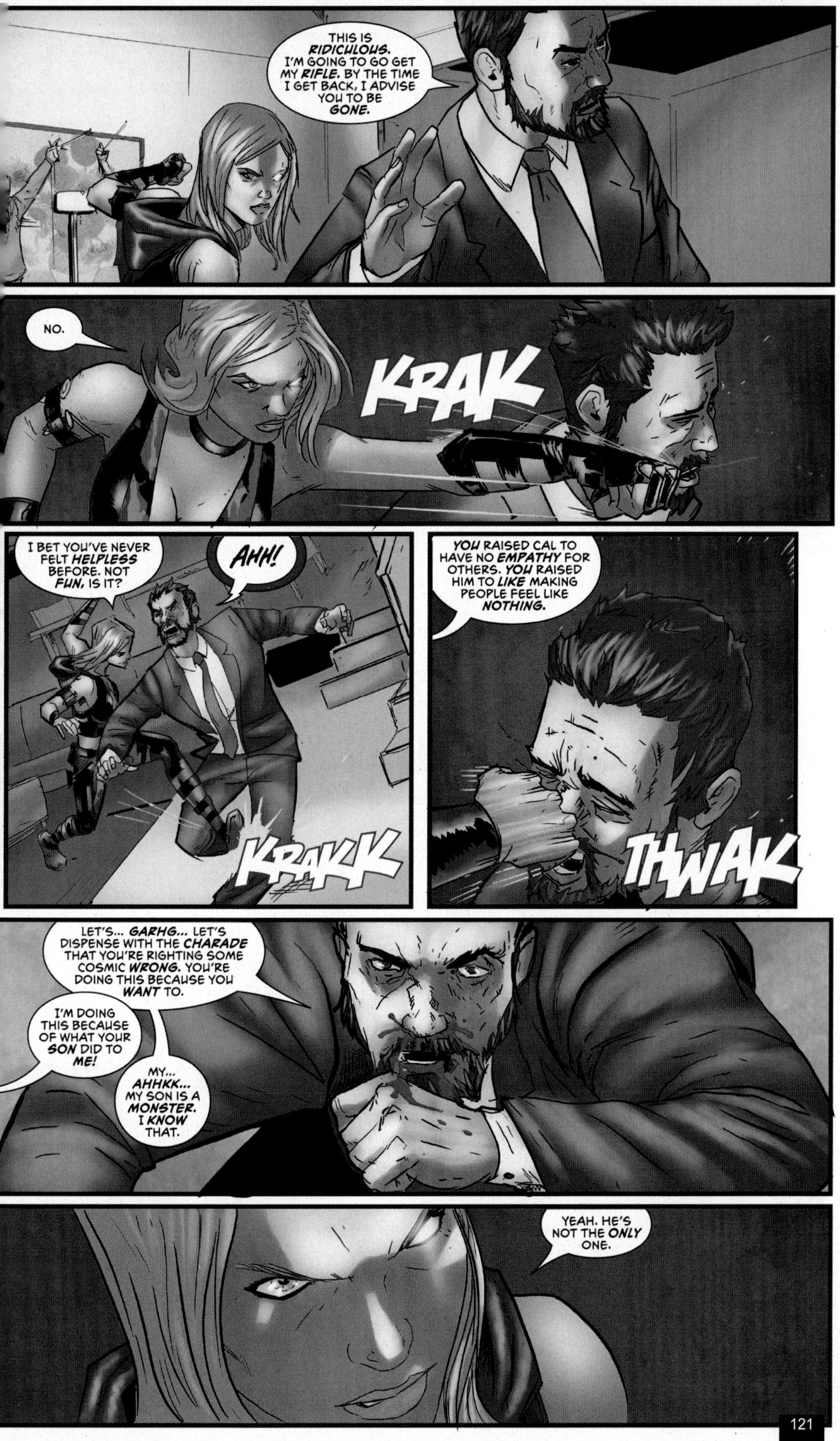
THIS IS RIDICULOUS. I'M GOING TO GO GET MY RIFLE. BY THE TIME I GET BACK, I ADVISE YOU TO BE GONE.
NO.
KRAK
I BET YOU'VE NEVER FELT HELPLESS BEFORE. NOT FUN, IS IT?
AHH!
KRAKK
YOU RAISED CAL TO HAVE NO EMPATHY FOR OTHERS. YOU RAISED HIM TO LIKE MAKING PEOPLE FEEL LIKE NOTHING.
THWAK
LET'S... GARHG... LET'S DISPENSE WITH THE CHARADE THAT YOU'RE RIGHTING SOME COSMIC WRONG. YOU'RE DOING THIS BECAUSE YOU WANT TO.
I'M DOING THIS BECAUSE OF WHAT YOUR SON DID TO ME!
MY... AHHKK... MY SON IS A MONSTER. I KNOW THAT.
YEAH. HE'S NOT THE ONLY ONE.

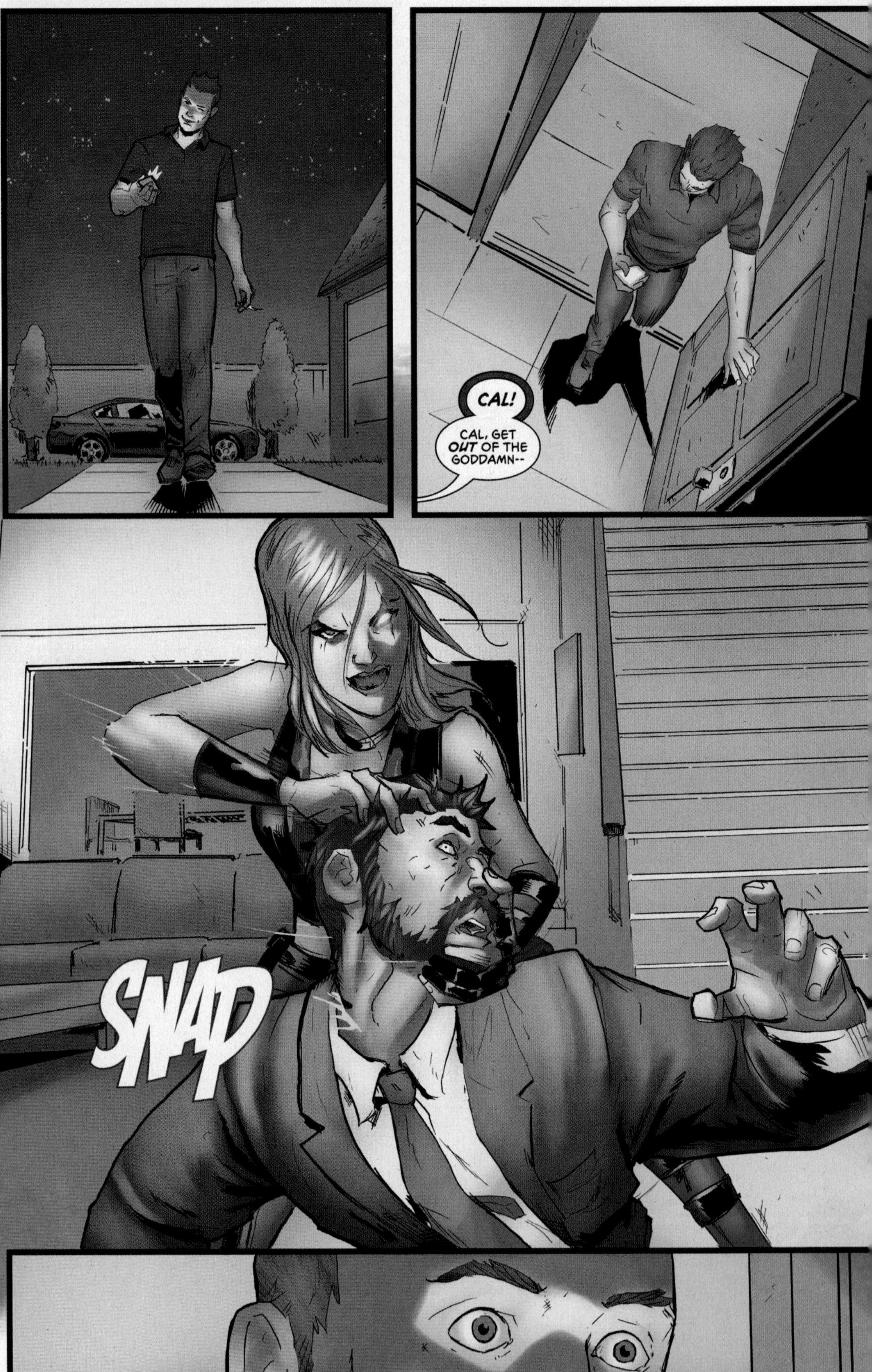
CAL!
CAL, GET OUT OF THE GODDAMN--
SNAP

WELL, LOOK WHAT YOU *DID*.
WHAT CAN I SAY BUT...
*THANKS.*
I WAS WONDERING WHEN I'D JUST GET *TIRED* OF WAITING FOR NATURE TO TAKE ITS COURSE AND SHOVE A *KNIFE* INTO THE BASTARD'S *THROAT,* BUT THEN *YOU* COME ALONG AND DO THE DIRTY WORK *FOR* ME!
THANK YOU. HOW CAN I REPAY YOU? *MONEY?* THAT'S PROBABLY WHY YOU'RE *HERE,* RIGHT? PROBABLY THOUGHT YOU'D ROB US, THAT I'D BE THE SAD, MOURNING SON... *HAH.* THAT'S A GOOD ONE.
I COULD'VE DONE WITHOUT YOU KILLING MY *BUDS* THOUGH -- THE HELL IS *THAT* ABOUT?
OH, GOD.
YOU... DON'T *REMEMBER* ME, DO YOU?

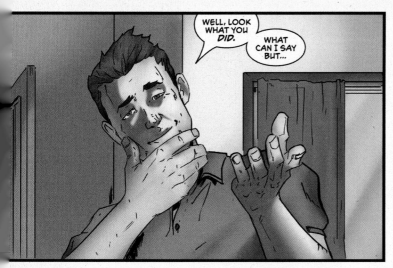

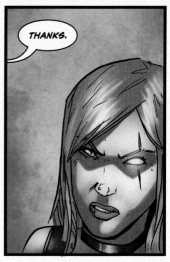

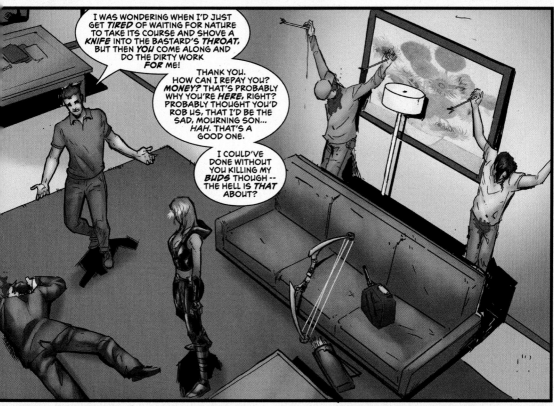

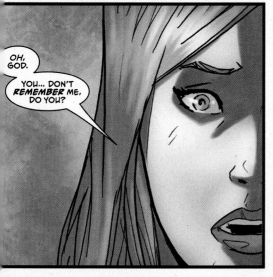

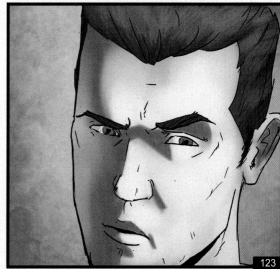

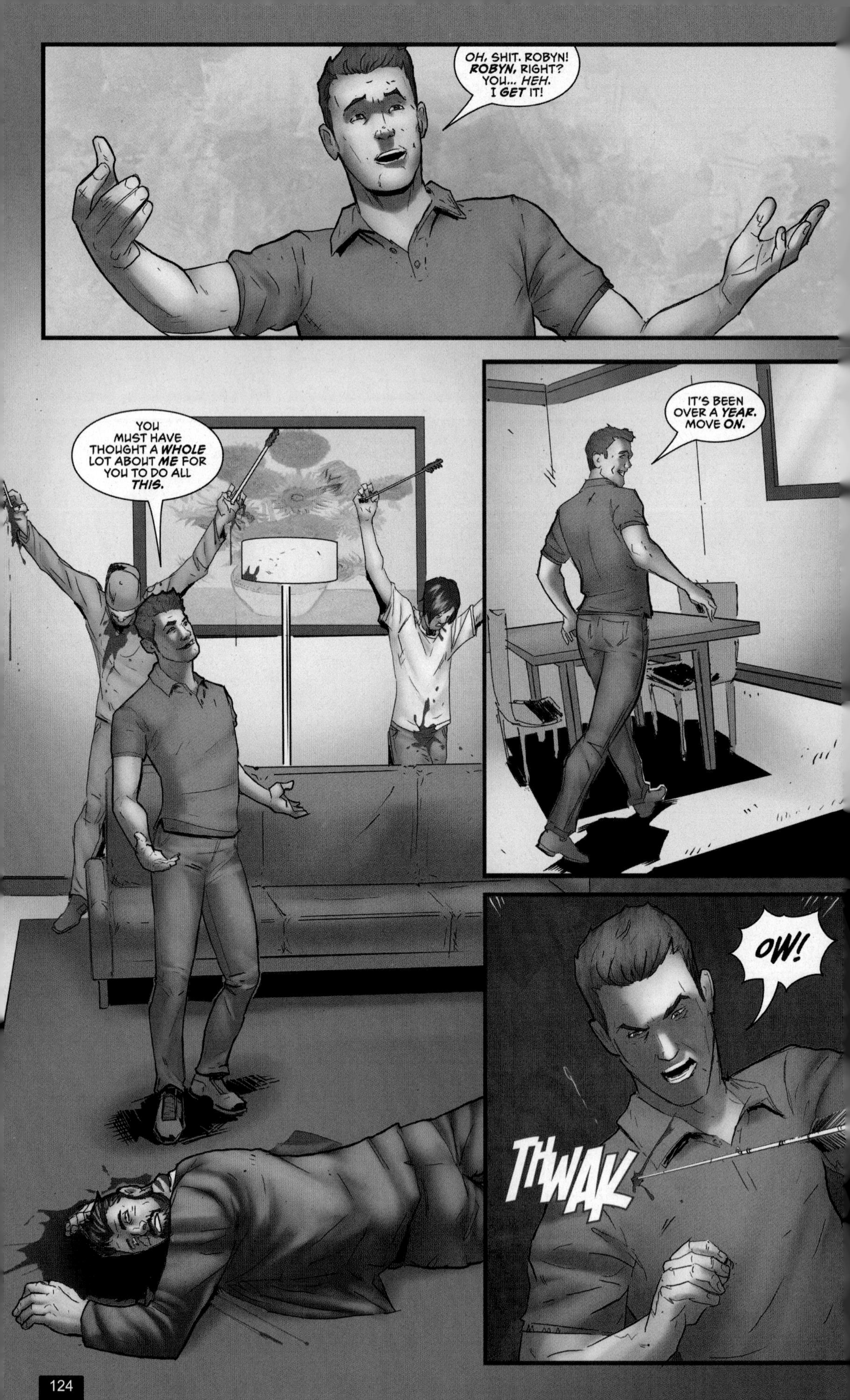
OH, SHIT. ROBYN! ROBYN, RIGHT? YOU... HEH. I GET IT!
YOU MUST HAVE THOUGHT A WHOLE LOT ABOUT ME FOR YOU TO DO ALL THIS.
IT'S BEEN OVER A YEAR. MOVE ON.
OW!
THWAK

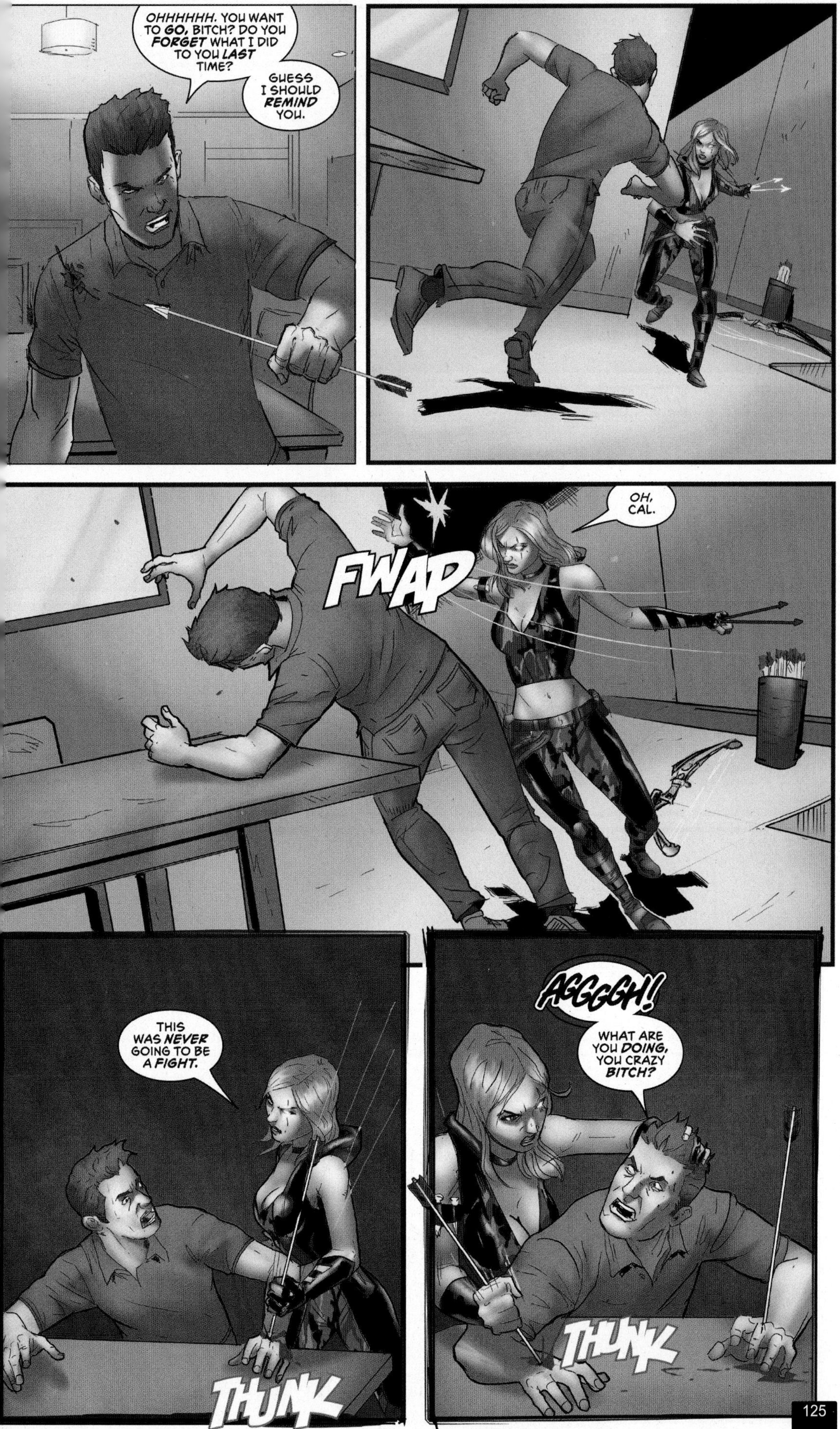
OHHHHHH. YOU WANT TO GO, BITCH? DO YOU FORGET WHAT I DID TO YOU LAST TIME?
GUESS I SHOULD REMIND YOU.
OH, CAL.
FWAP
THIS WAS NEVER GOING TO BE A FIGHT.
THUNK
AGGGGH!
WHAT ARE YOU DOING, YOU CRAZY BITCH?
THUNK

I'M TEACHING YOU *EMPATHY.*

OH, YOU *CAN'T* BE SERIOUS...

I REALLY, REALLY *AM.*

SKLTCH

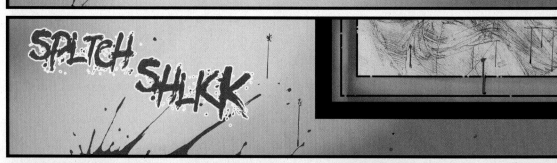

SPLTCH SHLKK

I'M... I'M...

DON'T YOU *DARE* APOLOGIZE.

NO, I... YOU...

I'M WONDERING... WHY YOU DIDN'T JUST... HIRE A GODDAMN *THERAPIST.*

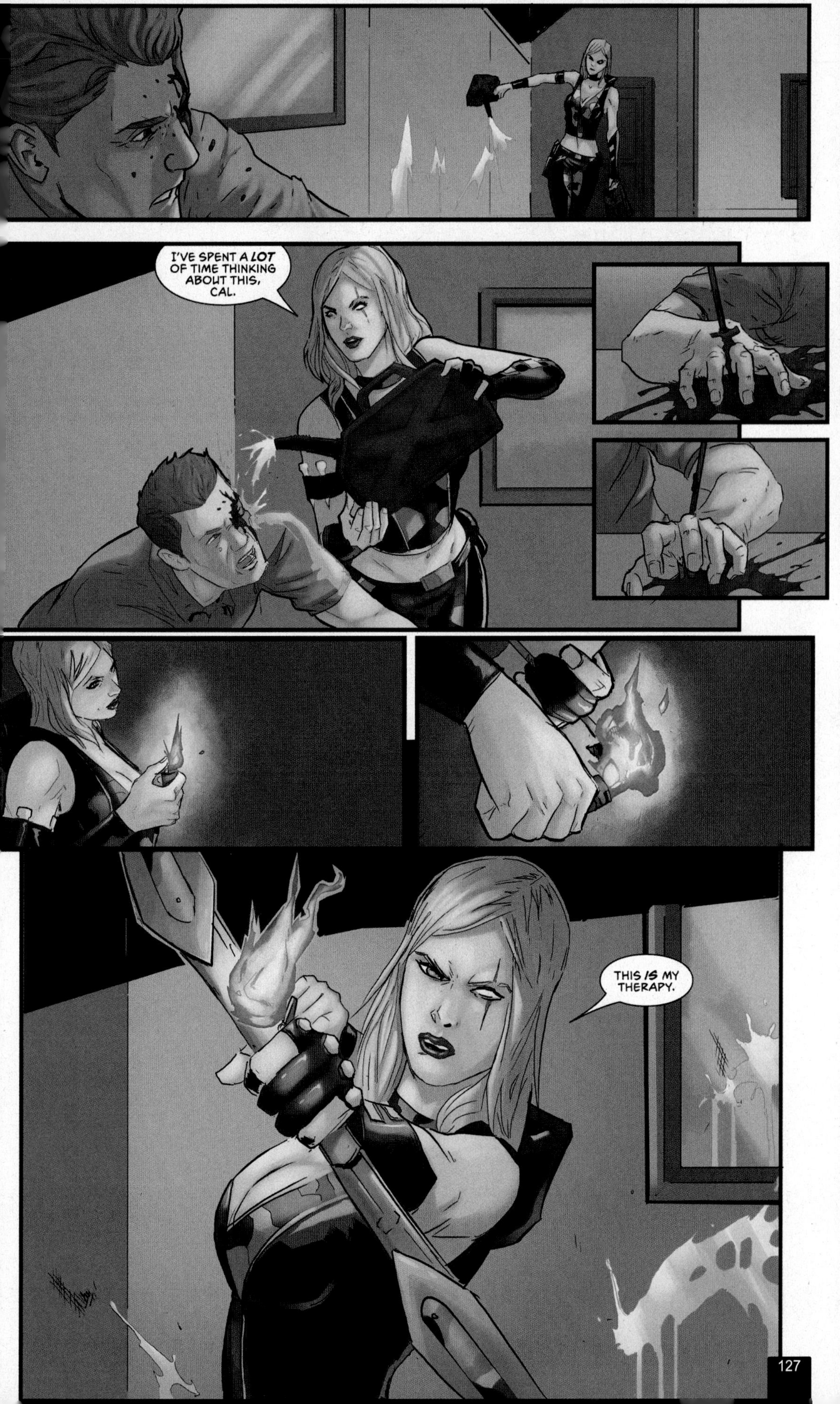
I'VE SPENT A *LOT* OF TIME THINKING ABOUT THIS, CAL.
THIS *IS* MY THERAPY.

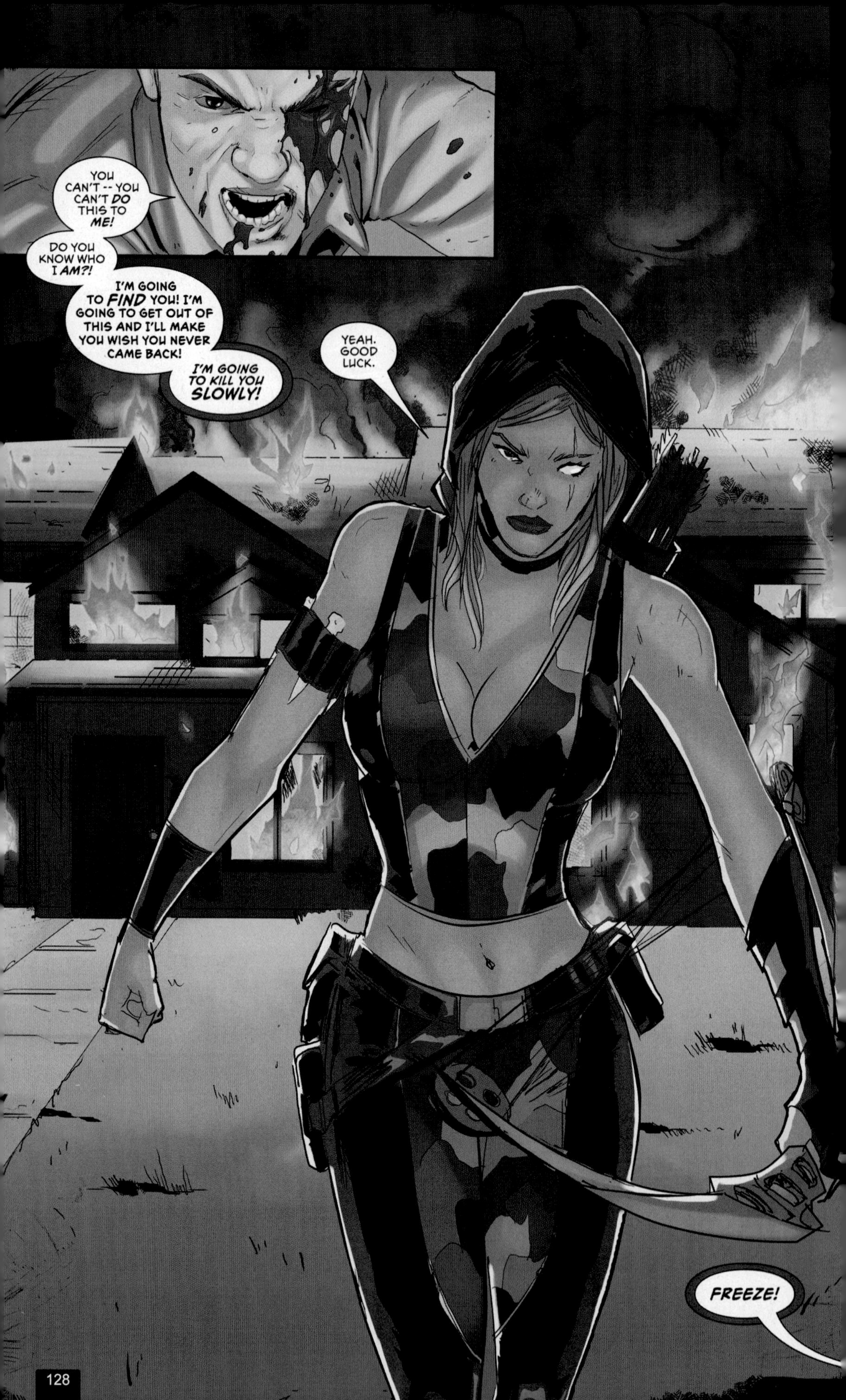
YOU CAN'T -- YOU CAN'T DO THIS TO ME!
DO YOU KNOW WHO I AM?!
I'M GOING TO FIND YOU! I'M GOING TO GET OUT OF THIS AND I'LL MAKE YOU WISH YOU NEVER CAME BACK!
I'M GOING TO KILL YOU SLOWLY!
YEAH. GOOD LUCK.
FREEZE!

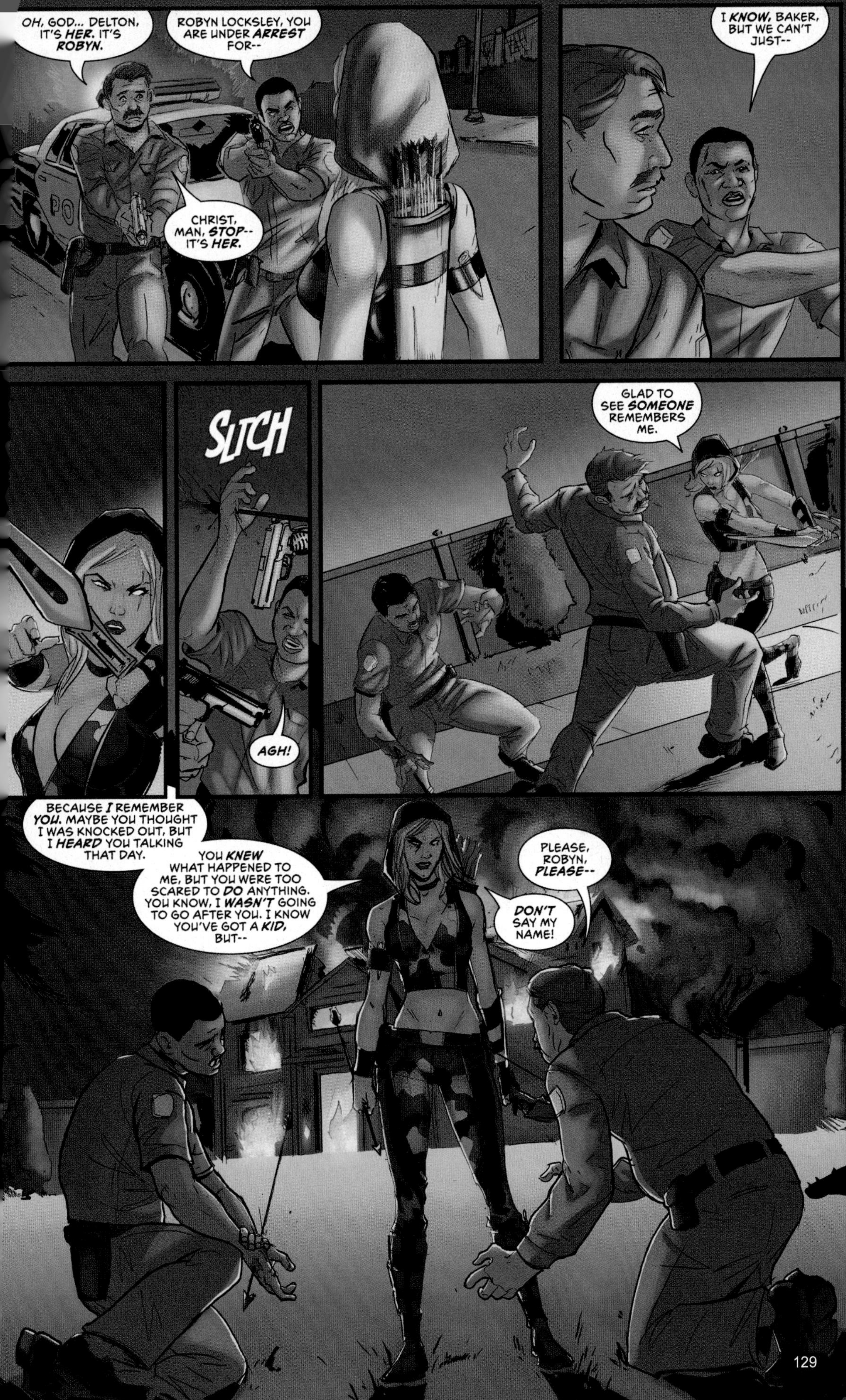

OH, GOD... DELTON, IT'S HER. IT'S ROBYN.
ROBYN LOCKSLEY, YOU ARE UNDER ARREST FOR--
CHRIST, MAN, STOP-- IT'S HER.
I KNOW, BAKER, BUT WE CAN'T JUST--
SLTCH
AGH!
GLAD TO SEE SOMEONE REMEMBERS ME.
BECAUSE I REMEMBER YOU. MAYBE YOU THOUGHT I WAS KNOCKED OUT, BUT I HEARD YOU TALKING THAT DAY.
YOU KNEW WHAT HAPPENED TO ME, BUT YOU WERE TOO SCARED TO DO ANYTHING. YOU KNOW, I WASN'T GOING TO GO AFTER YOU. I KNOW YOU'VE GOT A KID, BUT--
PLEASE, ROBYN, PLEASE--
DON'T SAY MY NAME!

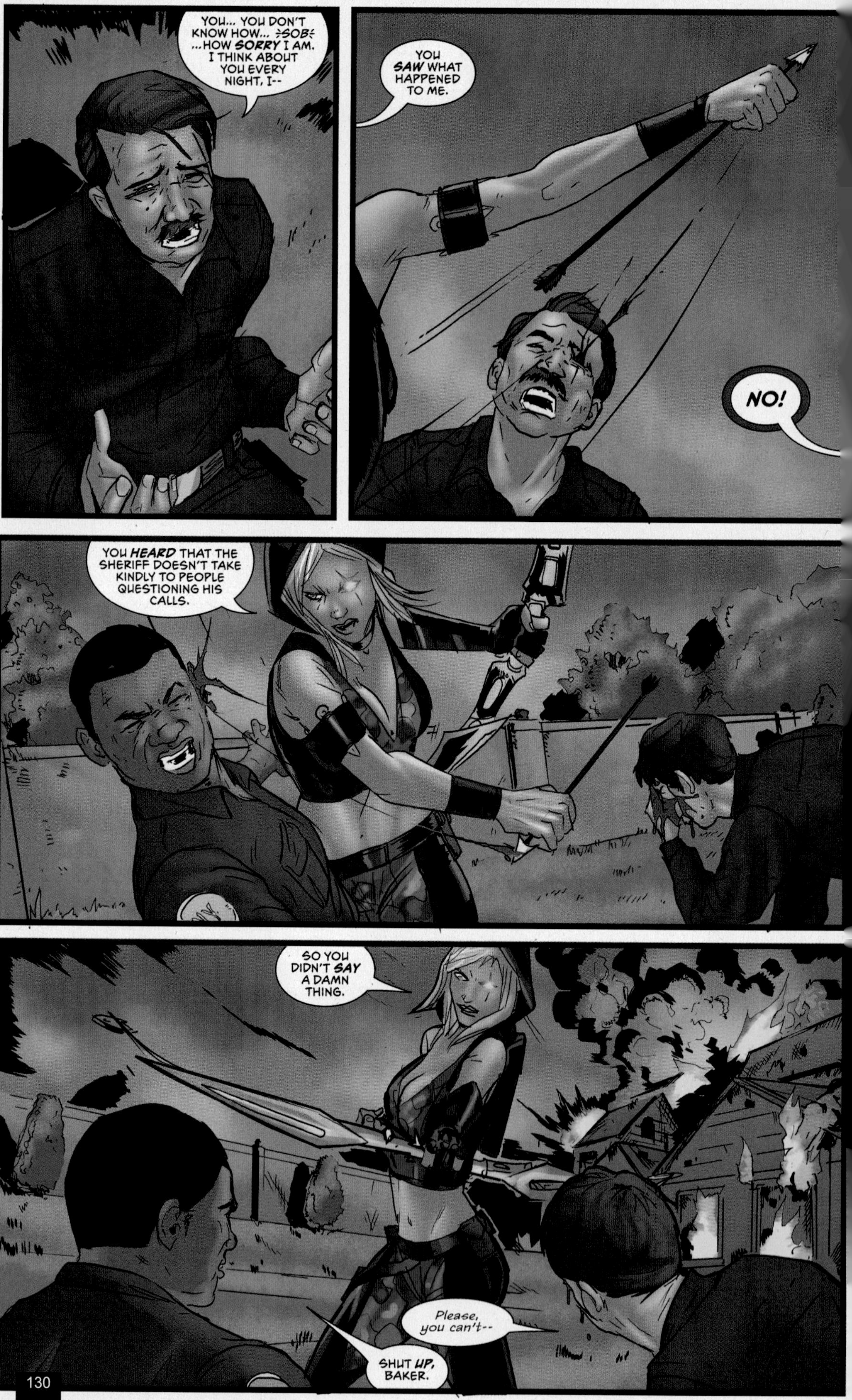
YOU... YOU DON'T KNOW HOW... ≠SOB≠ ...HOW SORRY I AM. I THINK ABOUT YOU EVERY NIGHT, I--
YOU SAW WHAT HAPPENED TO ME.
NO!
YOU HEARD THAT THE SHERIFF DOESN'T TAKE KINDLY TO PEOPLE QUESTIONING HIS CALLS.
SO YOU DIDN'T SAY A DAMN THING.
Please, you can't--
SHUT UP, BAKER.

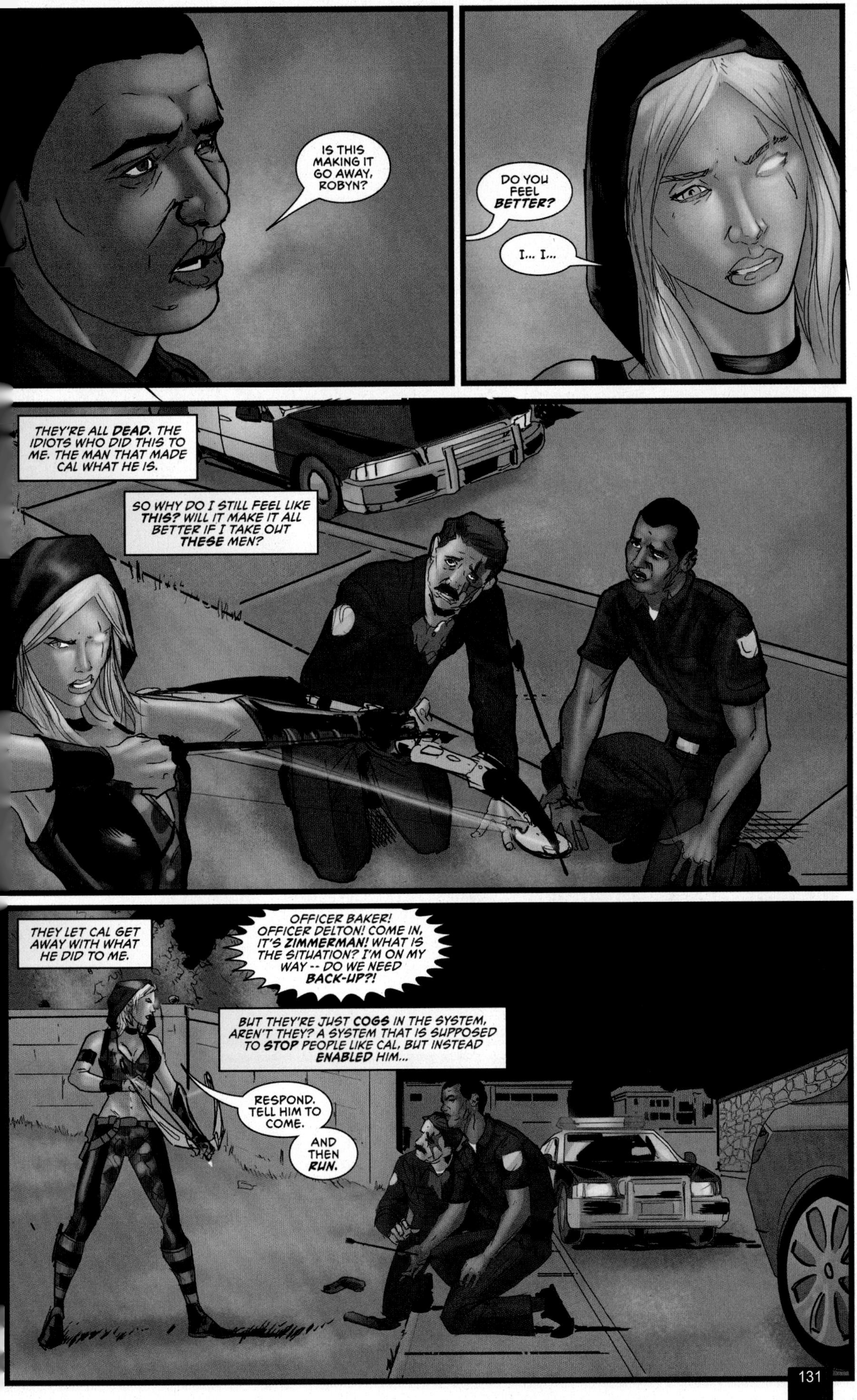
IS THIS MAKING IT GO AWAY, ROBYN?
DO YOU FEEL BETTER?
I... I...
THEY'RE ALL DEAD. THE IDIOTS WHO DID THIS TO ME. THE MAN THAT MADE CAL WHAT HE IS.
SO WHY DO I STILL FEEL LIKE THIS? WILL IT MAKE IT ALL BETTER IF I TAKE OUT THESE MEN?
THEY LET CAL GET AWAY WITH WHAT HE DID TO ME.
OFFICER BAKER! OFFICER DELTON! COME IN, IT'S ZIMMERMAN! WHAT IS THE SITUATION? I'M ON MY WAY -- DO WE NEED BACK-UP?!
BUT THEY'RE JUST COGS IN THE SYSTEM, AREN'T THEY? A SYSTEM THAT IS SUPPOSED TO STOP PEOPLE LIKE CAL, BUT INSTEAD ENABLED HIM...
RESPOND. TELL HIM TO COME.
AND THEN RUN.

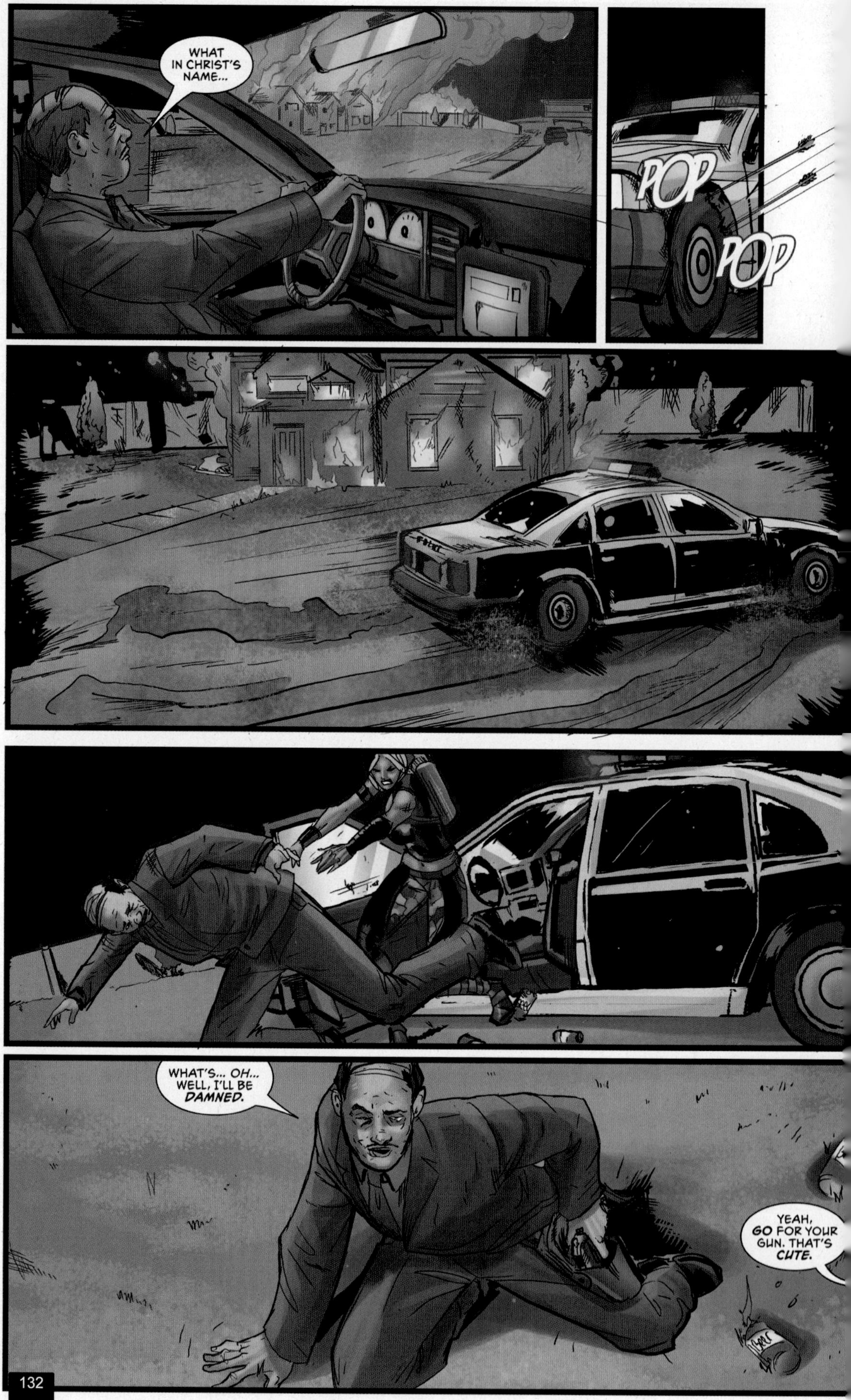
WHAT IN CHRIST'S NAME...
POP
POP
WHAT'S... OH... WELL, I'LL BE DAMNED.
YEAH, GO FOR YOUR GUN. THAT'S CUTE.

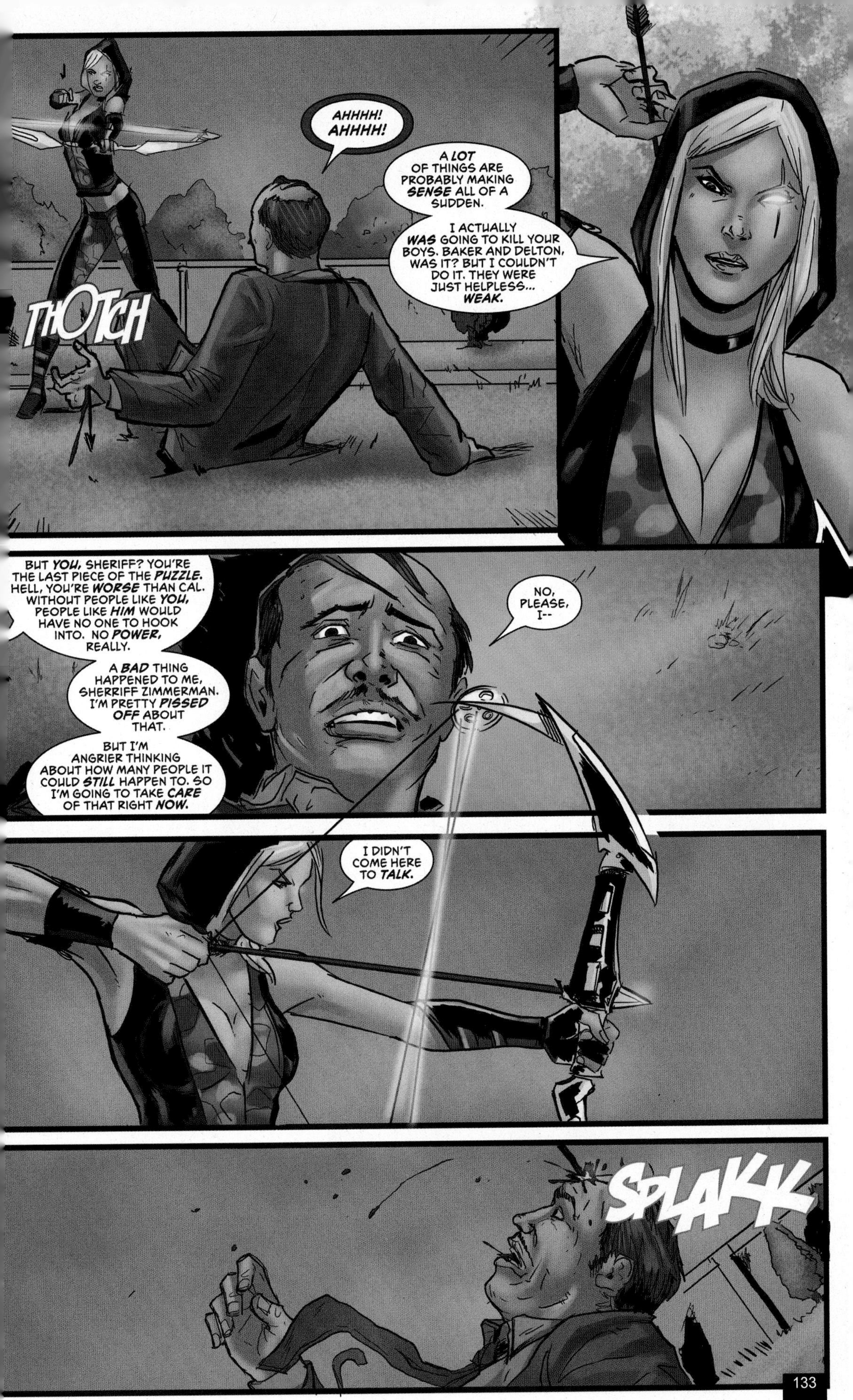
THOTCH
AHHHH! AHHHH!
A LOT OF THINGS ARE PROBABLY MAKING SENSE ALL OF A SUDDEN.
I ACTUALLY WAS GOING TO KILL YOUR BOYS. BAKER AND DELTON, WAS IT? BUT I COULDN'T DO IT. THEY WERE JUST HELPLESS... WEAK.
BUT YOU, SHERIFF? YOU'RE THE LAST PIECE OF THE PUZZLE. HELL, YOU'RE WORSE THAN CAL. WITHOUT PEOPLE LIKE YOU, PEOPLE LIKE HIM WOULD HAVE NO ONE TO HOOK INTO. NO POWER, REALLY.
NO, PLEASE, I--
A BAD THING HAPPENED TO ME, SHERRIFF ZIMMERMAN. I'M PRETTY PISSED OFF ABOUT THAT.
BUT I'M ANGRIER THINKING ABOUT HOW MANY PEOPLE IT COULD STILL HAPPEN TO. SO I'M GOING TO TAKE CARE OF THAT RIGHT NOW.
I DIDN'T COME HERE TO TALK.
SPLAKK

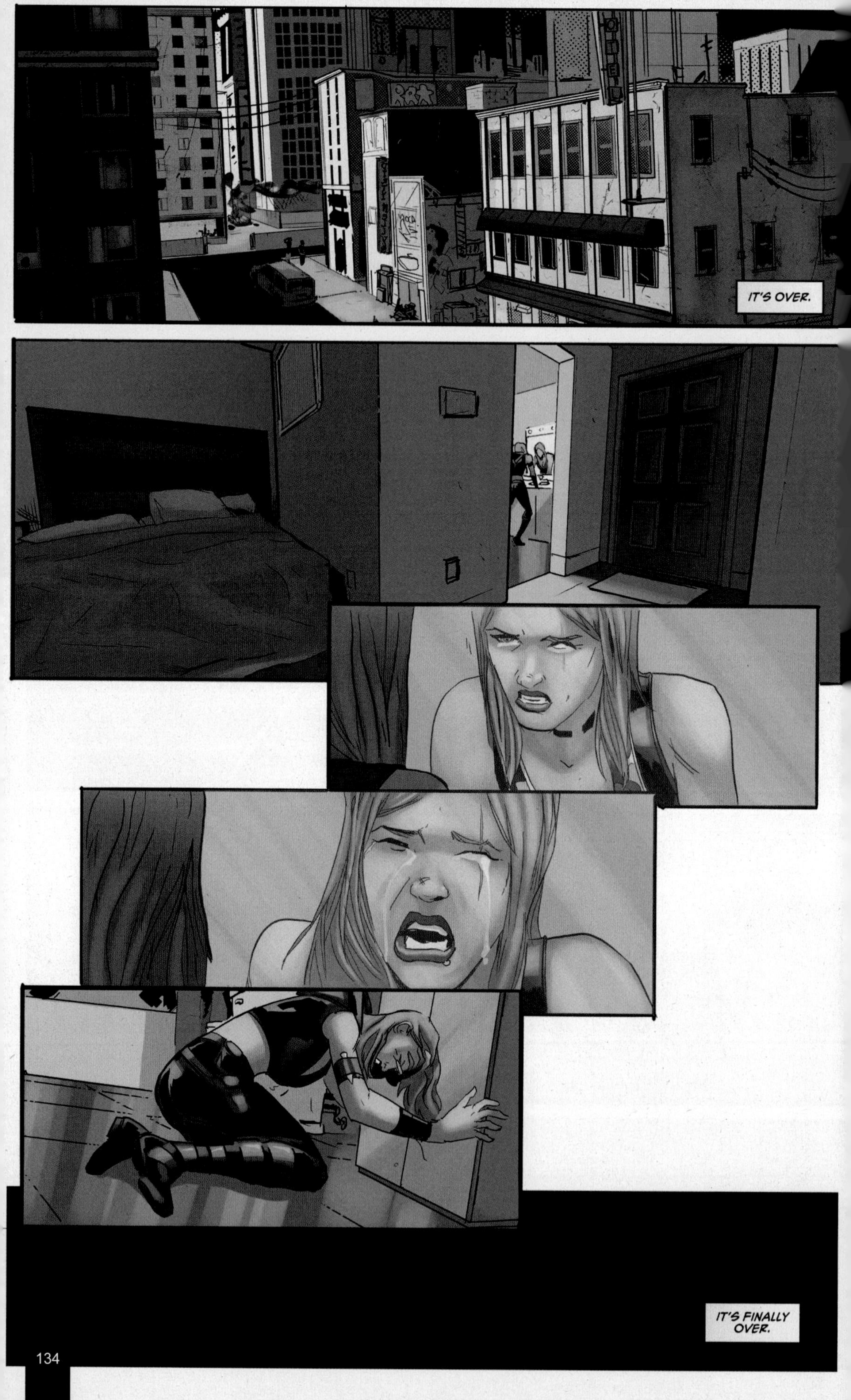
IT'S OVER.
IT'S FINALLY OVER.

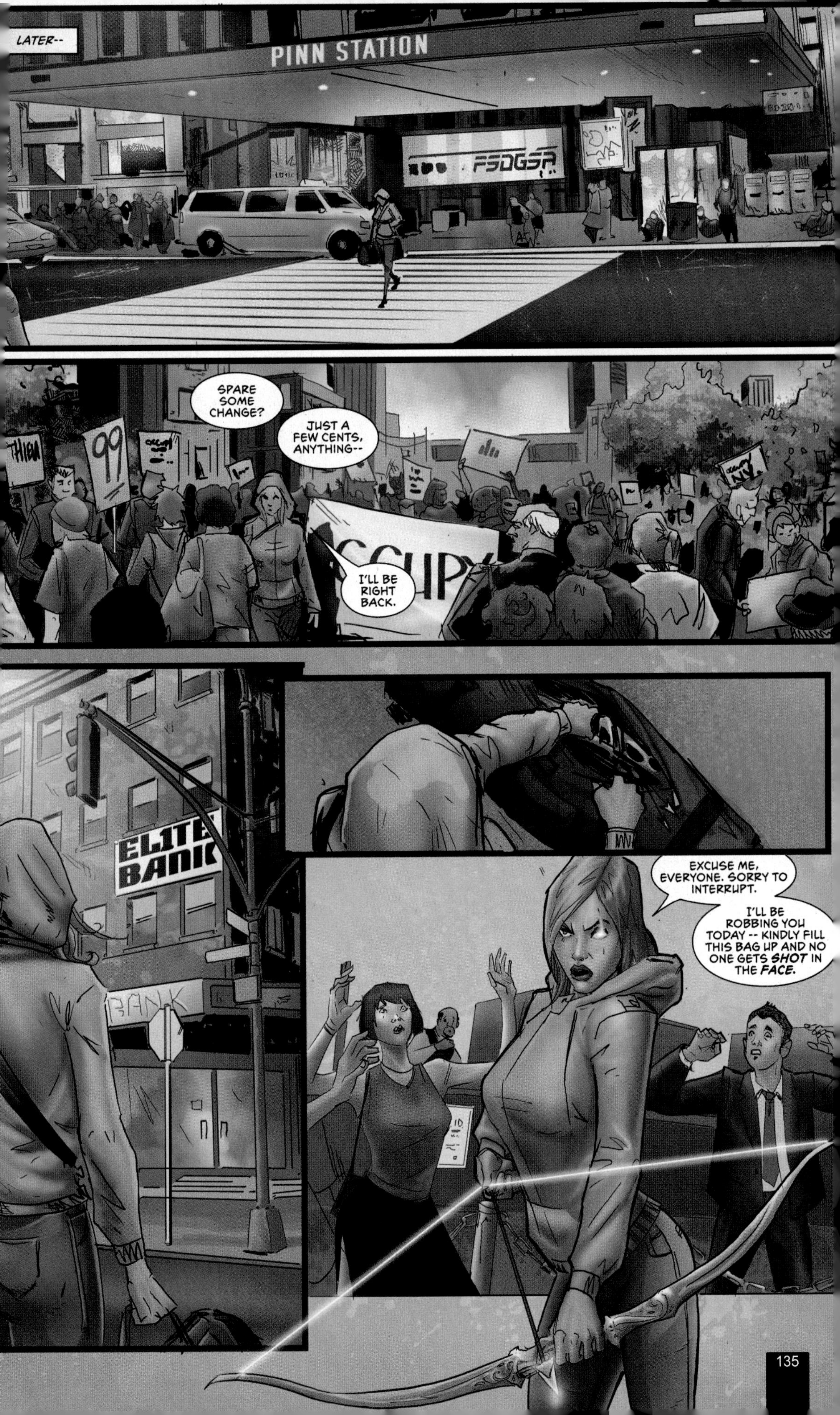
LATER--
PINN STATION
SPARE SOME CHANGE?
JUST A FEW CENTS, ANYTHING--
I'LL BE RIGHT BACK.
ELITE BANK
EXCUSE ME, EVERYONE. SORRY TO INTERRUPT.
I'LL BE ROBBING YOU TODAY -- KINDLY FILL THIS BAG UP AND NO ONE GETS *SHOT* IN THE *FACE*.

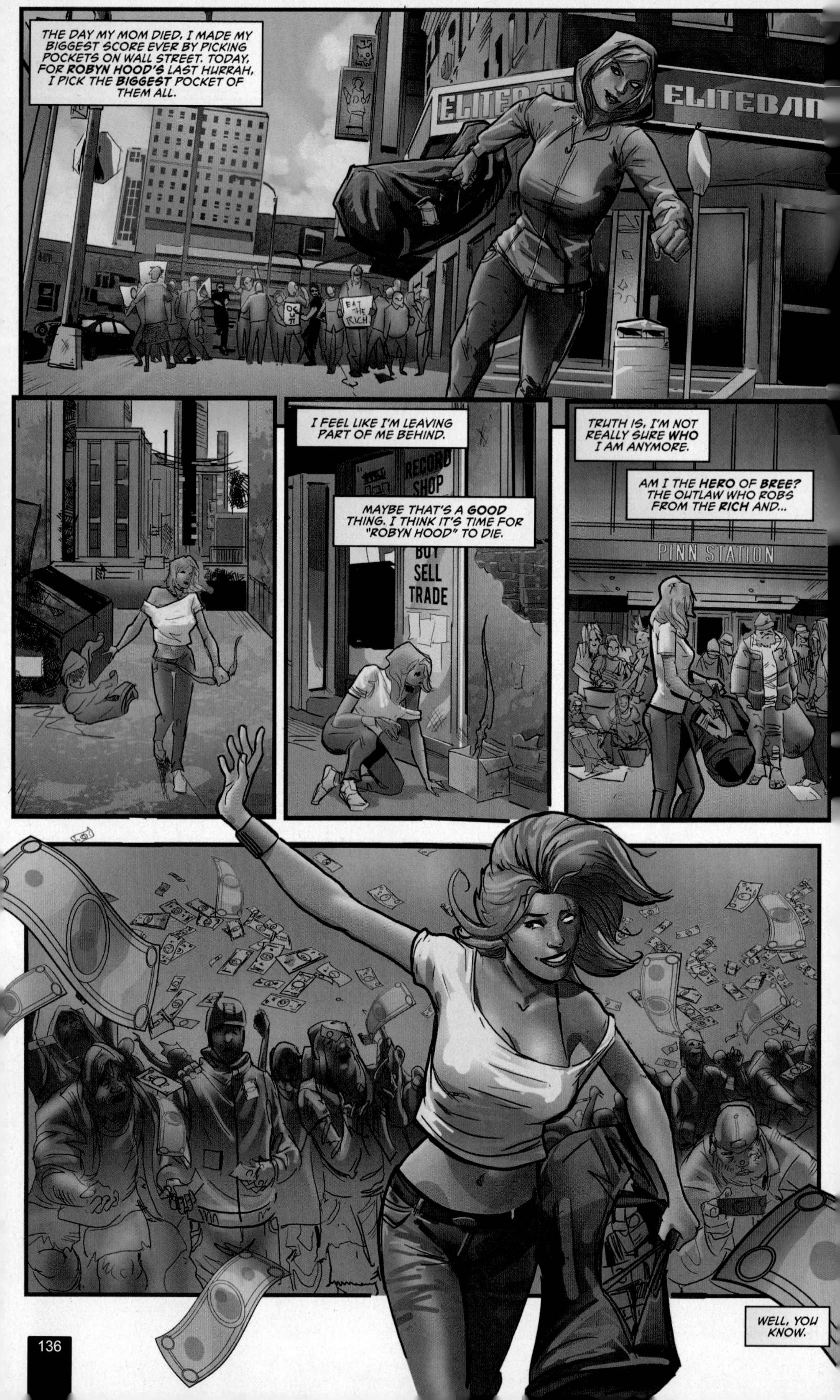
THE DAY MY MOM DIED, I MADE MY BIGGEST SCORE EVER BY PICKING POCKETS ON WALL STREET. TODAY, FOR ROBYN HOOD'S LAST HURRAH, I PICK THE BIGGEST POCKET OF THEM ALL.
ELITEBAN
EAT THE RICH
I FEEL LIKE I'M LEAVING PART OF ME BEHIND.
RECORD SHOP
MAYBE THAT'S A GOOD THING. I THINK IT'S TIME FOR "ROBYN HOOD" TO DIE.
BUY SELL TRADE
TRUTH IS, I'M NOT REALLY SURE WHO I AM ANYMORE.
AM I THE HERO OF BREE? THE OUTLAW WHO ROBS FROM THE RICH AND...
PINN STATION
WELL, YOU KNOW.

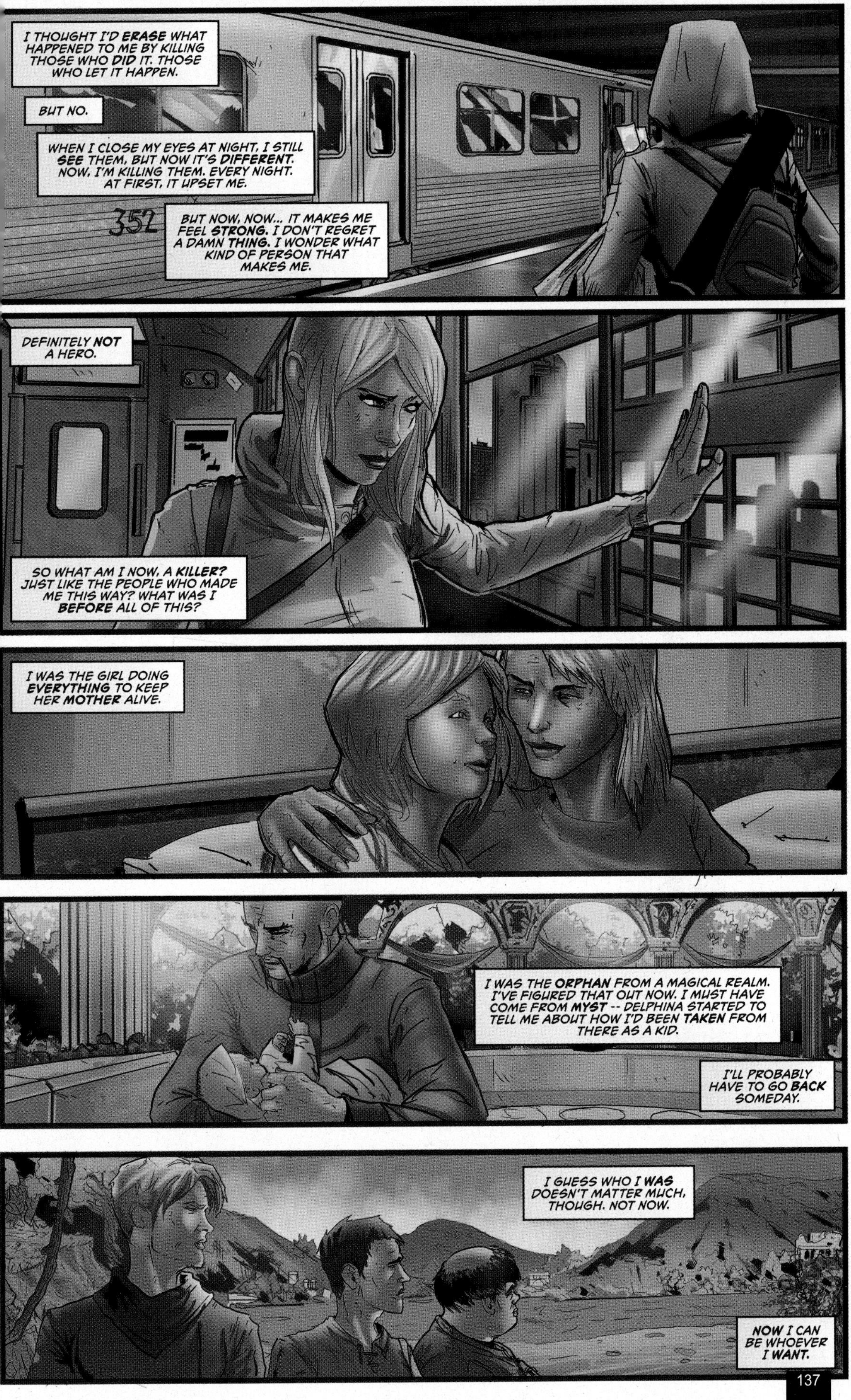
I THOUGHT I'D ERASE WHAT HAPPENED TO ME BY KILLING THOSE WHO DID IT. THOSE WHO LET IT HAPPEN.
BUT NO.
WHEN I CLOSE MY EYES AT NIGHT, I STILL SEE THEM, BUT NOW IT'S DIFFERENT. NOW, I'M KILLING THEM. EVERY NIGHT. AT FIRST, IT UPSET ME.
352
BUT NOW, NOW... IT MAKES ME FEEL STRONG. I DON'T REGRET A DAMN THING. I WONDER WHAT KIND OF PERSON THAT MAKES ME.
DEFINITELY NOT A HERO.
SO WHAT AM I NOW, A KILLER? JUST LIKE THE PEOPLE WHO MADE ME THIS WAY? WHAT WAS I BEFORE ALL OF THIS?
I WAS THE GIRL DOING EVERYTHING TO KEEP HER MOTHER ALIVE.
I WAS THE ORPHAN FROM A MAGICAL REALM. I'VE FIGURED THAT OUT NOW. I MUST HAVE COME FROM MYST -- DELPHINA STARTED TO TELL ME ABOUT HOW I'D BEEN TAKEN FROM THERE AS A KID.
I'LL PROBABLY HAVE TO GO BACK SOMEDAY.
I GUESS WHO I WAS DOESN'T MATTER MUCH, THOUGH. NOT NOW.
NOW I CAN BE WHOEVER I WANT.

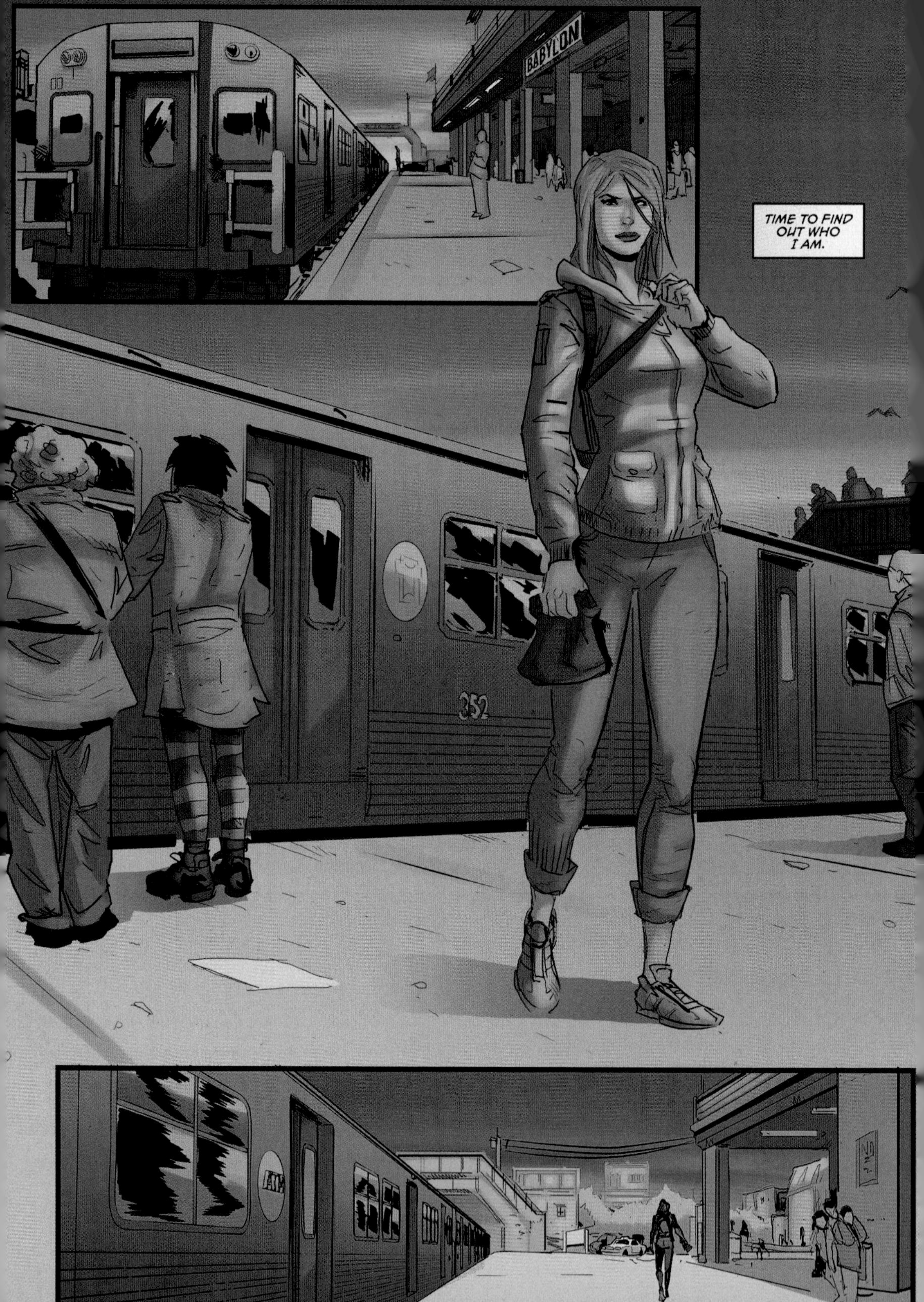
BABYLON
TIME TO FIND OUT WHO I AM.
352

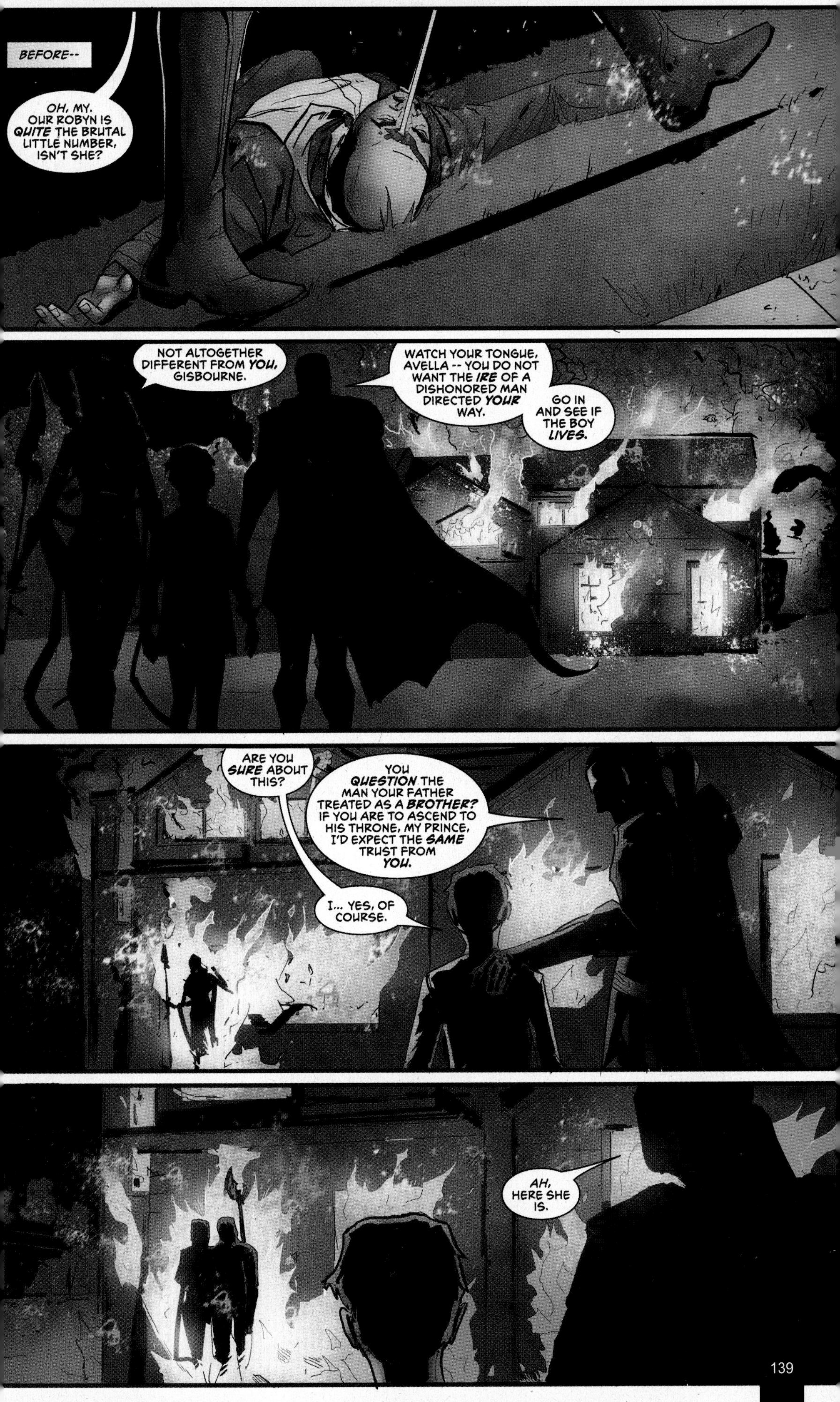
BEFORE--
OH, MY. OUR ROBYN IS QUITE THE BRUTAL LITTLE NUMBER, ISN'T SHE?
NOT ALTOGETHER DIFFERENT FROM YOU, GISBOURNE.
WATCH YOUR TONGUE, AVELLA -- YOU DO NOT WANT THE IRE OF A DISHONORED MAN DIRECTED YOUR WAY.
GO IN AND SEE IF THE BOY LIVES.
ARE YOU SURE ABOUT THIS?
YOU QUESTION THE MAN YOUR FATHER TREATED AS A BROTHER? IF YOU ARE TO ASCEND TO HIS THRONE, MY PRINCE, I'D EXPECT THE SAME TRUST FROM YOU.
I... YES, OF COURSE.
AH, HERE SHE IS.

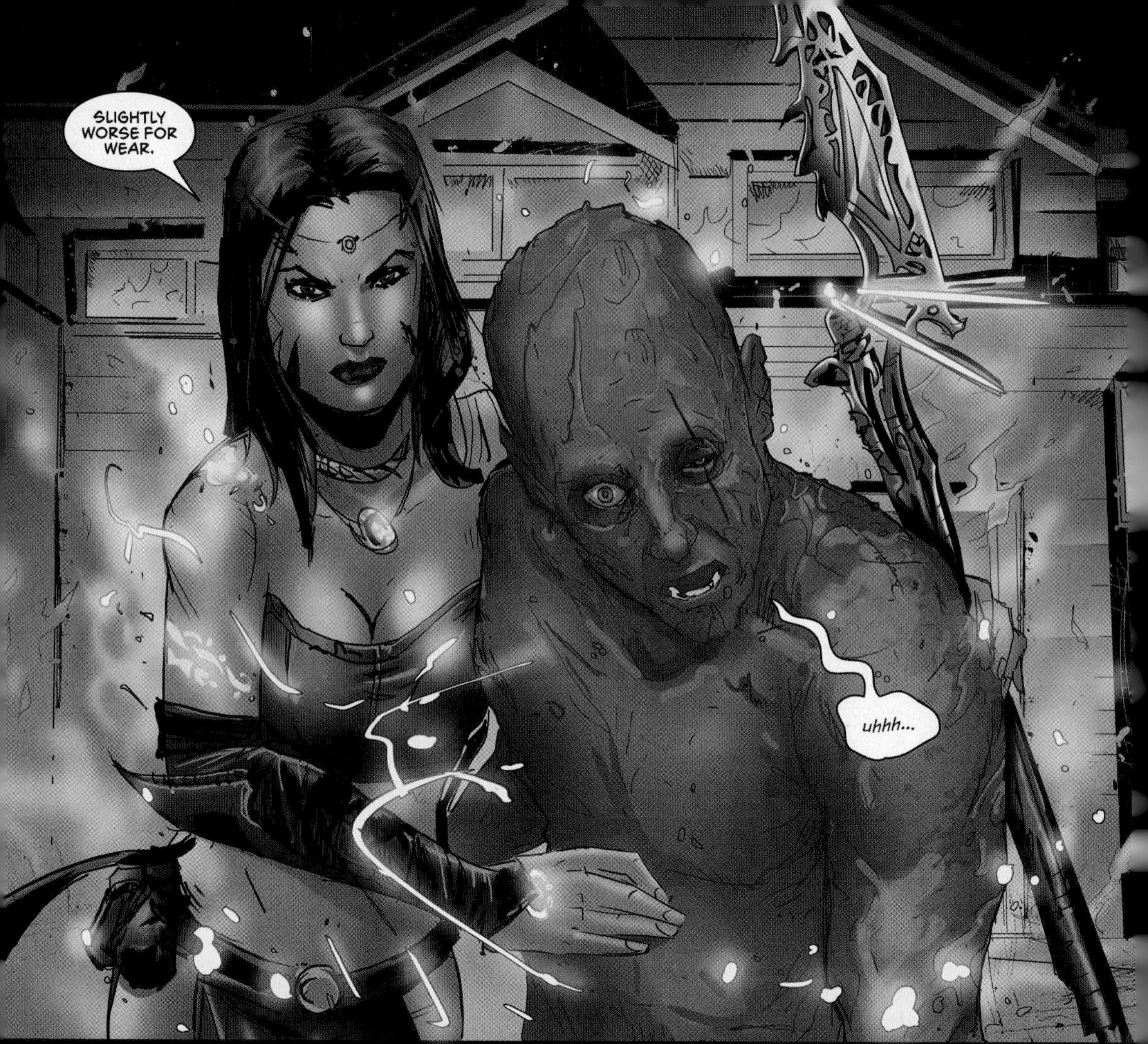
SLIGHTLY WORSE FOR WEAR.
uhhh...

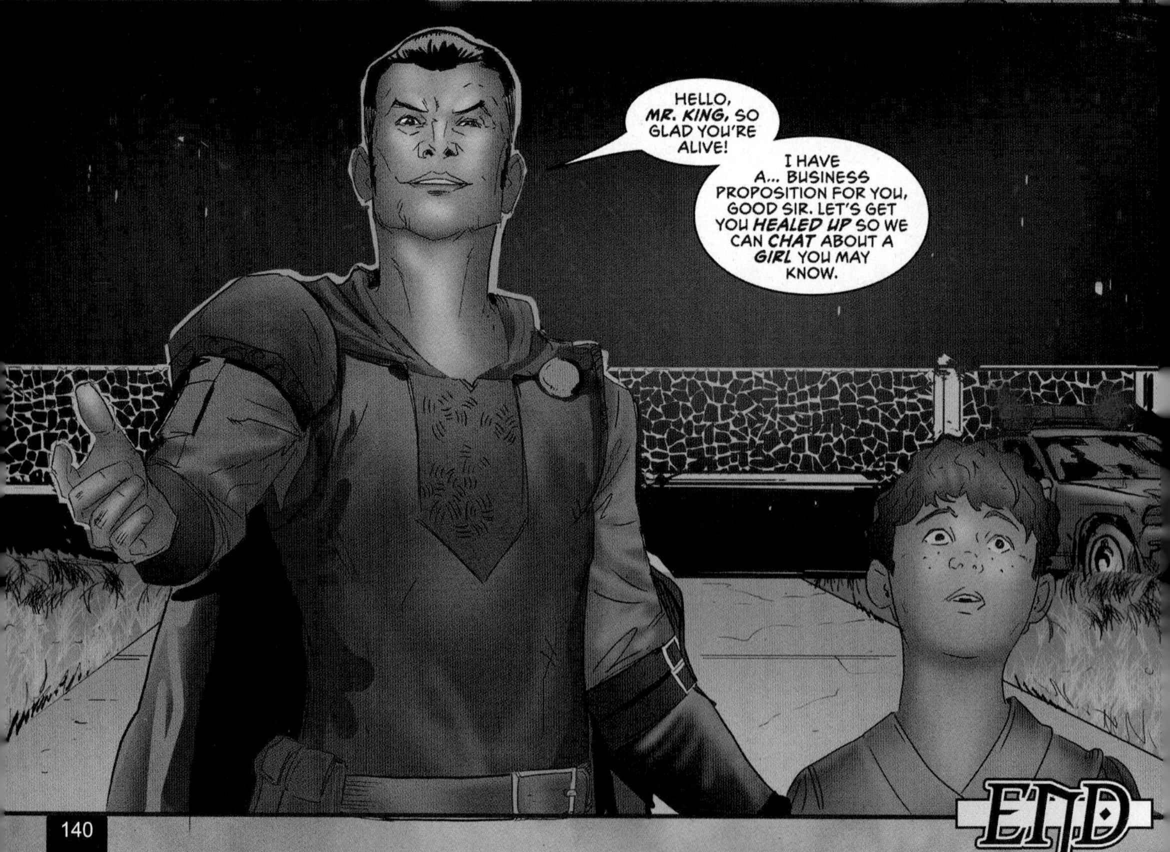
HELLO, MR. KING, SO GLAD YOU'RE ALIVE!
I HAVE A... BUSINESS PROPOSITION FOR YOU, GOOD SIR. LET'S GET YOU HEALED UP SO WE CAN CHAT ABOUT A GIRL YOU MAY KNOW.
END

# Grimm Fairy Tales presents:

# ROBYN HOOD ORIGIN

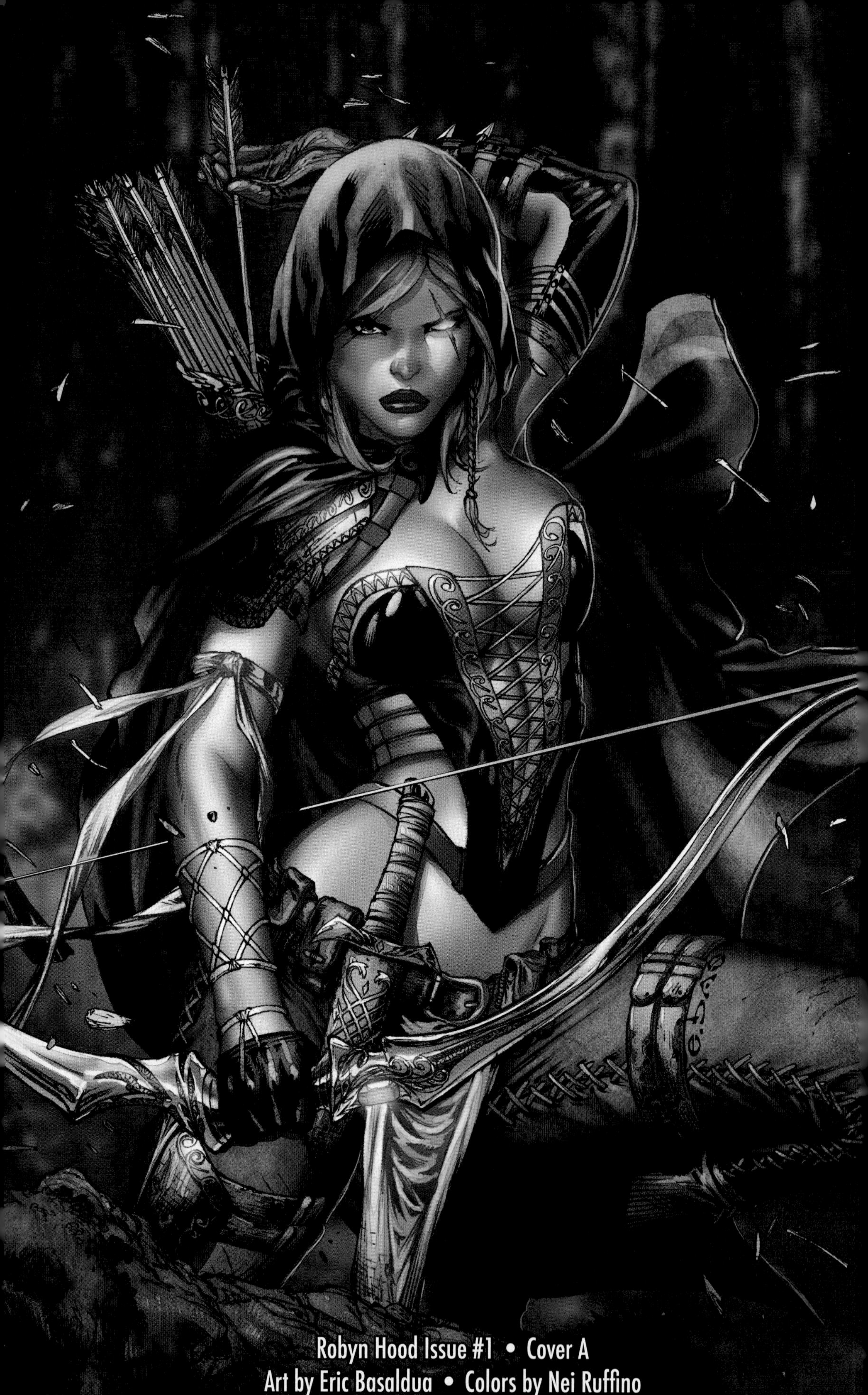

Robyn Hood Issue #1 • Cover A
Art by Eric Basaldua • Colors by Nei Ruffino

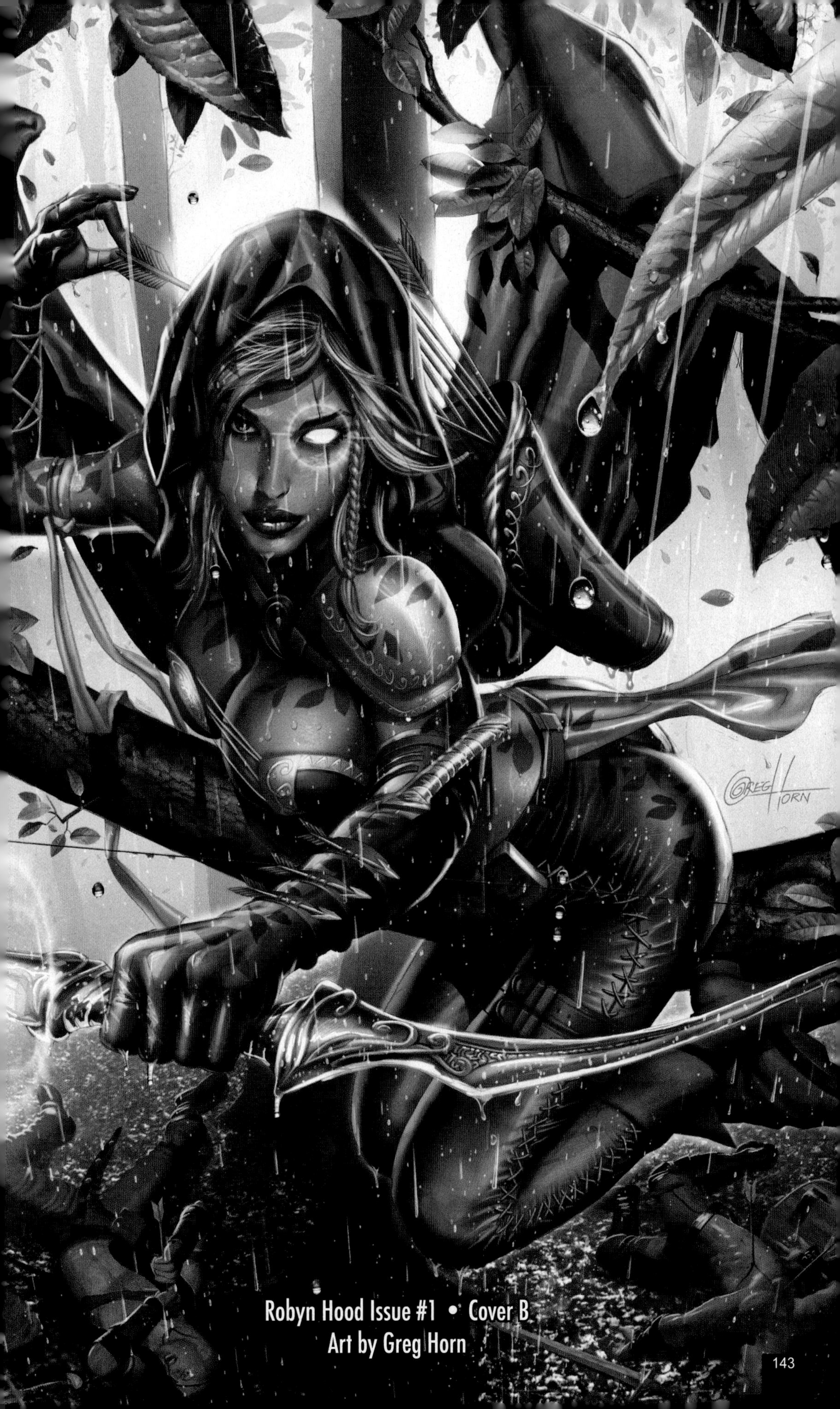

Robyn Hood Issue #1 • Cover B
Art by Greg Horn

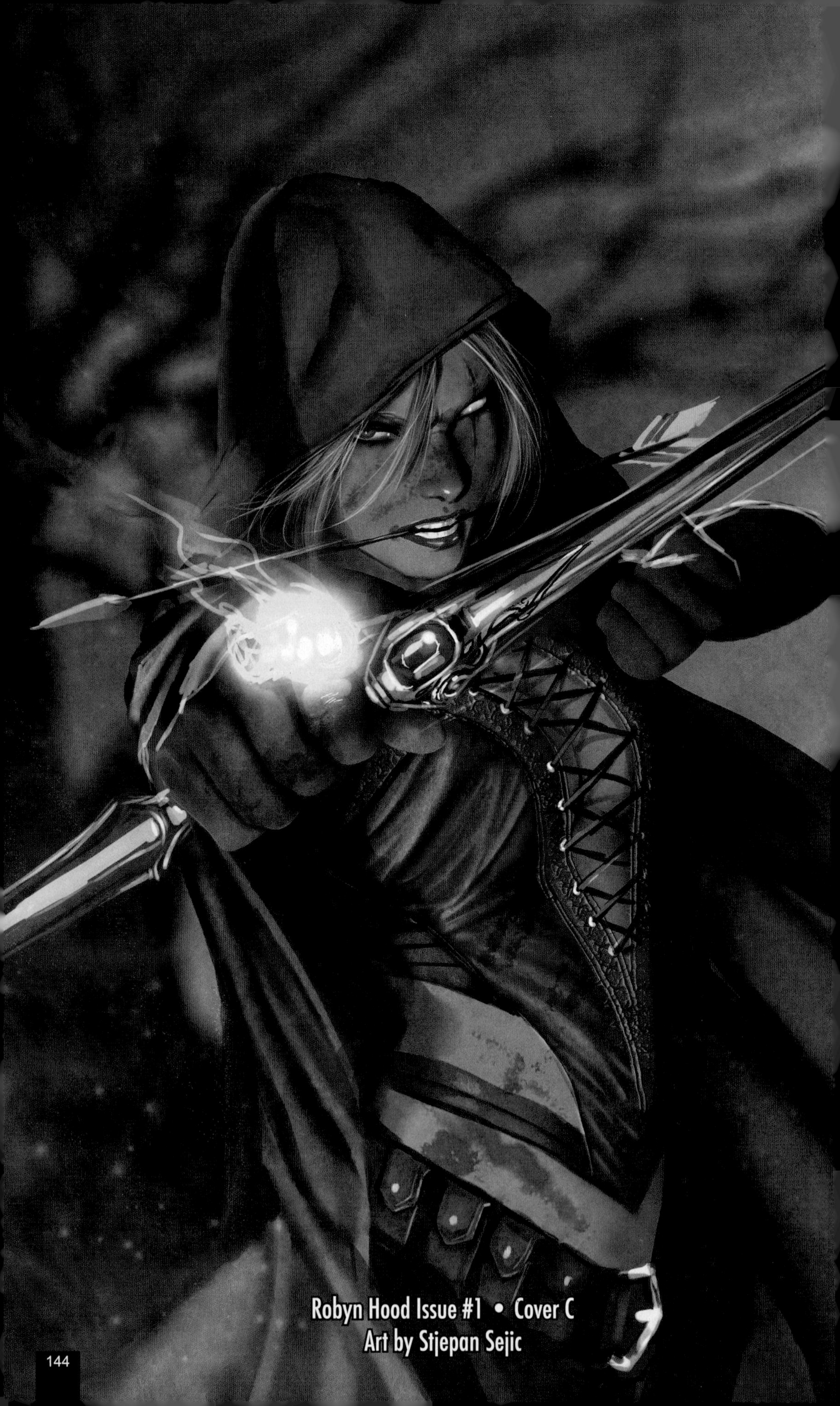

Robyn Hood Issue #1 • Cover C
Art by Stjepan Sejic

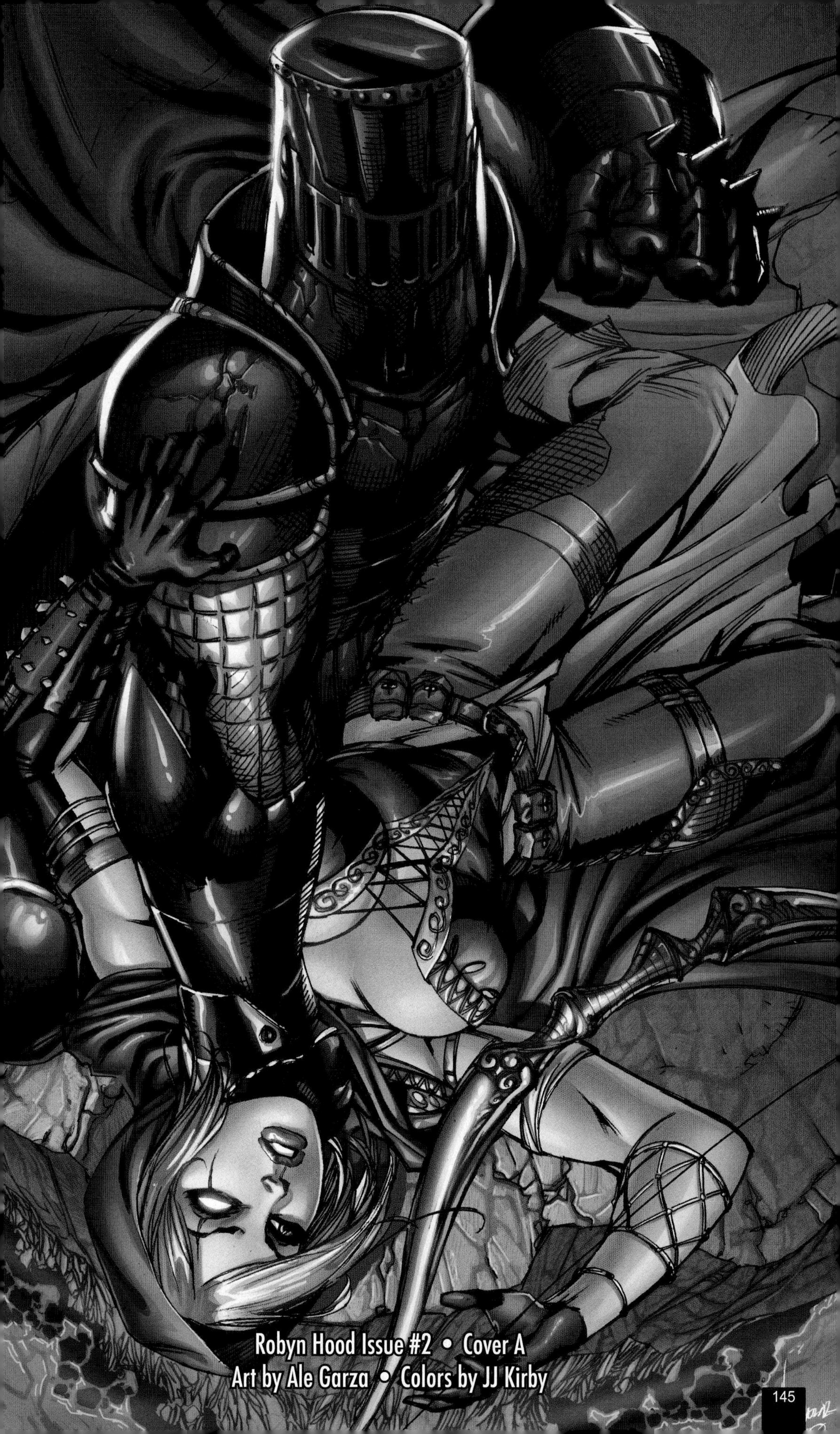

Robyn Hood Issue #2 • Cover A
Art by Ale Garza • Colors by JJ Kirby

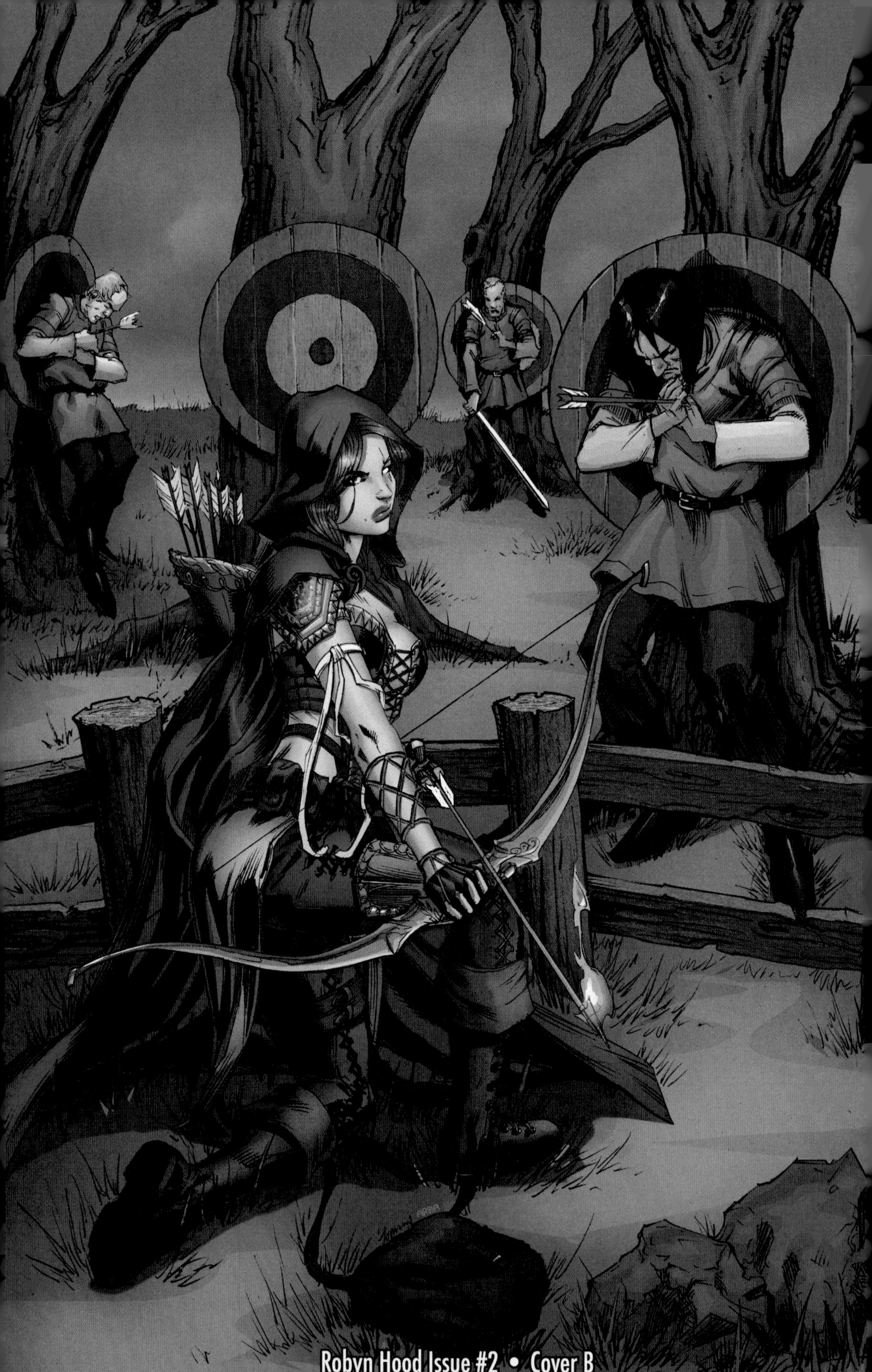

Robyn Hood Issue #2 • Cover B
Art by Tommy Patterson • Colors by Arsia Rozegar

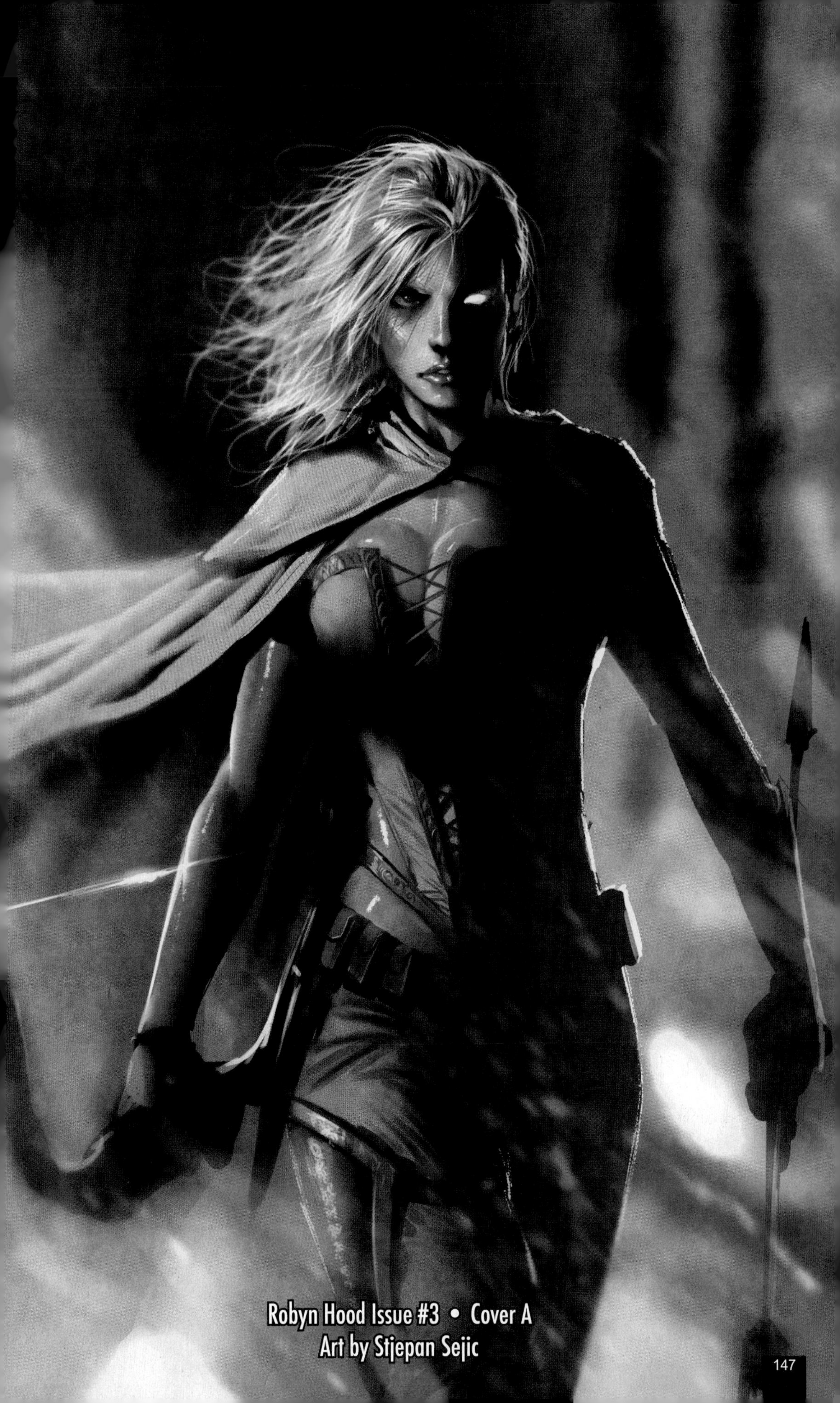

Robyn Hood Issue #3 • Cover A
Art by Stjepan Sejic

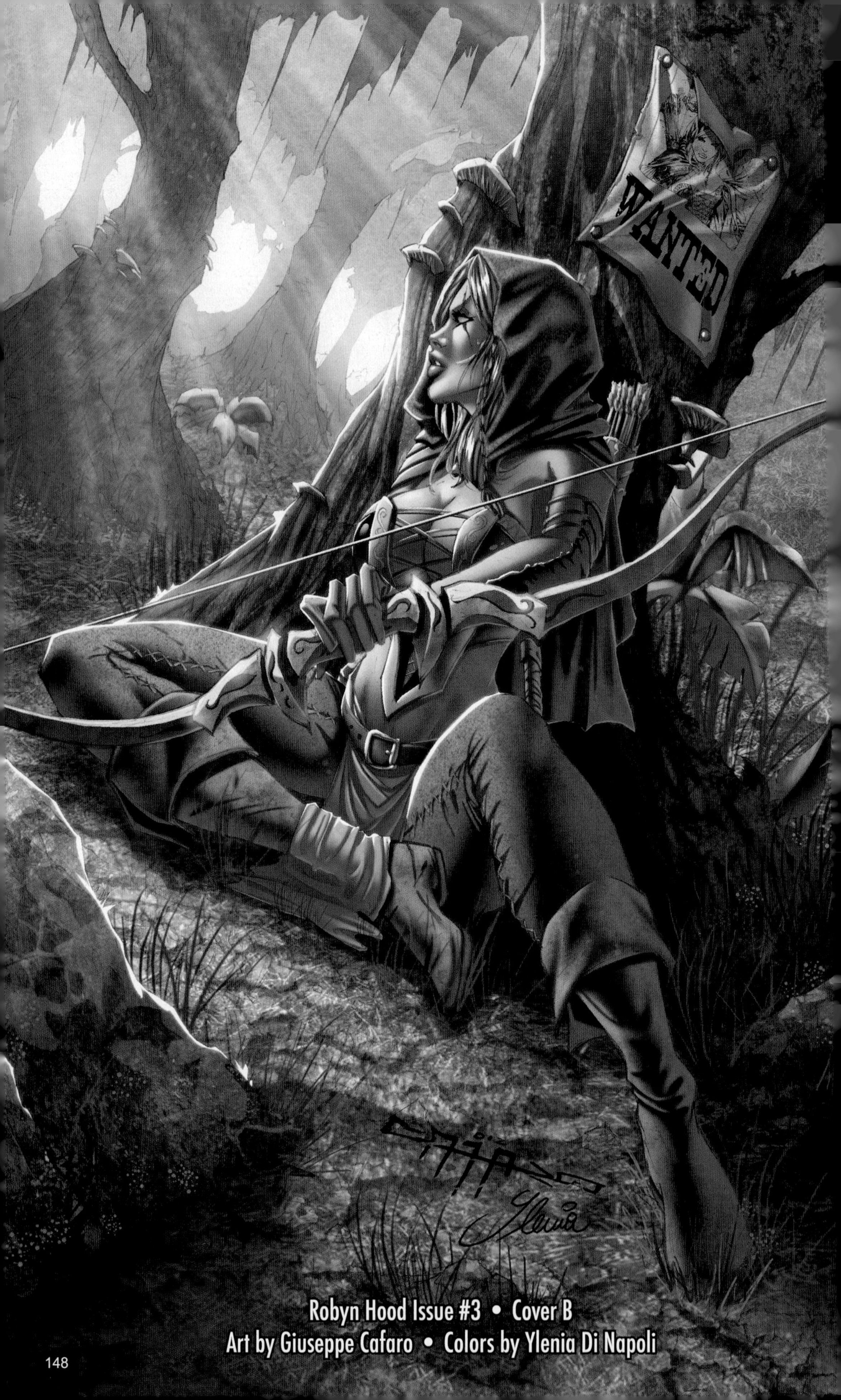
WANTED

Robyn Hood Issue #3 • Cover B
Art by Giuseppe Cafaro • Colors by Ylenia Di Napoli

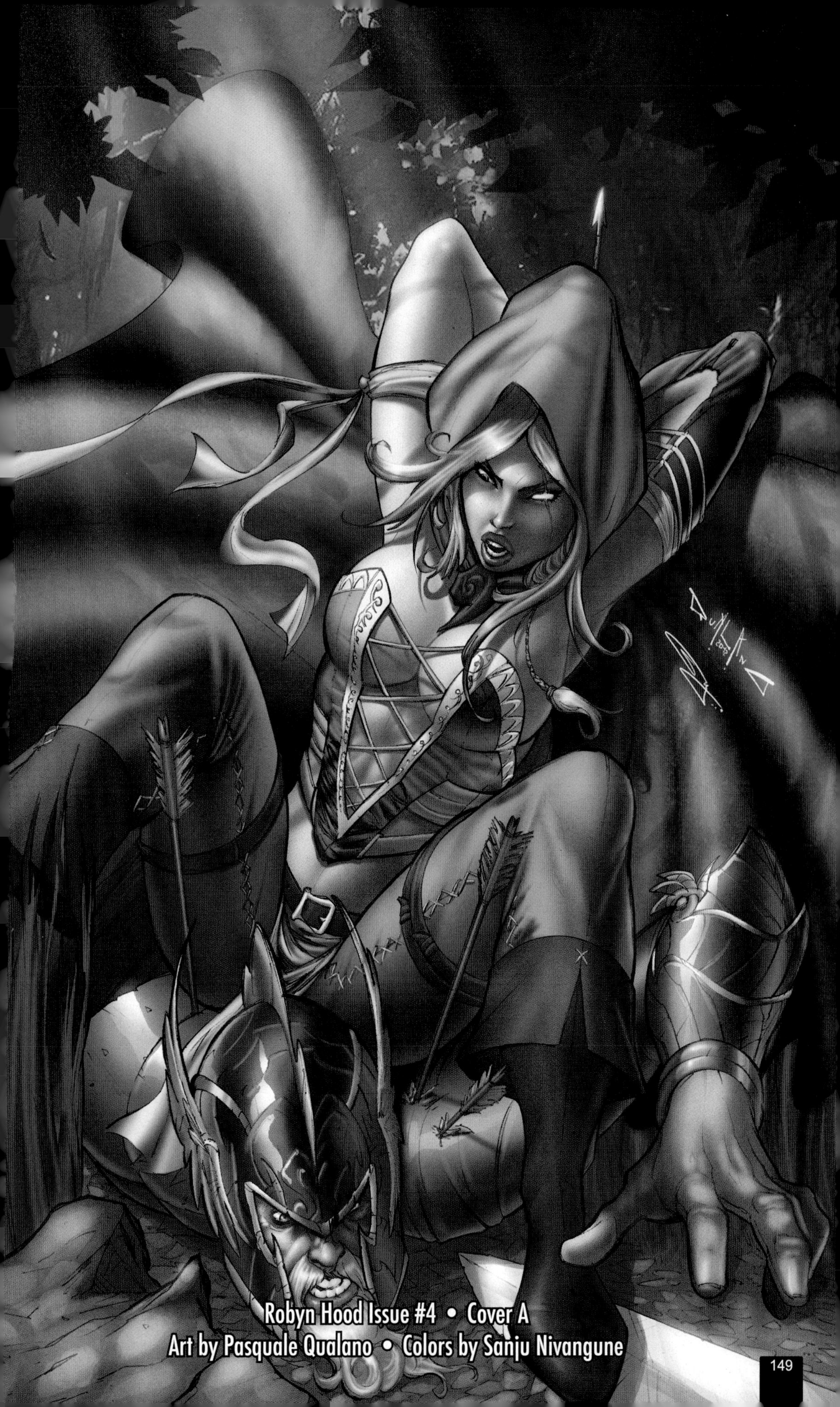

Robyn Hood Issue #4 • Cover A
Art by Pasquale Qualano • Colors by Sanju Nivangune

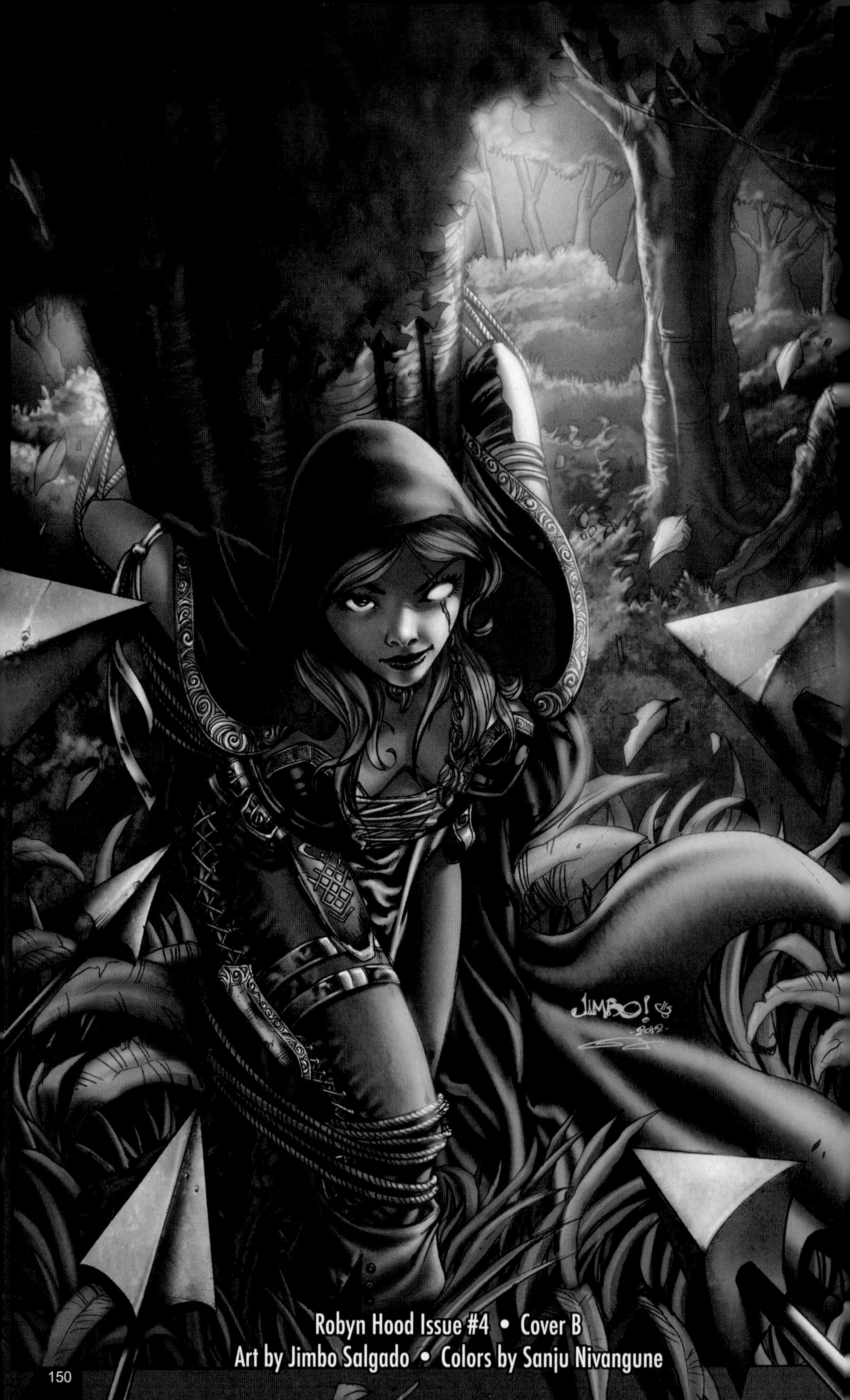
JIMBO!

Robyn Hood Issue #4 • Cover B
Art by Jimbo Salgado • Colors by Sanju Nivangune

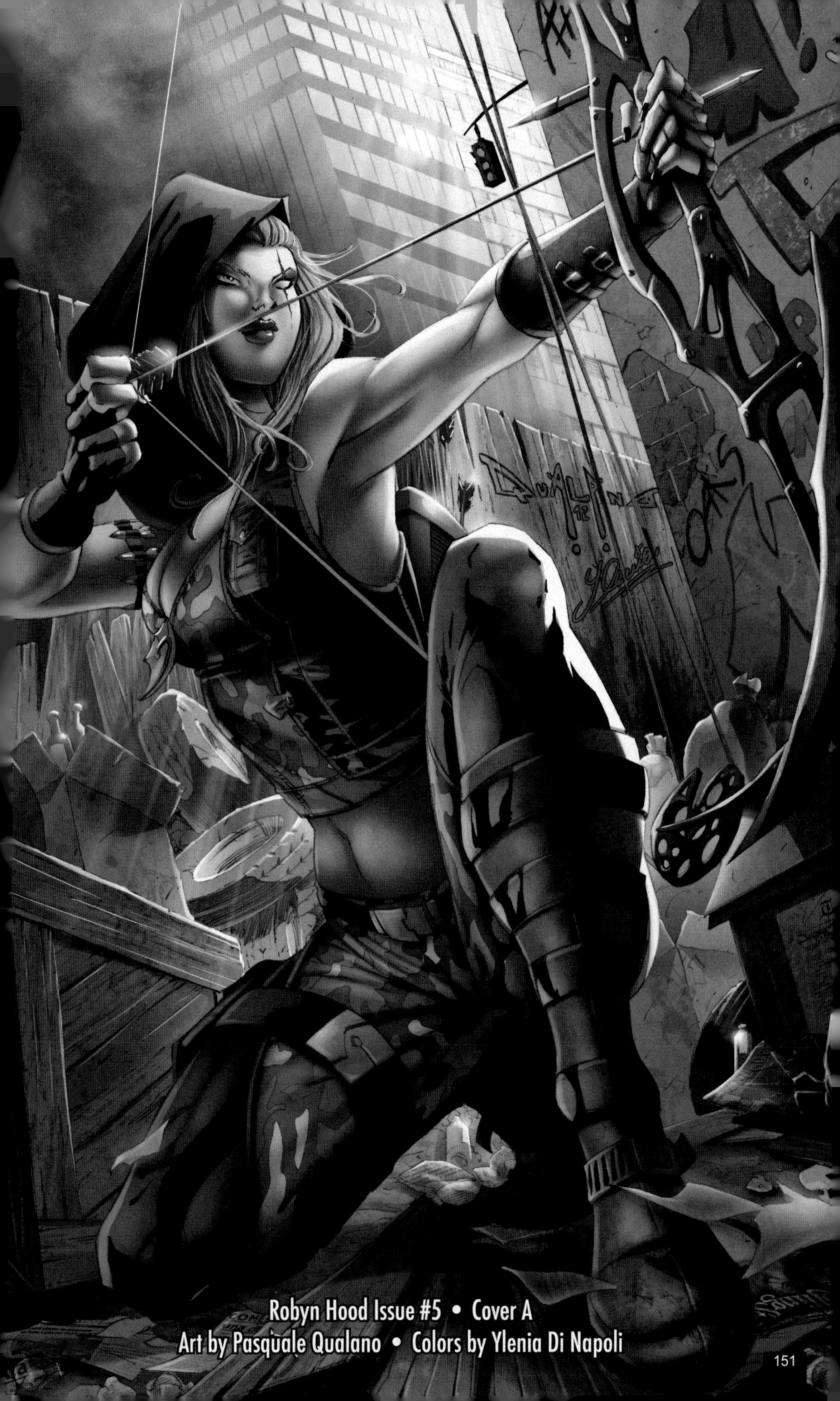

Robyn Hood Issue #5 • Cover A
Art by Pasquale Qualano • Colors by Ylenia Di Napoli

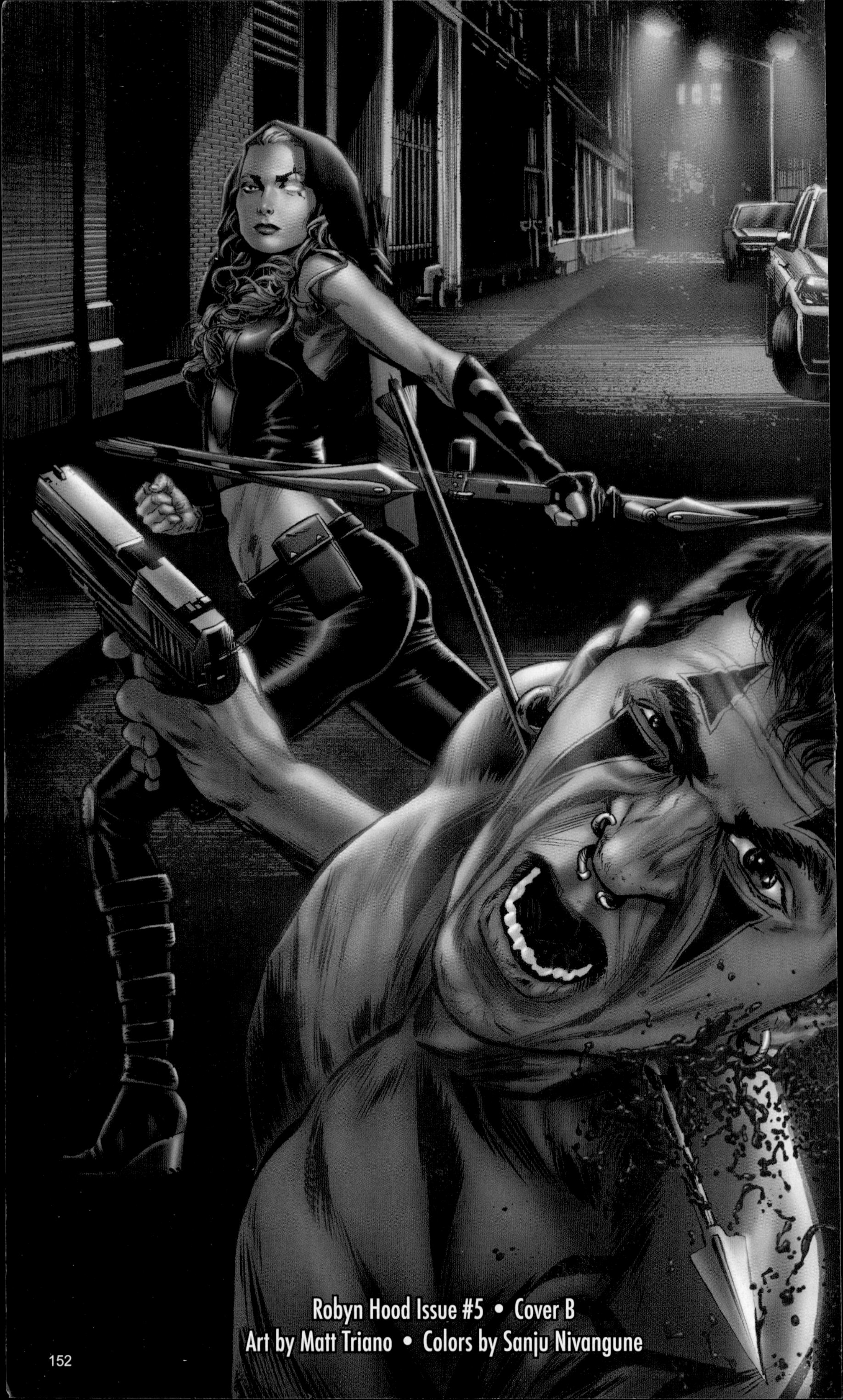

Robyn Hood Issue #5 • Cover B
Art by Matt Triano • Colors by Sanju Nivangune